# Melvin Charney

# Krzysztof Wodiczko

Published with the assistance of the Cultural Affairs Division of the Department of External Affairs, Canada.


PRINTED IN CANADA
ISBN 0-88884-540-5
Design: Peter Dorn, RCA, FDGC

CANADIAN CATALOGUING IN PUBLICATION DATA

Melvin Charney, Krzysztof Wodiczko.

Prepared by Diana Nemiroff.

Text in English, French, Italian.
Bibliography: p.

ISBN 0-88884-540-5

1. Art, Modern – 20th century – Canada – Exhibitions. 2. Art, Canadian – Exhibitions. 3. Architecture and society – Canada – Exhibitions. I. Charney, Melvin. II. Wodiczko, Krzysztof. III. Nemiroff, Diana. IV. National Gallery of Canada. V. Biennale di Venezia (42nd : 1986) VI. Title: Canada, Biennale di Venezia, 1986.

N6545 M4 1986 709'.71'0740531
CIP 86-099510-0E

COVER

Melvin Charney, *"Better if they think they are going to a farm ..."* (detail), 1982

Krzysztof Wodiczko, *The Swiss National Parliament Building Projection* (detail), 1985

Publié avec le concours de la Direction des affaires culturelles du ministère des Affaires extérieures du Canada.


IMPRIMÉ AU CANADA
ISBN 0-88884-540-5
Graphisme : Peter Dorn, ARAC, FGDC

DONNÉES DE CATALOGAGE AVANT PUBLICATION – CANADA

Melvin Charney, Krzysztof Wodiczko.

Préparé par Diana Nemiroff.

Texte en anglais, en français et en italien.
Bibliographie: p.

ISBN 0-88884-540-5

1. Art moderne – 20e siècle – Canada – Expositions. 2. Art canadien – Expositions. 3. Architecture et société – Canada – Expositions. I. Charney, Melvin. II. Wodiczko, Krzysztof. III. Nemiroff, Diana. IV. Musée des beaux-arts du Canada. V. Biennale di Venezia (42e : 1986). VI. Titre : Canada, Biennale di Venezia, 1986.

N6545 M4 1986 709'.71'0740531
CIP 86-099510-0F

ILLUSTRATIONS DE LA COUVERTURE

Melvin Charney, *« Il vaut mieux qu'ils croient aller à la ferme... »* (détail), 1982

Krzysztof Wodiczko, *Projection de l'édifice du Parlement fédéral de la Suisse* (détail), 1985

Catalogo pubblicato coll'assistenza finanziaria della Divisione per gli affari culturali del Ministero per gli Affari Esteri del Canadà.


STAMPATO IN CANADÀ
ISBN 0-88884-540-5
Disegni: Peter Dorn, RCA, FGDC

COPERTINA

Melvin Charney, *« E' meglio se pensano che stanno andando verso una tenuta agricola... »* (dettaglio), 1982

Krzysztof Wodiczko, *La proiezione del Palazzo del Parlamento nazionale svizzero* (dettaglio), 1985

# Contents



# Sommaire



# Indice

# Preface

The National Gallery of Canada is pleased to participate, for the seventeenth time, in the *Venice Biennale*. This year, Diana Nemiroff, Assistant Curator of Contemporary Art at the Gallery, has chosen Melvin Charney and Krzysztof Wodiczko, two artists with a common ground in architecture, to represent an important aspect of Canadian contemporary art.

Both artists try to situate architecture in space – Charney in a social context and Wodiczko in a bureaucratic and political one. In addition, their artistic comments on "built" things seek to depict the lives of human beings in the urban landscape.

The National Gallery of Canada wishes to thank the artists for their time and attention to the organization of the exhibition and for having conceived their works to fit into the space and location provided. Thanks are also due to the Centre Canadien d'Architecture/Canadian Centre for Architecture, Montréal, and The Ydessa Gallery, Toronto, for their help in providing photographs. As well, we would like to reiterate how much we appreciate the presence in Venice of our "guardian angel," Marietta-Stern Guetta. And we are deeply grateful to Guy Plamondon, Director of the Cultural Affairs Division of the Department of External Affairs, and Yves Pépin, Head of Visual Arts, who contributed generously to this exhibition through financial assistance to permit the active participation of the artists and publication of the catalogue. The efforts of our colleagues and friends at External Affairs have once again made it possible for Canadian contemporary art to be exhibited abroad.

*Joseph Martin*
Director, National Gallery of Canada
and Commissioner for Canada

# Introduction

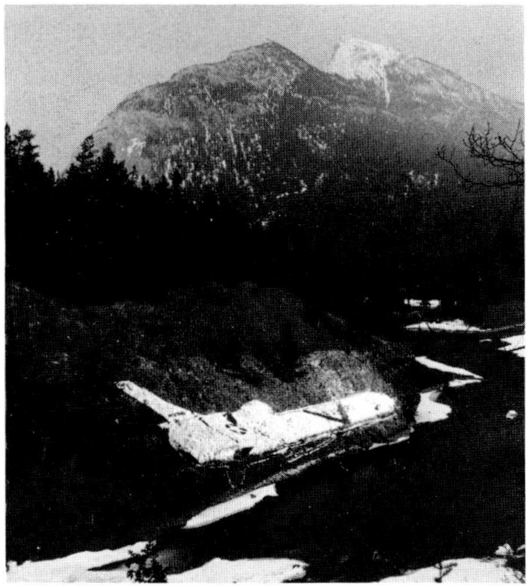

Fig. 1 Krzysztof Wodiczko
*The Bow Falls Projection,*
Banff, Alberta, 1983
The image of a cruise missile was projected on the cliff at Bow Falls

The debate about the role of public art (that is, any art work located outside of museum walls, whether intended to commemorate or decorate) has been renewed recently by the controversy surrounding Richard Serra's *Tilted Arc*, which culminated last summer in the decision to remove it from the plaza in front of the Federal Complex in lower Manhattan. The deeper implications of the debate go well beyond merely procedural questions of what kinds of consultations with the public about the choice and location outdoors of works of art are necessary and appropriate. They bring up the question of whether it is possible now to aspire to a broadly meaningful public art that is also artistically viable. At issue is the failure of modernism to address the problem of art's place in the forum of public discourse.

Yet if works like *Tilted Arc*, austerely uncompromising in their formalist ideals, have withdrawn or are being forced to retreat from the street, the iconographically dogmatic classical monuments that occupy the public squares of our cities are beyond revival. Their death was perhaps symbolized in the nineteenth century by Haussmann's destruction of Parisian working-class neighbourhoods in order to create the broad boulevards that provided distant lines of sight onto Napoleonic monuments such as the Arc de Triomphe. Haussmann approached the city as a void, a blank surface on which to draw the geometrical lines of his boulevards; he cut the monuments off from the organic vitality of the city, turning them into timeless memorials instead of living moments of the past.

A viable public art today will be one that challenges the monument at the same time as it seeks to recognize the intersection of discourses that makes up the reality of the public domain. Perhaps it is inevitable and even necessary, given the fragmented nature of contemporary society, that such a critical, anti-monumental art will be also an impermanent, marginal one.

Fig. 2 Melvin Charney
*A Stuttgart Façade,* 1983
Canvas construction, partially painted
7.6 × 39.4 × .40 m
Installed at Navy Pier, Chicago, for the exhibition *Chicago Sculpture International: Mile 2,* 1983 (Chicago International Art Exposition)
Collection of the artist, Montreal

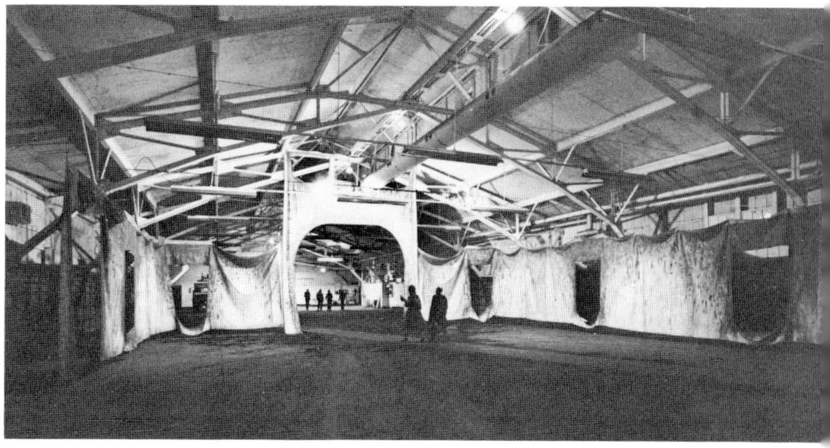

Both Melvin Charney and Krzysztof Wodiczko question the monument; Charney in an effort to recover what has been excluded from representation and Wodiczko in order to reveal what has been concealed. Architecture is the common link; each artist investigates the meanings of architectural language, both overt and symbolic and covert and ideological. As well, each uses existing buildings or monuments as the focus of work that is site-specific and ephemeral.

It is most likely no accident that both Charney and Wodiczko were trained in fields outside of art (art as narrowly defined): Charney in architecture, Wodiczko in industrial design. Neither practice, grounded of necessity in material realities, could afford to be as self-consciously idealist as the fine arts, yet a utopian, technologically-inspired idealism underlies both. Skeptical of this technological utopianism and aware of its social and political limitations, they nonetheless bring to their art habits of mind learned in disciplines with a strong social basis.

Charney "crossed over" into art from architecture at the beginning of the seventies. He is best known for his fragmentary, ghost-like architectural constructions and drawings, which examine how architecture occupies and defines social space. His art, like Wodiczko's, is grounded in certain fundamental ideas about collective experience. This has meant a questioning of the ahistorical bias of the modern movement in architecture. From the position of a minority culture in North America (that of French Canada) he has criticized those internationalist, anti-local premises, which have all but succeeded in effacing the traces of collective memory embedded in urban structures.

Wodiczko left his native Poland in 1977. His work had already begun to deal with systems, from the gallery proper to the larger cultural bureaucracy on which the gallery is founded. He has since become known for his "public projections." These transitory events, which take place at night, consist of images projected upon selected architectural monuments, images devised to unmask the hidden meanings of buildings and to give form to the invisible body of authority they represent. Wodiczko has sought to defend the public as the communal against the public as the private by exposing architecture's subservience to private interests. If architecture is the embodiment of the bureaucratic machine, the projection by contrast is a "communal, aesthetic counter-ritual ... an urban night festival."[1]

Charney and Wodiczko both situate their work in relationship to the social space of the street, affirming its collective rituals in the face of a hypnotic will-to-forget, manifest in the bland architecture of the contemporary city. Where Wodiczko uses humour in his projections to arrest the spectators and startle them into a sharpened recognition of the meanings behind the façades, Charney's ruined constructions and drawings evoke the history the buildings obscure, a history of the forgotten margins of society. Each seeks in his own way to uncover a vital aspect of the unconscious structure of architecture and in so doing reveals the metaphorical dimension of the everyday environment.

*Diana Nemiroff*
Commissioner for the exhibition

1 Krzysztof Wodiczko, "Public Projection," *Canadian Journal of Political and Social Theory* 7, no. 1–2 (Winter/Spring 1983): 186–87.

# Melvin Charney

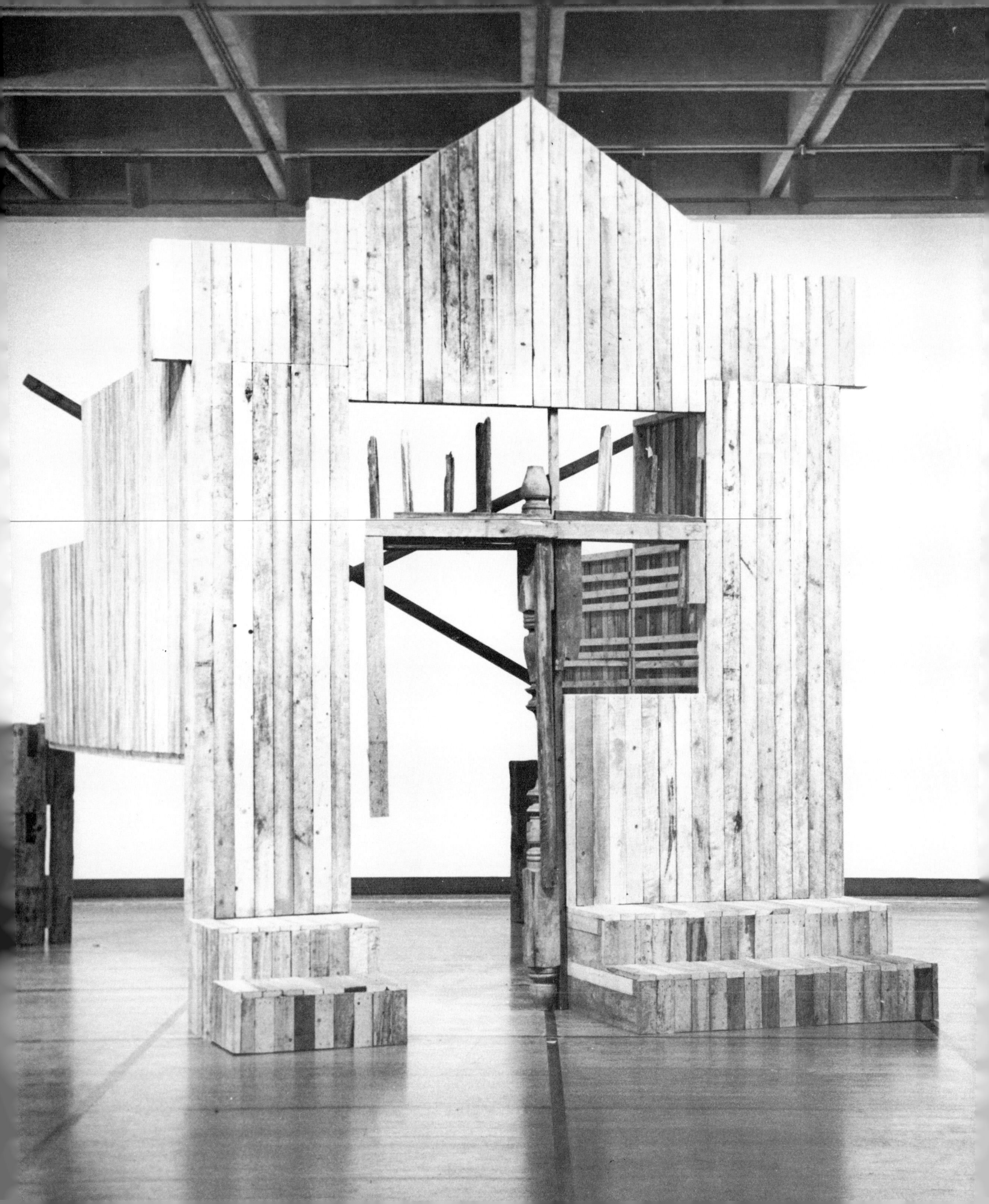

In *Civilization and Its Discontents,* Freud uses an analogy to illustrate his contention that "in mental life nothing which has once been formed can perish – everything is somehow preserved."[1] The image he draws is that of Rome, the Eternal City, in whose present outlines are preserved the traces of its past. "Now let us by a flight of imagination," he invites us, "suppose that Rome is not a human habitation but a psychical entity with a similarly long and copious past – an entity, that is to say, in which nothing that has once come into existence will have passed away and all the earlier phases of development continue to exist alongside the latest one."[2] Later Freud casts aside his metaphor, finding it unsuitable because the city, unlike the mind, is habitually subject to destructive influences such as the demolition and replacement of buildings, which render the traces of its past incomplete and fragmentary.

Yet if it is the city that we seek to know, as it is in the architectural constructions and drawings of Melvin Charney, Freud's metaphor of the city as a psyche with its conscious and half-buried unconscious layers, where primitive past and rational present coexist, is extraordinarily suggestive. Charney's constructions may be seen as a kind of excavation into the city's unconscious. They wilfully provoke a recuperation of forgotten strata of references, correspondences, and figurative allusions from that amnesiac terrain. The constructions constitute a series of diagrammatic disruptions in the landscape. Built of rough materials that recall the scaffolding and wooden forms of construction sites, they are unfinished and deliberately fragmentary in appearance. Most often, they are superimposed upon an existing building or site in order to revivify the history that informed it, thereby releasing through association and allusion a field of symbolic energy.

An early work, *Les Maisons de la rue Sherbrooke* [The Houses of Sherbrooke Street], 1976 (see pl. 2), reveals the richness of these references. Charney selected a ruined urban site common enough in North American cities, an empty lot in downtown Montreal, part of a large tract of land laid waste for re-development. It lay, significantly, at the intersection of two main streets, one of them the major artery and processional thoroughfare when Montreal became an important metropolitan centre, the other leading into the oldest part of the city, ending in a square before the cathedral. At this intersection he erected two full-size façades built of plywood formwork with rough-cut windows and doors, which mirrored the nineteenth-century greystone houses standing on the opposite corner. By this doubling he created a gate-like configuration, which served to formalize the meeting place of the two streets and to call up the figure of an urban square. Yet as mirror images, the façades go beyond historical reconstruction to ritual, the symmetrical repetition of their forms connoting the pleasure of all mimetic gesture.

Braced with tubular scaffolding like a fragment of a false-front street in a Hollywood set, this framework suggested, appropriately, a setting for the collective gestures of a street pageant. In fact, it was part of a parade-like itinerary of artworks, banners, and photographs along an eight-kilometre-length of Sherbrooke Street, which celebrated historically and poetically the life of the street. The exhibition, *Corridart*, had been created for the XXI Olympiad, held that summer in Montreal. But four days before the Games were to open, city crews came at night with orders to demolish this

1 Sigmund Freud, *Civilization and Its Discontents*, trans. Joan Riviere, ed. James Strachey (London: The Hogarth Press and the Institute of Psycho-analysis, 1930; rev. ed., 1963; reprint, 1969), 6.

2 Ibid., 7.

street-museum. Before long the traces of this monumental expression of communal libido, including *Les Maisons de la rue Sherbrooke*, were obliterated.

In the wake of this destruction the elegiac aspect of Charney's façade was revealed. But this reading is no more final than any other. Built in a gap (a tear) in the urban fabric, the appearance of the construction was ambiguous. It was at the same time a building under construction and a building in ruins, a text on urban renewal and destruction, and an artwork existing purely for delight.

Other more recent works, such as *A Toronto Construction*, 1982 (see pls. 8 and 9), and *A Kingston Construction*, 1983 (see pls. 10 and 11), have been built similarly upon vacant or open urban sites, reflecting in relative tranquility upon the theme of a collective memory that is given form in the urban fabric by archetypal architectural figures locally inflected. In these later constructions, however, Charney chose to penetrate the site through layers of reference projected inward from the surrounding buildings in order to turn the site outward again onto the street, as he had done with *Les Maisons*. Each work was unified by a processional axis that allowed the viewer to traverse the rebuilt layers of the site. Though both these constructions were denser and structurally more complex than *Les Maisons* (particularly *A Toronto Construction*), their figuration was more radically abstracted from their surroundings. In each the archetypal form of a small, gabled house (derived from vernacular domestic building) served as a link between the more monumental forms of a rectilinear grid or tower (reflecting the secular/commercial and sacred/ecclesiastical dimensions of the city) and the physical limits of the site.

The abstract vocabulary and the volumetric character of the Toronto and Kingston constructions may be traced back to a group of works that had occupied Charney during the six years following *Les Maisons*, and which involved building out from or directly into existing buildings. In these constructions he was engaged in deciphering the figurative content of several late-modernist buildings (and attempting thereby to restore to these pallid and bureaucratized examples of that style the memory of its heroic period of origin).

In the first of these, *Streetwork*, 1978 (see pl. 3), commissioned by the Art Gallery of Ontario, he built a wall that passed through an existing wall of the building and led from the interior, where it worked as a partition, to the exterior, where it became an arcade. The construction gave material form to the figure of two intersecting planes, a fundamental element in the syntax of building recalled, as it were, through the agency of a Suprematist composition by Malevich (see pl. 4). *Streetwork* realized physically the architectonic origins of Malevich's idealized abstraction, which was derived from a response to the dynamism of built form, and thus had a metaphorical as well as a structural meaning. As well, it breached the closed envelope of the building, denying its desire to exist as an autonomous entity separate from its surroundings, and thrust its contents (inasmuch as the construction was a work made for the museum although refusing to be contained by it) into the space of the street.

After *Edifice*, 1979 (see pl. 5), built in Montreal for the Musée d'art contemporain, and *Room 202*, 1979, created for P.S. 1 in New York, both continuing the ideas of *Streetwork*, Charney began *A Chicago Construction*, 1981–82 (see pls. 6 and 7). Here he proposed a considerably more elaborate analysis of a building, which took in its surroundings and local historical antecedents and integrated these traces with the representation of an abstract, idealized grid symbolic of the industrial landscape. The construction was built out from the façade of the Museum of Contemporary Art in Chicago, creating a layered, palimpsest effect related morphologically to the Toronto and Kingston constructions. Charney's allusions to the architectural history of Chicago were manifold: to the unbuilt tower diagrammed by the massive forms of the two-storey façade; to the structural form of such towers (the screen-wall design of the Chicago-style skyscraper) and to its idealized representation in the square grid; to the rows of pitched roof, gable-end houses that typified the working-class neighbourhoods in the 1920s and whose forms appeared, half-hidden and ornamental, in the truss work of the façade; to the structural necessities of wood-frame construction as reflected in those forms; and to the symbolic function of the façade itself as the place of passage from the building to the street. The construction was an assemblage of fragments meant to recall the sedimentary history of the building; tangibly material yet semi-transparent as in Freud's metaphor, so as to permit the simultaneous reading of the multiple layers.

Charney's most recent construction, built as part of an exhibition of site-specific installations held in an unfinished shopping arcade of a new apartment tower in Montreal, continued his examination of the origins of modern architecture. *From Laugier to Popova: A Construction in Parts*, 1985 (see pls. 21 and 22), reflected upon the trabeated, concrete slab-and-column construction of the contemporary loft building as a modern version of the "primitive hut" envisioned by Laugier and others who sought a generative model of architectural order. Charney outlined the basic elements of this reductive language of building – wall, column, and slab – by partially cladding them in plywood in order to evoke their original framework. Some were then displaced on rails, becoming, as it were, free-floating signifiers, fragments of a language to be manipulated into any configuration at will. The results of this playful deconstruction recalled the skeletal architecture of Popova's theatrical "machines" and, by association, Le Corbusier, whose theory of the house as a "machine for living" placed him in a tradition of utopian rationalism dating back to the eighteenth-century French *philosophes*.

At different points in his career Charney has built constructions relatively independent of a specific site, which come closer to the boundary between sculpture and architecture than is usual in his work. Two of these, *Le Trésor de Trois-Rivières* [The Treasury of Three Rivers], 1975 (see pl. 1), and *Pliny on My Mind No. 1 and No. 2*, 1983 (see pls. 14 and 15), were both built to be part of group exhibitions and housed inside a museum. Each of these works deals with the relationship of the classical and the vernacular in architecture and building, a theme that has served Charney as a vehicle for an exploration of archetypal architectural figures and the processes by which the significance of the built environment is communicated regardless of distinctions of scale and materials.

Found objects from the margins of society, those things usually regarded as crude, inferior, and expendable, have often provided Charney with a source of inspiration. Such an object was a photograph of a worker's shack in the Quebec mill town of Trois-Rivières, which he came across in the course of research on the early industrialization of Quebec. In this house built of inadequate materials he discovered a heroic aspect conveyed through the figural devices buried in its design. Ironically, given its humble construction, the form of the house specifically recalled a Greek treasury. *Le Trésor de Trois-Rivières* drew upon the fundamental ambivalence of the original structure: it was both monument and shack, temple and tomb. Charney's construction was no idealization, however, for it also plainly commemorated through its rudimentary material construction the particular conjunction of economic and social circumstances that produced this modest dwelling place.

In *Pliny on My Mind* Charney addressed the question of origins from a philosophical rather than a historicist point of view. In the context of an exhibition celebrating architectural classisicm in general and the antique villa in particular, he built two constructions. The first, a classical aedicule of post-and-lintel construction, stood at the top of a broad staircase at the entrance to the exhibition, recalling the museum's own ceremonial street entrance. The second, linked to the first by its assembly and its rough materials, was more shed than temple, though like *Le Trésor*, it contained clear echoes of the latter. Here he referred to the structure of the building as part of a city block, a construct seemingly antithetical to the rustic theme of the exhibition.

The scale of the two constructions and their brash though not inelegant materiality clearly expressed the conceptual nature of Charney's project. The classicism they evoked resided in the logic of rationally expressed tectonics. Furthermore, in drawing out the archetypal similarity of the two structures he emphasized their common origin in the need for shelter, a need whose ritual elaboration in architecture produces the material evidence of the social fabric.

An enduring record of otherwise transitory constructions, Charney's drawings have occupied a place throughout his work equal in importance to the constructions. Frequently they have been based on images he has collected of the built environment, images taken from newspapers, postcards, books, and film stills. Here built things are represented as events in everyday life making up the traces of a collective memory. This stock of images plays more than a documentary role in Charney's work. It comprises a mythic stratum out of which he constructs propositions that stand as countermyth, critique, and commentary on architecture as a cultural system.

The relationship between the drawings and the constructions is a fluid one; some drawings may precede, some follow a construction, while others stand as constructs in their own right. Such is a series of drawings on which Charney has been working since 1982, beginning with two proposals for façades to be built in Kassel, West Germany, for the unrealized Documenta-Urbana section of *Documenta 7*. Entitled "*Better if they think they are going to a farm ...*," 1982 (see pls. 12 and 13), the proposals called for the erection of an idealized farm façade in the Bahnhofplatz opposite the railway station or, alternatively, across the tramway tracks on one of Kassel's main streets. Throughout his work Charney has been aware of the double nature of the façade – partly structural, partly sham. The image of the idealized farm façade exhumed from recent German history the sinister deceit created by the SS architects who constructed a similar gateway as a bucolic camouflage for the railway entrance to the death camp at Auschwitz-Birkenau: "Better if they think they are going to a farm ..." This portal connects the present with the past; it is a monument to weeping and remembering, to be erected appropriately enough at a place of arrivals and departures.

After the specifically historical references of the Kassel drawings, Charney moved metaphorically through the gateway to find in the death camps the figure of a spectral city: a necropolis drawn in red and violet, a vision of the will-to-order run riot (see pls. 16–19). "Just imagine," says the innocent General Stumm with dawning realization in Robert Musil's *The Man without Qualities*, "a complete universal order embracing all humanity, in a word, a state of perfect civilian order. Take my word for it, it's sheer entropy, *rigor mortis*, a landscape on the moon, a geometrical plague!"[3] The city in Charney's visionary drawings is built on the model of the camp's barracks, laid out in intersecting rows of narrow buildings, doors open to reveal racks of shelves: cruel spaces for human lives. As in *Le Trésor*, Charney has collapsed into one the figure of the house and that of the mausoleum, recalling Adolf Loos's pronouncement that the ideal work of architecture is the tomb where the libido is finally at rest.

These drawings take to an extreme the logic governing all of Charney's propositions. In his work architecture is viewed as an "inscription by man in space," a text to be read and interpreted. The drawings and constructions dig out the traces of human will embedded in built things, proposing readings that are allusive, shifting, and open. Where the trauma of history has produced blockages, as in the experience of the Holocaust, Charney employs architecture as a key to unlock memory. By expiating the past in this way, the city (like the psyche) is permitted a new beginning. Thus it is not out of melancholy or nostalgia that his works recall the past, but out of a desire to ground the experience of the present in a fully historical sense of human order as expressed in architectural forms. Charney is fundamentally an allegorist, sketching out in materially rough and fragmentary constructions a monumental content.

*D.N.*

3 Robert Musil, *The Man without Qualities*, vol. 2 (London: Picador, 1954; reprint, 1979), 198.

# Biography / Exhibitions / Bibliography

## Biography

Melvin Charney was born in Montreal, Quebec, in 1935. After art studies at the School of Art and Design of the Montreal Museum of Fine Arts, he studied architecture at McGill University, Montreal, and at Yale University. He received his M. Arch. from Yale in 1959. From 1961 to 1964 he lived and worked in New York and Paris. Since 1964 he has lived in Montreal, where he is Professor at the School of Architecture of the University of Montreal. As well as teaching and exhibiting his own work he has also organized two exhibitions that dealt with the social and architectural landscape of the city of Montreal: *Montréal... plus ou moins* (1972) and *Corridart*, produced for the 1976 Olympic Games.

## One-person exhibitions

* indicates exhibition catalogue

1977
Cambridge, Massachusetts, Harvard University*

1978
Toronto, Art Gallery of Ontario

1979
Montreal, Musée d'art contemporain*
Long Island City, New York, Institute for Art and Urban Resources, P.S. 1

1980
Paris and Brussels, Canadian Cultural Centres

1982
Chicago, Museum of Contemporary Art*
Chicago, Richard Gray Gallery
New York, 49th Parallel, Centre for Contemporary Canadian Art

1983
Kingston, Ontario, Agnes Etherington Art Centre*

1985
Lethbridge, Alberta, Southern Alberta Art Gallery

## Major Group Exhibitions

1972
Montreal, The Montreal Museum of Fine Arts, *Montréal... plus ou moins**

1973
Paris, Musée d'art moderne de la ville de Paris, *Canada Trajectoires – '73**
Milan, *Triennale di Milano*, International Section

1975
Montreal, Institut d'art contemporain, circulated by the National Museums of Canada, *Québec 75**

1976
Montreal, Art and Culture Programme, Organizing Committee of the XXI Olympiad, *Corridart*

1977
Montreal, Institut d'art contemporain, 03 23 03*: Premières Rencontres internationales d'art contemporain**

1978
Toronto, A.C.T. Gallery, *Architectural Drawings*

1979
New York, John Weber Gallery, *Invitational IV*
Washington, D.C., Protech-McIntosh Gallery, *Art and Architecture: Space and Structure*

1980
Paris, Centre national d'art et de culture Georges Pompidou, *11e Biennale de Paris**
Los Angeles, Los Angeles Institute for Contemporary Art, *Architectural Sculpture**
Vancouver, Vancouver Art Gallery, *Architectural References**

1981
Quebec, Musée du Québec, *Art–Société/ 1975–1980**

1982
Toronto, Visual Arts Ontario and the Market Gallery of the City of Toronto Archives, *Citysite Sculpture**
Surrey, B.C., Surrey Art Gallery, *Drawings by Contemporary Sculptors**
Berlin, Akademie der Künste, *Canada in Berlin*

1983
Stuttgart, Württembergischer Kunstverein, *Künstler aus Kanada: Räume und Installationen**
Quebec, Musée du Québec, *Collection du gouvernement*
Montreal, Musée d'art contemporain, *Art et Bâtiment*
Chicago, International Art Exposition, *Chicago Sculpture International: Mile 2*
Como, Italy, Galleria Il Salotto, *Rendere visibile*
Montreal, The Montreal Museum of Fine Arts, *The Villas of Pliny and Classical Architecture in Montreal*

1984
Chicago, Museum of Contemporary Art, *Ten Years of Collecting*
Düsseldorf, Architektenkammer Nordrhein-Westfalen Akademie, *Festarchitektur**
Berlin, Internationale Bauausstellung, Martin Gropius Bau, *Idee, Prozess, Ergebnis*
Vancouver, Vancouver Art Gallery, *The Praxis Collection*

1985
Milan, *17ª Triennale di Milano*
Montreal, Musée d'art contemporain, *Vingt Ans de collection*
Quebec, Musée du Québec, *La Collection et l'Art du Québec au XXᵉ siècle*
Montreal, Centre international d'art contemporain, *Aurora Borealis**
Chicago, Museum of Contemporary Art, *Projects for Chicago*
Toronto, Evelyn Aimis Fine Art, *Environmental Concerns*

## Selected Writings on Melvin Charney


Banham, Reyner. *Megastructures – Urban Futures of the Recent Past.* London: Oxford University Press, 1976.

Barber, Bruce. "Architectural Reference: Post-modernism, Primitivism and Parody in the Architectural Image." *Parachute* 21 (Winter 1980): 5–12.

Battisti, Eugenio. "Contro l'International Style." *Casa del Libro* (January 1982): 24–27.

Bernstein, William and Ruth Cawker. "Corridart, Montreal." In *Contemporary Canadian Architecture*. Toronto: Fitzhenry and Whiteside, 1982.

Burkhardt, Lucius. "Melvin Charney." *Werk und Zeit* 4 (April 1981): 26.

Burns, James T. "A Gallant Try: Canadian National Pavilion Design Competition for 1970." *Progressive Architecture* 48, no. 8 (August 1967): 164–65.

Charbonneau, François, Marcel St-Pierre, and Esther Trépanier. "Pratiques artistiques d'opposition à Montréal." In *Art–Société/1975–1980*. Exhibition catalogue. Quebec: Musée du Québec in collaboration with Les Éditions Interventions, 1981.

"Corridart: The House of Sherbrooke Street." *Process: Architecture* 5 (March 1978): 124–27.

Déthier, Jean. "Melvin Charney: Deux Façades, une provocation." In *11ᵉ Biennale de Paris: L'Urbanité*. Exhibition catalogue. Paris, 1980.

Dompierre, Louise and Melvin Charney. *Melvin Charney 1981–1983*. Exhibition catalogue. Kingston, Ontario: Agnes Etherington Art Centre, 1983.

Forster, Kurt W. "Contradiction of Preservation and Destruction." *Architext* (December 1983): 3–5.

Freedman, Adele. "Building Metaphors – Literally." *The Globe and Mail* (Toronto) 13 December 1980.

Goldin, Amy. "Report from Toronto and Montreal." *Art in America* 65, no. 2 (March–April 1977): 35–47.

Grenville, Bruce. "Melvin Charney." *Parachute* 32 (November 1983): 36–37.

Hatch, Heather. *Citysite Sculpture*. Exhibition catalogue. Toronto: Visual Arts Ontario and the Market Gallery of the City of Toronto Archives, 1982.

Hould, Claudette. "Melvin Charney, ou les traces d'une mémoire collective." *Vie des Arts* 24, no. 98 (Spring 1980): 78–79.

Jacob, Mary Jane. *Melvin Charney: A Chicago Construction*. Exhibition catalogue. Chicago: Museum of Contemporary Art, 1982.

Lamoureux, Johanne. "Melvin Charney, ou l'illusion de la preuve." *Parachute* 17 (Winter 1979): 66–67.

Lippard, Lucy. *Architectural Sculpture*. Exhibition catalogue. Los Angeles: Los Angeles Institute for Contemporary Art, 1980.

McConathy, Dale. "Corridart: Instant Archeology in Montreal." *Artscanada* 33, no. 206/207 (July–August 1976): 36–45.

McDougall, Ian and Kathy Peake. "Melvin Charney." *Transition* (Melbourne) 2, no. 2 (June 1981): 7–10.

Merling, Mitchell. "Truth and Architecture." *The Fifth Column* 4, no. 1 (Fall 1983): 5–6.

Needham, Gerald. "Melvin Charney: Constructs and Concepts." *Artscanada* 37, no. 234/235 (April–May 1980): 24–26.

Nixon, Virginia. "Melvin Charney – Architectural Sculpture." *The Canadian Forum* 63, no. 728 (May 1983): 18–19, 41.

Oechslin, Werner. *Festarchitektur*. Exhibition catalogue. Akademie der Architektenkammer Nordrhein-Westfalen. Stuttgart: Verlag Gerd Hatje, 1984.

Osterwold, Tilman and Bruce Ferguson. Interview. In *Künstler aus Kanada: Räume und Installationen*. Exhibition catalogue. Stuttgart: Württembergischer Kunstverein, 1983.

Pagé, Suzanne. "Melvin Charney: quelques monuments nationaux." *Canada Trajectoires – '73*. Exhibition catalogue. Paris: Musée d'art moderne de la ville de Paris, 1973.

Patton, Andrew. "Melvin Charney at the Art Gallery of Ontario." *Artists Review* (Toronto) 13 (April 1978): 12–13.

Pontbriand, Chantal. "Melvin Charney: Entretien avec Melvin Charney." *Parachute* 13 (Winter 1978): 26–30.

____, Normand Thériault, and Thierry de Duve. 03 23 03: *Premières Rencontres internationales d'art contemporain*. Exhibition catalogue. Montreal: Institut d'art contemporain, 1977.

"Progetto canadese per Osaka '70." *L'Architettura* 13, no. 8 (December 1967): 526–28.

"Self-Constructing Exhibition Pavilion." *Design* (London) 231 (March 1968): 54–56.

Shapiro, Babs. *Architectural References*. Exhibition catalogue. Vancouver: Vancouver Art Gallery, 1980.

Thériault, Normand. "Melvin Charney." In *Québec 75*. Exhibition catalogue. Montreal: Institut d'art contemporain, 1975.

Toupin, Gilles. "Charney: L'Architecture archéologique." *La Presse* (Montreal) 10 November 1979.

Tzonis, Alexander. "Un monument contre les massacres et la terreur." *Le Carré bleu* (January 1972): 13–16.

____ and Melvin Charney. *Melvin Charney: Œuvres 1970–1979*. Exhibition catalogue. Montreal: Musée d'art contemporain, 1979.

## Selected Writings by Melvin Charney

"The Grain Elevators Revisited." *Architectural Design* (London) 37, no.7 (July 1967): 328–31.

"A Self-Erecting Exhibition System: Project for the Canadian Pavilion, Osaka Expo '70." *Architecture Canada* 46, no.3 (March 1969): 34–36.

"Experimental Strategies: Notes for Environmental Design." *Perspecta: The Yale Architectural Journal* 12 (March 1969): 21–32. Translated and reprinted in *Deutsche Bauzeitung* 103, no.8 (August 1969): 574–81, and in *Formalism, Realism, Contextualism*, edited by Hajime Yatsuka. Tokyo: Shokokusha Publishing Co., 1979.

"On the Liberation of Architecture: Memo Series on an Airforce Memorial." *Artforum* 9 (May 1971): 34–37.

"Pour une définition de l'architecture au Québec." In *Architecture et urbanisme au Québec*, conférences J.-A. de Sève 13–14. Montreal: Les Presses de l'Université de Montréal, 1971. Translated and reprinted in part in "Towards a Definition of Quebec Architecture." *Progressive Architecture* 53, no. 9 (September 1972): 104–07.

With Serge Carreau and Colin H. Davidson. *The Adequacy and Production of Low Income Housing in Canada*. Ottawa: Canada Mortgage and Housing Corporation, 1972. Excerpts in "Low Income Housing." *Architectural Design* (London) 43, no. 1 (January 1972): 7–8, and in *Montréal... plus ou moins*.

Exhibition catalogue. Montreal: The Montreal Museum of Fine Arts, 1972.

"Quelques monuments nationaux." *Architectural Design* (London) 44, no.4 (April 1974): 241–43.

"Dead End Choices: Housing in Canada." *Architectural Design* (London) 46, no.4 (April 1976): 202–06.

*Melvin Charney: Other Monuments 1970–1976*. Exhibition catalogue. Harvard University, 1977. Reprinted in *Vanguard* 6, no. 2 (March 1977): 3–8.

"Corridart: Melvin Charney on Art as Urban Activism." *Architectural Design* (London) 47, no. 7–8 (July–August 1977): 545–47.

"Modern Movements in French-Canadian Architecture." *Process: Architecture* 5 (March 1978): 15–25.

"Monuments Now: On Contemporary Architecture and the Avant-Garde." In *Avant-Garde: A History of Innovation and Invention in Architecture*, edited by Geert Bekaert. Eindhoven, The Netherlands: University of Technology, 1978.

*Melvin Charney: Œuvres 1970–1979*. Exhibition catalogue. Montreal: Musée d'art contemporain, 1979.

"The Montrealness of Montreal: Formations and Formalities in Urban Architecture." *Architectural Review* 167, no. 999 (May 1980).

"On Architecture: A Statement about Statement." In *Building with Words*, edited by William Bernstein and Ruth Cawker. Toronto: Coach House Press, 1981.

"À qui le droit: au sujet d'architecture contemporaine au Québec." *Architecture/Québec* (January–February 1982): 12–24.

"Of Temples and Sheds." *Architecture/Québec* (October 1983): 11–15.

"Signs of Recognition, Ciphers of Deception." *Parachute* 36 (September–November 1984): 38–42.

"Aus einem Wörterbuch der Architektur ... über 'Clients' und 'Models'." In *Idee, Prozess, Ergebnis*. Berlin: Internationale Bauausstellung, 1984.

# Krzysztof Wodiczko

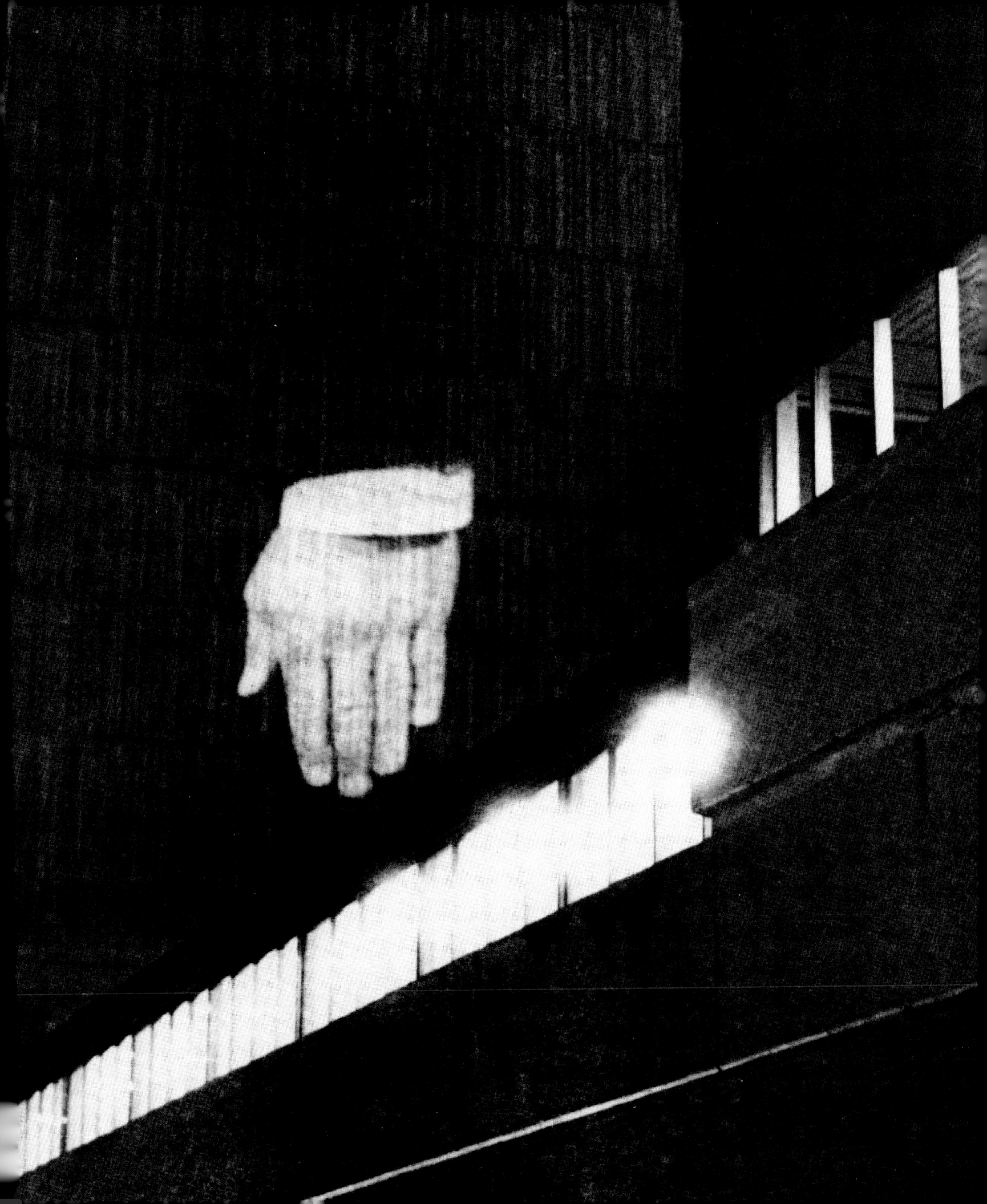

Fig. 3 *Vehicle 1*, Warsaw, 1973

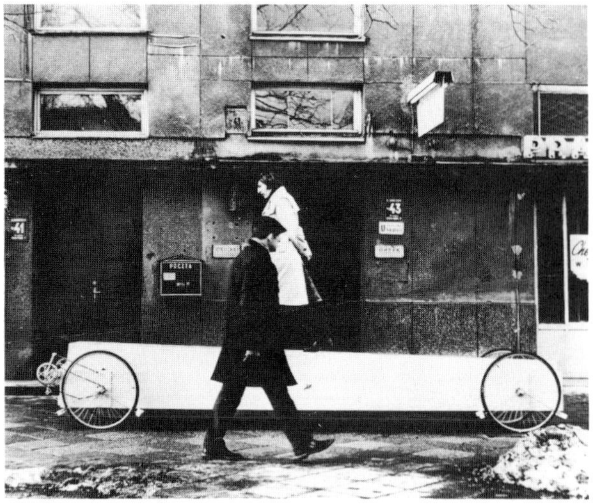

Before us we have three photographs. The first (fig. 3) shows a young man intently walking along the gently inclined surface of an unfamiliar vehicle. The vehicle is long, low, and presumably home-made; slender bicycle wheels at each end and a system of gears and pulleys suggest its means of propulsion. An older man strolling in the opposite direction glances at the vehicle and its driver but otherwise controls his curiosity. The second (fig. 4) is an image from a newspaper, greatly enlarged and drastically cropped. Two men in business suits, one decorated with medals, clasp hands. The free hand of the one loosely cradles the other's arm; behind them the front fender of a waiting car is visible. The gesture, cut loose from its surroundings, takes on weight and suggestiveness, as if we were glimpsing in this fragment the sign of some momentous pact. In the third photograph (fig. 5) a large disembodied eye casts a sidelong gaze from the pediment of the Swiss parliament building. This projected image lends the building a startlingly human mien that undermines the solemn dignity of its neo-classical façade. The building makes a spectacle of itself.

The three photographs, though they depict projects widely separated in time (*Vehicle 1* was made in 1973 when Krzysztof Wodiczko was still living in Poland, whereas the projection in Bern took place in 1985), give evidence of some common links in Wodiczko's work. In each instance there is a disruption of context: a surprising confrontation with the work occurs in a public, urban environment; or a fragment, an image from the media at once banal and politically loaded, is exposed through insertion into the gallery. As well, the body is designated as the privileged site or instrument of the inscription of meaning. In particular, attention is focussed on the act as it is abstracted into symbolic gesture. From the photographs it may be inferred that the works are transitory events, conterminous with their reception. Thus the meaning and purpose of the works are bound up with the address to an audience and with the response of this largely unpredictable factor.

Within this framework Wodiczko has elaborated an analysis of the bureaucratic institutions whereby power is formalized in contemporary society: the state, the military, the financial and cultural establishments. His aim is to unmask and demythify the authority and power concretized by these institutions through subjecting their edifices – the literal, physical body of myth – to a sudden, brief glare of public scrutiny.

Since 1980 his instrument has been the public projection, a large-scale, evanescent montage of image and architecture, conducted outdoors and at night while the everyday functions of the building are suspended. With the aid of powerful Xenon-arc slide projectors, images that speak the unmistakable language of power are beamed onto the sleeping body of a building whose ideological meaning Wodiczko seeks to divest of its mystery. Aroused from the torpor of its static and timeless verity, the building begins to gesticulate and reveals the unconscious fantasies concealed by its façade, like the wearer of that garment in the fairytale, which compels him to act out the naked truth of his desires. This public performance takes place in the street, before an audience that has become, for its duration, a collective body. Formed haphazardly, its response will be heterogeneous, but the audience as a public body, insofar as it is stimulated by the projection to respond consciously and critically to the covert message of the architecture, challenges what Michel Foucault calls, "the great fantasy ... of a social body constituted by the universality of wills."[1] Wodiczko's desire to

1 Michel Foucault, "Body/Power," in *Power/Knowledge: Selected Interviews and Other Writings 1972–1977* (New York: Pantheon Books, 1980), 55.

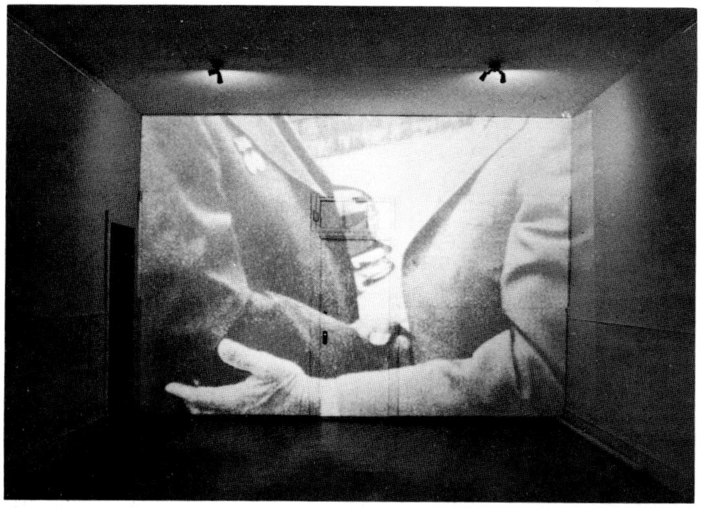

Fig. 4 *Projection* (Leonid Brezhnev and Erich Honecker), Eye Level Gallery, Halifax, Nova Scotia, April 1979

unmask this myth as it is embodied in public buildings by exposing the private interests invested in them follows Foucault's understanding that, "the phenomenon of the social body is the effect not of a consensus but of the materiality of power operating on the very bodies of individuals."[2]

In its strategic use of easily recognizable popular imagery associated with mass media, in its appropriation of non-art contexts, and in its theatricality, Wodiczko's work may be associated with several of the critical strategies of postmodernism. The shaping influence of his life and work as an artist in Poland until 1977 should not be overlooked, however. The relatively independent cultural policy of the Polish state has made it the most liberal in the Eastern Bloc. Since the late fifties the Polish cultural bureaucracy has readily tolerated the most abstruse expressions of modernism; only politics in art is taboo. Yet as Andrzej Ostrowski and Karl Beveridge have observed:

> Most artists in Poland lead a double life.... The necessity of disengaging art from politics is juxtaposed in the day-to-day life of the artist with the necessity to be engaged in official politics through the production of art and design for the state's propaganda system.... On one hand, the state needs to develop effective propaganda to consolidate its power, but it also needs to develop the illusion of cultural freedom as part of the same propaganda.[3]

In sharp contradistinction to the political disablement of the artist in present-day Poland lies the memory of the Russian and Polish Constructivists' aspirations for art as an instrument of social change. Though in the Polish reality it is

2 Ibid.
3 Andrzej Ostrowski (a.k.a. Krzysztof Wodiczko) and Karl Beveridge, "West/East: The Depoliticization of Art," *Fuse* (March 1980): 141.

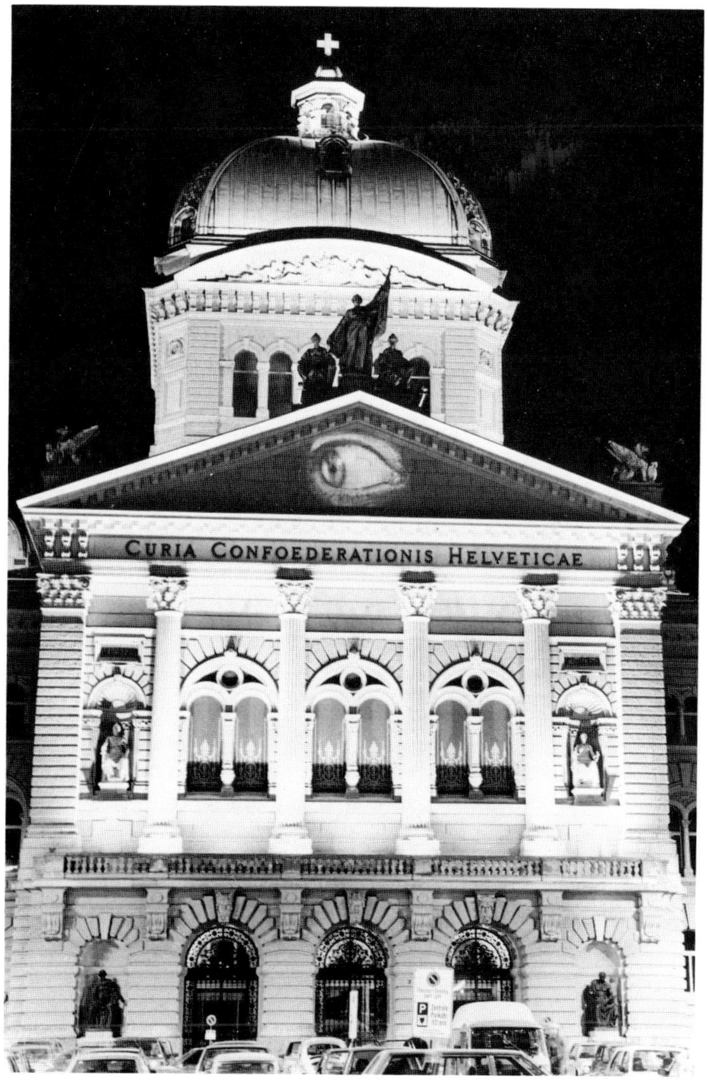


Fig. 5 *The Swiss National Parliament Building Projection,* Bern, Switzerland, 12–14 April 1985

impossible even to dream of these heroic and utopian ideals, some of the strategies of Constructivism were retained and transmitted to Wodiczko and others through their design training. Thus the necessity to think in terms of the total environment combined with their actual political impotence to produce a powerful inducement to elaborate a critique of the policies of the cultural bureaucracy. Yet the danger of a continual state of theoretical opposition in the absence of any imaginable concrete action (a danger all the greater as the ideological apparatus of the state adopts apparently more liberal strategies) lay in the artist's vulnerability to seduction and absorption by bureaucratic reason.

While still in Poland Wodiczko began to respond to this problematic situation with design proposals for several vehicles that could be read as analytical models of the political mechanisms of the state. *Vehicle 1*, 1973, was the only one for which a prototype was built. Made for the exclusive use of the artist, this elegant machine was propelled by the action of the artist walking in an attitude of philosophical contemplation back and forth along the tilting platform. The resulting seesaw movement allowed the energy generated to be transmitted by a system of cables and gears to the wheels. For all the labour expended, however, the vehicle could move in a straight line in one direction only. Other proposals included vehicles for the worker, for a casual assembly of citizens (on the line of a public square), and even for coffee-shop debaters. Though the vehicles varied in the kind of action permitted – from obvious, futile repetition to relative absence of constraint – all were limited to linear, unidirectional motion.

The strategy of these constructions is clearly allegorical, prompted by the need "to speak publicly with hidden meaning as a response to the prohibition of public speech."[4] They inform us obliquely and with a keen sense of irony that the measure of individual freedom lies not only in the degree of movement permitted, but also in the effect of that movement; in the absence of a steering mechanism whereby the state's direction might be influenced, the individual's ability to change his condition is nominal.

Wodiczko subsequently extended his use of allegorical strategies with the introduction of montage in a group of works on line, produced between 1976 and 1978. These works, which proceed from an analytical presentation of the properties of line (line as theory, object, image, and reality) to a tentative exploration of the comparable linear element in gestures in art and propaganda, represent a further attempt to associate art with social and political realities. As transitional works they constitute a point of interrogation of the gallery. Dependent on montage techniques of confiscation, superimposition, and fragmentation common to both political allegory and advertising, they are of interest chiefly for their demonstration of how the structure of one system may be used to give structure to or to translate the structure of another, thereby effecting a transference of meaning.

The lessons learned from this work were transferred to the *Public Projections*, which marked Wodiczko's definitive rupture with the gallery as a structural support for his work. The logic of the movement from gallery space to the public space of the urban architectural environment as a screen for his projections was inherent in his appropriation of the strategy of montage from his avant-garde predecessors of the early twentieth century. As Benjamin Buchloh remarks:

> Even though these activities originated in the socially isolated institution of the "avant-garde" and high art practice, it was an essential feature of these activities from their inception to address those instances of ideological domination at the material site of their function, i.e. within the very system of representation where they occur and exert their power. And it was equally essential that the formal operation within the ideological constructs had to be structured materially ... in ways that guaranteed the work's capacity to re-enter the very same discourse, its circulation form and distribution system.[5]

Consonant with Wodiczko's opposition to the burying of the avant-garde,[6] the *Public Projections* may be viewed as an attempt at a model of a public sphere of production that still remains visible and persuasive as art. The effect of his provocative montage of slide images upon the bodies of public buildings and monuments is to expose the discrepancies between the sensual, material experience of the projection and the normal, "official" language of the architecture as *ruptures* in the mythic fabric of the social body represented by the edifice.

What is the nature of this mythic social body that architecture represents? According to Wodiczko, it is a "disciplined/disciplining body" based on the regulated relationship of the whole to the parts and of each part to the others. Unchanging and universal, its spirit is the spirit of the name of the father, the Law that seduces "by its structural ability to embody ... our intimate, unspoken drive for the disciplined collaboration with its power." The building is not only the physical site of the institutions of power, but is also a "spatial medium for the continuous and simultaneous symbolic re-

4 Benjamin H.D. Buchloh, "Montage and Allegorical Deconstruction," in *Vocation/Vacation*, exhibition catalogue, Walter Phillips Gallery (Banff, Alberta, 1981), unpaginated.

5 Ibid.

6 Krzysztof Wodiczko, "For the De-Incapacitation of the Avant-Garde," *Parallelogramme* 9 (April–May 1984): 22–26.

production of both the general myth of power and of the universal desire for power."[7]

The *Public Projections* deconstruct the myth by making visually concrete the implicit ideology of the building and then superimposing these images upon the myth's very body, that is, at the material site of its function. Suddenly the building is personified. Let us consider briefly several recent projections. On the grey breast of the tall AT & T building in downtown Manhattan (see pl. 31) a hand in a starched cuff makes the American pledge of allegiance: to the democratic ideals of the United States of America, or to its own multinational interests, which have aided in crushing those ideals elsewhere? At the broad base of Place Ville-Marie's cruciform tower in Montreal, seat of the financial operations of The Royal Bank of Canada (and also home to the South African consulate, which rents office space in the tower), a pair of bloodied fists appears (see pl. 34). The political clout of the international banking community and the apartheid policies of the South African government are linked in this single image of violence. The projection interrupts the bland functionalism of the buildings like a commercial message from the sponsor. The form of the projection is similarly fragmentary and its duration brief, but where the commercial's seductive language seeks consent, the projection speaks of private property and private interests in order to arouse recognition and argument.

Similarly, on classical monuments commemorating the timeless glory of past victories he projects images of contemporary military hardware. On the memorial arch at Brooklyn's Grand Army Plaza an American and a Soviet warhead stand joined by a chain and padlock (see pl. 32). The reality of the ideals of justice and freedom connoted by the classical language of the architecture (appropriated by every nation as its own) lies in fact in the deadly locked battle for military superiority waged by the two powers. At the foot of the Duke of York column in London are projected the parading figures of Britain's striking coal miners, while above them the base of the column has been temporarily mobilized by the body of a rolling tank (see pl. 35). Two male hands cross themselves defensively over the bottom of this phallic protrusion, as if the monument sensed its need for protection from present-day unrest and were willing to turn its forces upon domestic fields. By confronting the rhetorical monument with evidence of contemporary realities, the projection exposes the sham of its humanistic idealism and re-centres the focus on the power relations such idealism masks.

Since the *Public Projections* are not merely didactic, however, it is necessary to inquire into their effect as art, particularly their theatrical effect. They operate as spectacular interruptions in the mystifying ritual of architecture: at a selected moment the gaze of the projectors is turned upon a building or monument, and the hypnotized edifice begins its performance. Each interruption, calculated to startle the spectators by its incongruity and unexpectedness, creates an interval, an opening for critical reflection. Thus the projection-as-interruption functions as an alienating mechanism designed to disturb the audience's readiness for empathy with the building by making suddenly visible its ideological foundations.

Wodiczko's use of interruption as a fundamental structuring device invites a consideration of some parallels between the *Public Projections* and Brecht's theory of an epic theatre. Though the effect of each projection is devised in relation to a specific work of architecture, the projections collectively take on the character of an epic narrative. Unlike the dramatic theatre, whose effect depends upon the cumulative

7 Wodiczko, "Public Projection," *Canadian Journal of Political and Social Theory* 7, no. 1–2 (Winter/Spring 1983): 185.

progress of the action, an epic work may be broken up or interrupted, each segment remaining fully capable of life. Walter Benjamin has observed that the result of this process of interruption is to privilege the gesture, hence: "Epic theatre is by definition a gestic theatre."[8] The appropriateness of this observation to the *Public Projections* is obvious: it is literally through gesture that the "journey-in-fiction" of architecture is interrupted and that the conditions for ideological absorption masked by its physical authority are made recognizable. The unmasking that Wodiczko seeks through the humorous incongruity of the montaged gesture may be seen as analogous to the process of alienation (giving the "natural" the force of what is startling) that Brecht thought necessary to all understanding.

One final parallel should be made clear. The public projection is a performance that exposes the apparatus of its production. Not only are the projectors and wiring clearly on view, but Wodiczko himself appears working with the apparatus and available to participate in debate. This relaxed atmosphere extends to the spectators, who are free to discuss the events and come and go as they please. In contrast to dramatic narrative (in contemporary terms best represented by the entertainment film), Wodiczko's epic narrative substitutes realism of production for realism of representation. Not only is the artist's role demystified through this interaction, but the work of art is redefined as the site of an exchange that is dialectical, rather than economic in nature. Thus the narration of the projection fuses with its reception to create a critical model for the reintegration of art into social life.

*D.N.*

8 Walter Benjamin, "What is Epic Theater?" in *Illuminations* (New York: Shocken Books, 1969), 151.

# Biography / Projections / Exhibitions / Bibliography

## Biography

Krzysztof Wodiczko was born in Warsaw, Poland, in 1943. He studied art and design at the Academy of Fine Arts in Warsaw, receiving an MFA in Industrial Design in 1968. From 1968 until 1977 he worked as an industrial designer and taught at Warsaw Polytechnic. In 1975 he was invited to be artist-in-residence at the University of Illinois, followed in 1976 by a similar invitation from the alternative gallery A Space in Toronto. Wodiczko immigrated to Canada in 1977, teaching first at the University of Guelph, Ontario, and later at the Ontario College of Art, Toronto, the Nova Scotia College of Art and Design, Halifax, and Trent University, Peterborough, Ontario. Since 1983 Wodiczko has divided his time between New York, where he teaches at the New York Institute of Technology, and Canada, where he continues to teach at the Nova Scotia College of Art and Design. He became a Canadian citizen in 1984. Wodiczko is represented by The Ydessa Gallery, Toronto, and by the Hal Bromm Gallery, New York.

## Public Projections

1980
Toronto, University of Toronto, Power Plant
Toronto, Toronto subway

1981
Boston, Massachusetts Institute of Technology
Halifax, Nova Scotia, Dalhousie University, School of Architecture
Halifax, Nova Scotia, Nova Scotia Power Corporation Plant
Halifax, Nova Scotia, Scotia Square Towers
Peterborough, Ontario, City Hall
Toronto, Art Gallery of Ontario

1982
Adelaide, Australia, War Memorial
Adelaide, Australia, Festival Centre Complex
Sydney, Art Gallery of New South Wales
Sydney, MLC (Mutual Life and Citizens Assurance Company) Centre Tower
Sydney, Qantas International Centre
Sydney, American Express Building (in conjunction with the *Sydney Biennale*

1983
Banff, Alberta, Bow Falls, projection on cliff
Dayton, Ohio, Memorial Hall
Dayton, Ohio, Old Courthouse
Dayton, Ohio, Community College Complex
Regina, Museum of Natural History
Stuttgart, Main train station
Stuttgart, Victory Column
Toronto, South African War Memorial (concurrent with The Ydessa Gallery exhibition)

1984
Columbus, Ohio, International Conference of Humanities on George Orwell's *1984*
London, Ontario, Federal Courthouse
New York, *Completing Façades*, projections on Washington Memorial Arch, Washington Square, and AT & T Building
New York, Tower Gallery (in conjunction with *Body Politic* exhibition)
New York, The Astor Building/New Museum (in conjunction with the exhibitions *On View* and *Difference: Representation and Sexuality*)
Seattle, Washington, Seattle Art Museum

1985
Brooklyn, Grand Army Plaza, Memorial Arch
Bern, Switzerland, Parliament Building
Montreal, Place Ville-Marie, Royal Bank of Canada (in conjunction with *Aurora Borealis* exhibition)
Purchase, New York, State University of New York, Performing Arts Center
Halifax, Nova Scotia, Grand Parade War Memorial
London, Trafalgar Square, Nelson's Column
London, Waterloo Place, Duke of York Column
Derry, Northern Ireland, Guildhall

## One-Person Exhibitions

* indicates exhibition catalogue

1970, 1972
Warsaw, Gallery Wspolczesna

1973, 1975, 1976
Warsaw, Gallery Akumulatory 2

1973, 1974, 1975, 1976, 1977
Warsaw, Gallery Foksal

1975
Chicago, NAME Gallery
Urbana, Illinois, University of Illinois

1976
Lund, Sweden, Gallery St. Petri
Montreal, Véhicule

1976, 1977
Toronto, A Space

1977
New York, P.S. 1
Toronto, York University

1977, 1979, 1981
Halifax, Nova Scotia, Eye Level Gallery

1977, 1978, 1980, 1984
New York, Hal Bromm Gallery

1978
New York, Artists Space

1979
Montreal, Optica
Toronto, Gallery 76

1981
Charlottetown, Prince Edward Island, Great George Street Gallery
New York, Franklin Furnace
Peterborough, Ontario, Artspace

1982
Adelaide, Australia, Gallery of the South Australian College of Advanced Education*

1983, 1985
Toronto, The Ydessa Gallery

1985
Purchase, New York, State University of New York, Neuberger Museum
London, Canada House
Oshawa, Ontario, Robert McLaughlin Gallery
Derry, Northern Ireland, Orchard Gallery
Halifax, Nova Scotia, Nova Scotia College of Art and Design, Anna Leonowens Gallery*

## Major Group Exhibitions

1969, 1975
Paris, *Biennale de Paris*

1977
Kassel, Federal Republic of Germany, *Documenta 6*

1979
Lisbon, *Drawing Biennal*
Rome, Museum of Rome, *Polish Avant-Garde*

1979, 1982
Sydney, *Sydney Biennale*

1981
Vienna, Erweiterte Fotografie, *5 Biennial*

1983
Paris, Centre national d'art et de culture Georges Pompidou, *Présence polonaise*
Stuttgart, Württembergischer Kunstverein, *Künstler aus Kanada: Räume und Installationen**
Banff, Alberta, Walter Phillips Gallery, *Social Space*

1984
New York, Tower Gallery, *Body Politic*
Seattle, Washington, COCA (Center on Contemporary Art), *Public Comments*
New York, 49th Parallel, Centre for Contemporary Canadian Art, *New York/ Canada*

1985
New York, *Eastern Europeans in New York*
Montreal, *Aurora Borealis**
São Paulo, Brazil, *São Paulo Biennal*
Bern, Switzerland, Kunstmuseum, *Alles und Noch Viel Mehr**

## Selected Writings on Krzysztof Wodiczko

*Alles und Noch Viel Mehr: das poetische ABC*. Exhibition catalogue. Bern, Switzerland: Benteli, 1985.

Borsa, Joan. "Krzysztof Wodiczko: Power and Ideology." *Vanguard* 12 (November 1983): 14–17.

Coutts-Smith, Kenneth. "Vehicles: Krzysztof Wodiczko at Optica, Montreal, and Eye Level, Halifax." *Artists Review* (Toronto) 2 (April 1979): 2–4.

Fleming, Martha. "Künstler aus Kanada." *Artforum* 22 (Fall 1983): 81–82.

Horne, Stephen. "Krzysztof Wodiczko: Grand Parade Memorial Projection." *Vanguard* 14 (November 1985): 30.

Hume, Christopher. "Not Your Average Slide Show." *Toronto Star*, 16 April 1983.

Maxwell, Ailsa. *Poetics of Authority: Krzysztof Wodiczko*. Exhibition catalogue. Adelaide, Australia: South Australian College of Advanced Education, 1982.

Monk, Philip. "Künstler aus Kanada." *Parachute* 31 (June, July, August 1983): 46–47.

____. "Krzysztof Wodiczko." *Parachute* 32 (September, October, November 1983): 45–46.

Nemiroff, Diana. "Identity and Difference: Canadians at Stuttgart." *Vanguard* 12 (Summer 1983): 18–21.

Osterwold, Tilman and Bruce Ferguson. Interview. In *Künstler aus Kanada: Räume und Installationen*. Exhibition catalogue. Stuttgart: Württembergischer Kunstverein, 1983.

"Unmasking Monuments: Krzysztof Wodiczko." *Section a* 2 (February–March 1984): 2.

## Selected Writings by Krzysztof Wodiczko

Ostrowski, Andrzej (a.k.a. Krzysztof Wodiczko) and Karl Beveridge. "West/East: The Depoliticization of Art." *Fuse* (March 1980): 140–43.

"Public Projection." *Canadian Journal of Political and Social Theory/Revue canadienne de théorie politique et sociale* 7, no. 1–2 (Winter/Spring 1983): 185–87.

"For the De-Incapacitation of the Avant-Garde." *Parallelogramme* (Toronto) 9, no. 4 (April–May 1984): 22–26.

"The Wall." *Krzysztof Wodiczko Public Projection*. Exhibition leaflet. Halifax, Nova Scotia: Nova Scotia College of Art and Design, Anna Leonowens Gallery, 1985.

# Préface

Le Musée des beaux-arts du Canada est heureux de participer pour la dix-septième fois à la *Biennale* de Venise. Cette année, Diana Nemiroff, conservatrice adjointe de l'art contemporain au Musée, a choisi pour représenter un aspect important de l'art contemporain canadien deux artistes liés l'un à l'autre par l'architecture. Le premier est Melvin Charney et le second, Krzysztof Wodiczko.

Tous les deux essaient de situer l'architecture dans l'espace. Charney essaie de le faire dans l'espace social et Wodiczko dans le contexte bureaucratique et politique. Dans chaque cas, la critique du « bâti » cherche à révéler la vie des êtres humains dans le paysage urbain.

Le Musée des beaux-arts du Canada tient à remercier les artistes, qui se sont dépensés généreusement lors de l'organisation de l'exposition, et qui ont conçu la présentation de leurs œuvres en fonction de l'espace et du lieu qui leur étaient fournis. Le Centre Canadien d'Architecture/Canadian Centre for Architecture de Montréal et The Ydessa Gallery de Toronto ont également droit à notre reconnaissance pour avoir aidé à rassembler la documentation photographique de cet ouvrage. Nous disons de nouveau à Marietta Stern-Guetta, fidèle gardienne du pavillon canadien, combien sa présence à Venise nous est précieuse. Nous exprimons notre vive gratitude à Guy Plamondon, directeur des Affaires culturelles au ministère des Affaires extérieures du Canada, et au chef des Arts visuels, Yves Pépin, qui ont contribué généreusement à l'organisation de cette exposition en aidant financièrement à la participation active des artistes et à la publication du catalogue. Les efforts de nos collègues et amis des Affaires extérieures rendent de nouveau possible la présence, à l'étranger, de l'art canadien contemporain.

*Joseph Martin*
Directeur du Musée des beaux-arts du Canada
et commissaire du Canada

# Introduction

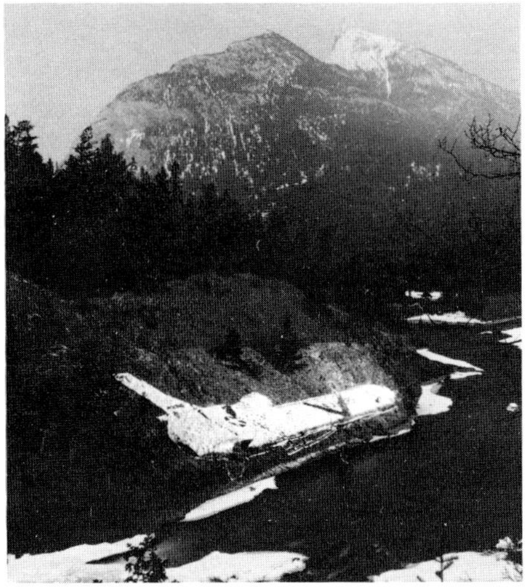

Fig. 1 Krzysztof Wodiczko
*Projection des chutes de la rivière Bow*,
Banff (Alberta), 1983
On a projeté l'image d'un missile Cruise sur la falaise des chutes de la Bow.

La controverse qui a fait rage à propos de *Tilted Arc*, par Richard Serra, et qui a entraîné l'été dernier son retrait de la devanture du complexe fédéral du centre de Manhattan, a relancé le débat sur le rôle de l'art public (c'est-à-dire de toute œuvre d'art commémorative ou décorative exposée hors des musées). Dans ce débat, il ne s'agit pas simplement de déterminer les mécanismes de consultation publique relativement au choix et à la localisation des œuvres d'art devant être exposées hors des musées. En fait, il faut se demander si d'ores et déjà on peut tendre vers un art public à la fois signifiant pour la majorité et viable sur le plan artistique. L'échec du modernisme, qui n'a pas su aborder la question de la place de l'art sur la tribune publique, demeure au centre du débat.

Néanmoins si des œuvres comme *Tilted Arc*, dont le style est sans concessions, ont disparu des rues ou en sont chassées, les monuments classiques à l'iconographie dogmatique qui occupent les places publiques de nos villes ne risquent pas de réapparaître. Leur mort a peut-être été symbolisée au siècle dernier par la démolition, sur les ordres du baron Haussmann, d'un grand nombre de taudis parisiens, en vue de percer les grands boulevards qui accédaient à des monuments commémoratifs de la grandeur napoléonienne, comme l'arc de triomphe par exemple. Haussmann considérait la ville comme un espace vierge, vide, où il pouvait dessiner les lignes géométriques de ses boulevards; il coupa les monuments de la vie organique de Paris, leur donnant un caractère intemporel au lieu d'en faire des souvenirs vivants du passé.

L'art public de notre temps sera viable, pour sa part, s'il se fait antimonumental et s'il cherche en même temps à reconnaître les points de recoupement des idées sous-jacents à la réalité du domaine public. Il est peut-être inévitable, et même nécessaire, étant donné la nature fragmentaire de la société contemporaine, qu'un tel art, critique et antimonumental, s'avère également provisoire et marginal.

Melvin Charney et Krzysztof Wodiczko s'interrogent tous deux sur les monuments, Charney pour retrouver ce qui a été exclu de la représentation, et Wodiczko pour révéler ce qui en a été caché. L'architecture est le dénominateur commun; chaque artiste étudie les significations, tant déclarées et symboliques que voilées et idéologiques, du langage architectural. De même, chacun vise des édifices ou des monuments existants par sa présentation d'une œuvre éphémère et particulière à un lieu.

Le fait que Melvin Charney et Krzysztof Wodiczko aient tous deux été formés dans des disciplines autres que l'art (tel qu'on le définit au sens strict), le premier en architecture et le second en design industriel, ne tient sans doute pas du hasard. Ni l'une ni l'autre de ces spécialités, fortement ancrées dans le réel, ne peut se permettre l'idéalisme plus ou moins affecté des beaux-arts, et pourtant un idéalisme utopique inspiré par la technologie est à la base de l'une et de l'autre. Sceptiques face à cet utopisme technologique et conscients de ses limites sur les plans social et politique, Charney et Wodiczko conservent néanmoins dans leur art des formes de pensée acquises dans des disciplines à forte assise sociale.

Charney est passé de l'architecture à l'art au début des années soixante-dix. Il est surtout connu pour ses constructions et ses dessins architecturaux fragmentaires et fantomatiques, qui étudient comment l'architecture occupe et définit l'espace social. Son art, comme celui de Wodiczko, est fondé sur certaines idées fondamentales concernant l'expérience collective. Ceci l'a amené à remettre en question le préjugé ahistorique du modernisme en architecture. Épousant le point de vue d'une culture minoritaire en Amérique du Nord (celle du Canada français), il a critiqué les prémisses internationalistes et antilocales qui ont presque réussi à effacer les traces de la mémoire collective fixées dans les structures urbaines.

Wodiczko a quitté sa Pologne natale en 1977. Déjà, son œuvre avait commencé à traiter les systèmes, tant ceux du musée même que ceux de la bureaucratie culturelle dont dépend ce dernier. Maintenant, il est surtout connu par ses « projections publiques ». Ces manifestations transitoires, qui ont lieu de nuit, consistent en projections d'images sur des monuments architecturaux choisis, les images étant conçues de façon à dévoiler les significations cachées des édifices et à donner forme à l'invisible autorité qu'ils représentent. Wodiczko a essayé de défendre le public-collectivité contre le public-privé en dénonçant l'asservissement de l'architecture aux intérêts privés. Si l'architecture est l'incarnation de la machine bureaucratique, la projection est, par contraste, « un contre-rite communautaire et esthétique... une fête de nuit urbaine[1] ».

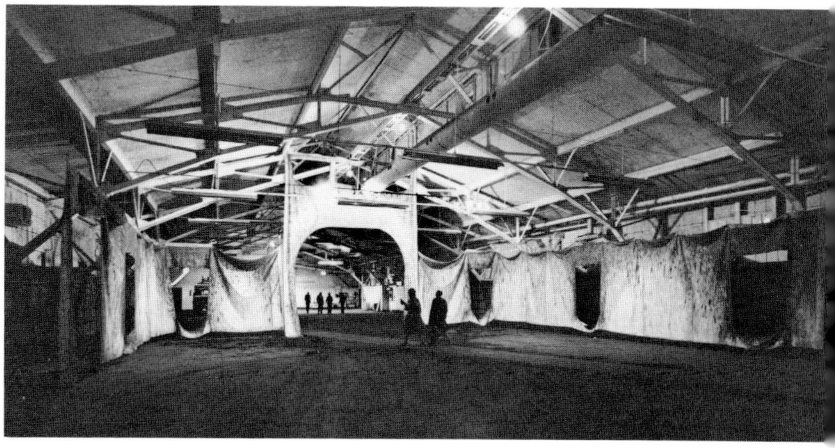

Fig. 2 Melvin Charney
*Une façade de Stuttgart*, 1983
Construction en toile, partiellement peinte
7,6 × 39,4 × 0,4 m
Œuvre installée à l'embarcadère de la Marine, à Chicago, dans le cadre de l'exposition *Chicago Sculpture International : Mile 2*, 1983 (Chicago International Art Exposition)
Collection de l'artiste, Montréal

Charney et Wodiczko situent leur œuvre par rapport à l'espace social de la rue, affirmant ses rites collectifs devant une volonté d'oublier hypnotique, manifeste dans l'architecture insipide de la ville contemporaine.

Tandis que Wodiczko se sert de l'humour dans ses projections pour captiver les spectateurs et les étonner afin qu'ils perçoivent mieux les significations masquées par les façades, les constructions en ruines et les dessins de Charney évoquent l'histoire que les édifices ont voilée, l'histoire d'un groupe marginal oublié de la société. Chacun à leur manière, les deux artistes cherchent à révéler un aspect essentiel de la structure inconsciente de l'architecture et, du même coup, à mettre en lumière la dimension métaphorique de notre milieu quotidien.

*Diana Nemiroff*
Commissaire de l'exposition

1 Krzysztof Wodiczko, « Public Projection », *Revue canadienne de théorie politique et sociale,* vol. 7, n° 1–2 (hiver/printemps 1983), p. 186–187.

# Melvin Charney

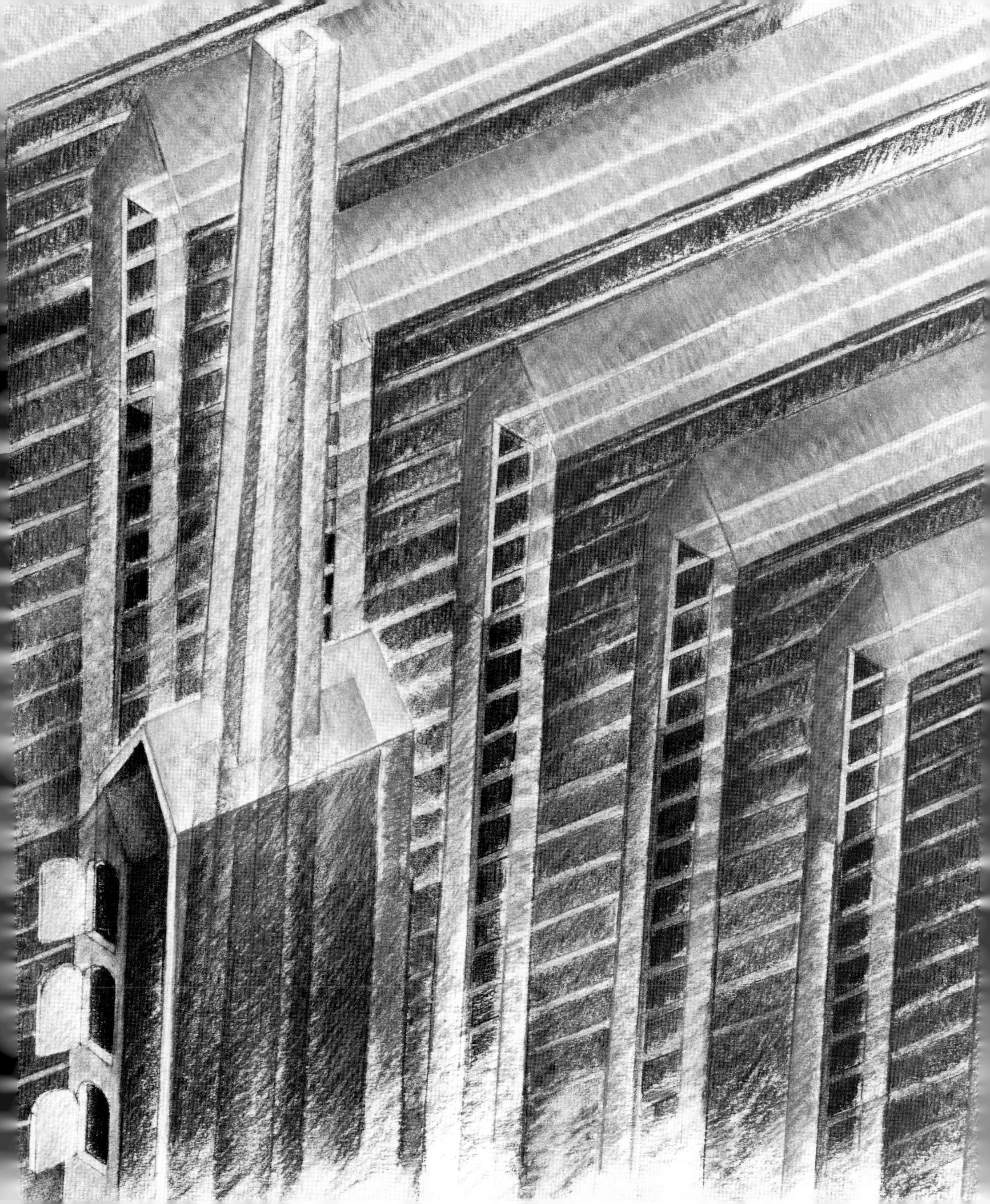

Dans *Malaise dans la civilisation*, Freud affirme que « rien dans la vie psychique ne peut se perdre [...], tout est conservé d'une façon quelconque[1] », et illustre cette assertion au moyen d'une analogie. Il compare l'âme humaine à Rome, la Ville éternelle dont la configuration actuelle porte les traces visibles du passé. « Imaginons », dit Freud, « qu'elle ne soit point un lieu d'habitation humaine, mais un être psychique au passé aussi riche et aussi lointain, où rien de ce qui s'est une fois produit ne se serait perdu, et où toutes les phases récentes de son développement subsisteraient encore à côté des anciennes[2]. » Par la suite, Freud écarte cette métaphore, qu'il juge inadéquate, car la ville, contrairement à l'esprit, est habituellement soumise à des influences destructrices, ses édifices étant démolis pour être remplacés par d'autres, de sorte que le passé n'y laisse que des traces incomplètes et fragmentaires.

Cependant, si c'est la ville que nous cherchons à connaître, comme c'est le cas pour les constructions et les dessins d'architecture de Melvin Charney, la métaphore de Freud s'avère fort évocatoire quand elle assimile la ville à la psyché, avec ses couches inconscientes à demi enfouies, où le passé primitif coexiste avec le présent rationnel. Les constructions de Charney peuvent en quelque sorte être perçues comme fouillant l'inconscient de la ville. Elles provoquent une quête délibérée des couches de références, des correspondances et des allusions figurées oubliées dans ce terrain amnésique où elles constituent une série d'interruptions schématiques. Constituées de matériaux grossiers qui rappellent les échafaudages et les coffrages en bois des chantiers de construction, elles sont inachevées et offrent volontairement un aspect fragmentaire. Le plus souvent, elles viennent s'ajouter à un édifice ou à un terrain existant pour revivifier l'histoire dont elles sont issues et libérer du même coup un champ d'énergie symbolique par un jeu d'associations et de renvois.

La richesse de ces références s'est manifestée dans une des premières œuvres de Charney, *Les Maisons de la rue Sherbrooke* (voir pl. 2), de 1976. Charney sélectionna un emplacement dévasté comme on en voit partout dans les villes nord-américaines, un grand terrain désolé au centre-ville de Montréal, parcelle d'une grande bande de terrain rasée en vue d'un réaménagement. Fait à relever cependant, ce terrain était situé à l'intersection de deux rues principales, dont l'une fut une grande artère et servit de parcours d'honneur à l'époque où Montréal devenait métropole, tandis que l'autre menait dans la plus vieille partie de la ville, débouchant sur une place devant la cathédrale. À cette intersection, Charney érigea deux façades grandeur nature en contre-plaqué, qui étaient des répliques des maisons de briques grises du XIX^e siècle situées en face, et dans lesquelles il perça des portes et des fenêtres grossières. Ce dédoublement créait un effet de portail qui donnait un caractère solennel au point de rencontre des deux rues, et évoquait une place publique. Cependant, comme les images reflétées dans les miroirs, les façades dépassaient la reconstitution historique pour atteindre au rituel; le caractère répétitif symétrique de leurs formes connotait le plaisir que procure tout geste mimétique.

Soutenue par un échafaudage tubulaire comme un décor de film western, cette structure faisait songer opportunément à la scène d'un spectacle de rue collectif. En fait, elle faisait partie d'une fête mettant en scène, sur plus de huit kilomètres le long de la rue Sherbrooke, un véritable défilé d'œuvres d'art, de bannières et de photographies pour célébrer poétiquement et historiquement la vie de la rue. Cette manifestation artistique intitulée *Corridart* précédait l'ou-

1 Sigmund Freud, *Malaise dans la civilisation*, trad. par Ch. et J. Odier, Presses universitaires de France, Paris, 1971, p. 11.

2 *Ibid.*, p. 13

verture imminente des Jeux de la XXI^e Olympiade, accueillis cette année-là par Montréal, mais, quatre jours avant leur inauguration, des équipes d'ouvriers de la ville vinrent nuitamment démolir cette rue-musée. Bientôt, il ne restait pratiquement aucune trace de cette expression monumentale de libido collective dont faisait partie *Les Maisons de la rue Sherbrooke*.

Au lendemain d'une telle destruction, les façades de Charney faisaient figure d'élégie. Cette interprétation n'est pas plus définitive que les autres. Construite dans une trouée du tissu urbain (une déchirure), la structure avait un aspect indéfini. C'était à la fois un édifice en construction et une ruine; une réflexion concrète sur le renouveau et la destruction des villes, et une œuvre d'art sans autre finalité que la pure jouissance.

D'autres œuvres plus récentes, comme *Une construction de Toronto* (voir pl. 8–9), de 1982, et *Une construction de Kingston* (voir pl. 10–11), de 1983, ont également été construites sur des terrains vagues ou dégagés et constituaient une réflexion dans une atmosphère de calme relatif sur le thème d'une mémoire collective que l'artiste façonne dans le paysage urbain en infléchissant localement les archétypes architecturaux. Avec ces dernières constructions, Charney choisit d'investir le terrain en projetant des couches de références vers l'intérieur à partir des édifices adjacents, pour pouvoir ensuite tourner le terrain de l'intérieur vers la rue, comme il l'avait fait pour *Les Maisons de la rue Sherbrooke*. Chaque construction était unifiée par un axe processionnel qui permettait aux spectateurs de franchir les couches reconstituées de l'emplacement. Quoique ces constructions aient été de plus grande envergure et d'une organisation plus complexe que *Les Maisons de la rue Sherbrooke* (particulièrement *Une construction de Toronto*), elles faisaient plus radicalement abstraction de leur entourage. On remarque dans les deux œuvres la forme archétype d'une petite maison à pignons, réminiscence des habitations populaires, qui fait le lien entre les formes plus monumentales d'une grille ou d'une tour rectiligne (correspondant au caractère profane/commercial et sacré/ecclésiastique de la ville) et les limites réelles du terrain.

Le vocabulaire abstrait et le caractère volumétrique des constructions de Toronto et de Kingston peuvent être rapprochés d'un groupe d'œuvres réalisé par Charney dans les six années qui suivirent *Les Maisons de la rue Sherbrooke*, ouvrages construits à l'intérieur d'édifices existants ou s'y greffant. Avec ces constructions, Charney s'efforçait de déchiffrer les figures que recèlent les édifices modernes récents (tentant du même coup de restituer à ces pâles rejetons bureaucratisés du modernisme le souvenir de la période héroïque de ce style).

Pour la première de ces œuvres, *Streetwork* (voir pl. 3), de 1978, conçue et réalisée pour le Musée des beaux-arts de l'Ontario, il construisit une paroi traversant un mur de l'édifice, et faisant figure de cloison à l'intérieur de celui-ci et d'arcade à l'extérieur. La construction concrétisait la figure formée par l'intersection de deux plans, un élément fondamental dans la syntaxe de l'édifice, dont une composition suprématiste de Malevitch lui avait laissé le souvenir (voir pl. 4). *Streetwork* rendait concrètement les origines architectoniques de l'abstraction idéalisée de Malevitch, conçue en réaction au dynamisme des formes bâties, et revêtait par conséquent une signification à la fois métaphorique et structurale. De plus, elle brisait la coquille de l'édifice, lui refusant la possibilité d'exister indépendamment de son voisinage, et projetait son contenu dans la rue (dans la mesure où la construction était réalisée expressément pour le musée mais refusait de s'y cloîtrer).

Après *Édifice* (voir pl. 5), de 1979, construit à Montréal pour le Musée d'art contemporain, et *Pièce 202* de 1979, pour P.S. 1 à New York, qui reprenaient la réflexion amorcée avec *Streetwork*, Charney entreprit *Une construction de Chicago* (voir pl. 6–7) en 1981–1982. Avec cette œuvre, il proposait une analyse beaucoup plus poussée d'un édifice, intégrant l'espace environnant et ses antécédents historiques locaux pour les incorporer avec la représentation d'un de ces cadres abstraits et idéalisés qui symbolisent le paysage industriel. La construction, qui se greffait sur la façade du Museum of Contemporary Art à Chicago, créait un effet de stratification, de palimpseste, la reliant morphologiquement aux constructions de Toronto et de Kingston. Les références de Charney à l'histoire architecturale de Chicago étaient multiples : la tour inexistante suggérée par le coffrage massif de la façade à deux étages; l'ossature de ce type de tour (le murécran des gratte-ciel retrouvés à Chicago) et sa représentation idéalisée dans le quadrillage; les rangées de maisons à pignons, typiques des quartiers ouvriers de Chicago au début du XX^e siècle et dont la forme transparaît, à demi cachée et ornementale, dans les fermes de la façade; les contraintes structurales des constructions à ossature de bois illustrées par ces formes; et enfin, le rôle symbolique de la façade elle-même comme lieu de transition entre l'édifice et la rue. La construction était un assemblage de fragments destiné à évoquer l'histoire sédimentaire de l'édifice, tangible mais à demi transparente, comme dans la métaphore de Freud, afin de permettre une lecture simultanée des différentes couches.

La construction la plus récente de Charney a été créée dans le cadre d'une exposition d'installations conçues en fonction de l'espace environnant, en l'occurrence un centre commercial inachevé dans une nouvelle tour d'habitation à Montréal; avec cette œuvre, l'artiste continuait sa réflexion sur les origines du modernisme en architecture. *De Laugier à Popova : Une construction en parties* (voir pl. 21–22) réalisée en 1985, méditait sur l'architecture à piliers et à dalles de béton de l'immeuble commercial contemporain, considéré comme la version moderne de la hutte primitive envisagée par Laugier et d'autres, qui cherchaient un archétype de l'évolution architecturale. Charney souligna les éléments fondamentaux de ce lexique réduit de la construction – mur, pilier et dalle – en les revêtant partiellement de contreplaqué, de façon à évoquer leur charpente originelle. Certains des éléments furent ensuite montés sur rails coulissants, devenant de ce fait des signifiants mobiles, fragments d'un langage dont la forme variait à volonté. Cette déconstruction badine évoquait l'architecture squelettique des machines de théâtre de Popova et, par association, Le Corbusier, qui, avec son concept de la maison envisagée comme « machine à habiter », se situait dans la tradition du rationalisme utopique des philosophes français du XVIIIe siècle.

À différentes étapes de sa carrière, Charney a réalisé des constructions relativement indépendantes du milieu et se rapprochant d'une manière inusitée dans son œuvre, de la frontière qui sépare la sculpture de l'architecture. Deux d'entre elles, *Le Trésor de Trois-Rivières* (voir pl. 1), de 1975, et *Pline en tête n^o^ 1 et n^o^ 2* (voir pl. 14–15), de 1983, sont deux œuvres destinées à des expositions collectives tenues dans un musée. Ces deux œuvres traitent de la relation entre le style populaire et le style classique en architecture et en construction; c'est là un thème qui a servi de véhicule à Charney pour explorer les figures archétypes de l'architecture et la façon dont cet art communique la signification du milieu bâti sans distinction d'échelle ou de matériaux.

Les objets trouvés, mis au ban de la société, ces choses que l'on considère habituellement comme grossières, inférieures et irrécupérables, ont souvent servi de source d'inspiration à Charney. Il en est ainsi d'une photographie figurant une cabane d'ouvrier dans la ville industrielle de Trois-Rivières, trouvée par Charney au cours de ses recherches sur les origines de l'industrialisation au Québec. Dans cette maison faite de mauvais matériaux, Charney découvrit l'image d'un temple classique qui lui donnait un caractère d'archétype. Chose ironique, vu son architecture modeste, le portique de la maison faisait songer précisément à un trésor grec. *Le Trésor de Trois-Rivières* jouait sur l'ambivalence fondamentale de la structure originale : à la fois monument et cabane, temple et tombe. La construction de Charney n'était pas une idéalisation cependant, car son aspect rudimentaire évoquait sans fard les circonstances économiques et sociales particulières dans lesquelles cette modeste habitation avait été construite.

Avec *Pline en tête*, Charney aborda le problème de l'origine d'un point de vue philosophique plutôt qu'historique. Il réalisa deux constructions dans le cadre d'une exposition consacrée de façon générale à l'architecture classique et, de façon plus précise, à la villa de l'Antiquité. La première construction était un édicule classique fait de piliers et de linteaux, édifié sur le palier supérieur d'un vaste escalier à l'entrée de l'aire d'exposition, et rappelant l'entrée principale du musée. La deuxième, qui n'était pas sans rappeler la première dans son assemblage et ses matériaux bruts, était plus près de la cabane que du temple, dont elle gardait pourtant des échos sensibles, comme *Le Trésor de Trois-Rivières*. Avec cette œuvre, Charney faisait référence à la structure de l'édifice comme partie intégrante du pâté urbain, une construction en apparence antithétique si l'on considère que le thème de l'exposition était la rusticité.

De par leurs dimensions, leur matérialité crue mais non pas inélégante, ces deux constructions exprimaient clairement la nature conceptuelle du projet de Charney. Leur évocation du classicisme reposait sur la logique d'une structure tectonique exprimée rationnellement. En outre, en mettant en évidence le caractère commun d'archétype des deux structures, Charney soulignait la fonction primitive de l'abri, fonction dont le développement rituel en architecture sert de témoignage concret sur le tissu social.

Les dessins de Charney, qui sont le report fidèle et permanent de ses constructions, occupent une place tout aussi importante dans son œuvre. Ils sont souvent réalisés à partir d'images du milieu bâti collectionnées par l'artiste; elles sont tirées indifféremment de journaux, de cartes postales, de livres et de films. Les constructions y font figure d'événements quotidiens, les traces d'une mémoire collective. Ce répertoire d'images ne joue pourtant pas qu'un rôle documentaire dans l'œuvre de Charney. Il comporte un gisement mythique de représentations à partir desquelles Charney construit des propositions qui font office de contre-mythe, de critique et de commentaire par rapport à l'architecture comme système culturel.

La relation entre les dessins et les constructions n'est pas rigide; certains dessins précèdent des constructions, d'autres viennent après, et d'autres encore sont des réalisations en soi. Il en est ainsi pour une série de dessins sur lesquels Charney travaille depuis 1982, dont les premiers sont deux projets de façades à édifier à Kassel en 1982 dans le cadre de *Documenta 7*, et plus précisément pour la section Documenta-Urbana, qui ne devait pas voir le jour. Intitulé *« Il vaut mieux qu'ils croient aller à la ferme... »* (voir pl. 12–13), le projet consiste à construire la façade idéalisée d'une ferme sur la Bahnhofplatz en face de la gare, ou encore de l'autre côté des voies du tramway, dans l'une des rues principales de Kassel. Tout au long de son œuvre, Charney n'a jamais perdu de vue la nature ambivalente de la façade, en partie structure et en partie simulacre. Avec l'image de la façade de la ferme idéalisée, Charney a exhumé du passé récent de l'Allemagne l'affreux mensonge des architectes SS, qui construisirent un portail semblable pour camoufler derrière un décor bucolique l'entrée du camp d'extermination d'Auschwitz-Birkenau : « Il vaut mieux qu'ils croient aller à la ferme ». Ce portail relie le présent au passé; il s'agit d'un monument aux larmes et au souvenir, à ériger fort opportunément dans un lieu d'arrivées et de départs.

Après les allusions historiques des dessins de Kassel, Charney franchit métaphoriquement le portail pour découvrir dans les camps d'extermination l'image d'une cité spectrale (voir pl. 16–19) : nécropole peinte de rouge et de violet, vision d'une volonté rationnelle d'ordre qui aurait perdu toute mesure. « Mais imagine-toi maintenant », dit le naïf général Stumm qui commence à voir clair dans le roman de Robert Musil *L'Homme sans qualités*, « un ordre humain total, universel, en un mot, l'ordre civil parfait : parole d'honneur ! C'est la mort par le froid, la rigidité cadavérique, un paysage lunaire, une épidémie géométrique[3] ! » Les dessins visionnaires de Charney montrent une ville bâtie sur le modèle des baraquements du camp, étroits bâtiments disposés en rangées perpendiculaires, leurs portes ouvertes laissant voir des étagères : espaces cruels où confiner des vies humaines. Comme dans *Le Trésor de Trois-Rivières*, Charney a fondu la figure de la maison et celle du mausolée en une seule, rappelant Adolf Loos, selon qui l'œuvre architecturale idéale est la tombe où la libido trouve le repos.

Ces dessins poussent à l'extrême la logique qui gouverne tous les projets de Charney. Charney envisage l'architecture comme une « inscription humaine dans l'espace », texte que l'on doit lire et interpréter. Les dessins et les constructions révèlent les traces de volonté humaine enfouies dans les choses fabriquées, dont l'artiste propose des lectures allusives, changeantes et ouvertes. Lorsque les traumatismes de l'histoire ont causé des blocages, comme ceux produits au moment de l'Holocauste, Charney se sert de l'architecture comme d'une clé servant à déverrouiller la mémoire. Par cette expiation du passé, la ville (comme la psyché) peut se permettre une existence nouvelle. Ce n'est donc pas par mélancolie ou par nostalgie que ses œuvres rappellent le passé, mais plutôt par désir d'enraciner l'expérience du présent dans le sens historique de l'ordre humain tel qu'il est exprimé dans les formes architecturales. Charney incarne fondamentalement l'auteur d'allégories, esquissant un contenu monumental dans des constructions grossières et fragmentaires.

*D.N.*

3 Robert Musil, *L'Homme sans qualités*, Éditions du Seuil, Paris, 1956, tome 1, p. 555–556.

# Biographie / Expositions / Bibliographie

## Biographie

Melvin Charney est né à Montréal (Québec) en 1935. Après des études de beaux-arts à la School of Art and Design du Musée des beaux-arts de Montréal, il a étudié l'architecture à l'université McGill, à Montréal, et à l'université Yale. Il a obtenu une maîtrise en architecture de Yale en 1959. De 1961 à 1964, il a habité et travaillé à New York et à Paris. Depuis 1964, il habite à Montréal, où il enseigne à l'École d'architecture de l'Université de Montréal. En plus d'enseigner et d'exposer ses propres travaux, il a également organisé deux expositions traitant du paysage social et architectural de la ville de Montréal : *Montréal... plus ou moins* (1972) et *Corridart*, réalisée pour les Jeux olympiques de 1976.

## Expositions solo

* publication d'un catalogue d'exposition

1977
Cambridge (Massachusetts), Université Harvard *

1978
Toronto, Musée des beaux-arts de l'Ontario

1979
Montréal, Musée d'art contemporain *
Long Island City (New York), Institute for Art and Urban Resources, P.S. 1

1980
Paris et Bruxelles, Centre culturel canadien

1982
Chicago, Museum of Contemporary Art *
Chicago, Richard Gray Gallery
New York, 49e Parallèle/Centre d'art contemporain canadien

1983
Kingston (Ontario), Agnes Etherington Art Centre *

1985
Lethbridge (Alberta), Southern Alberta Art Gallery

## Principales expositions collectives

1972
Montréal, Musée des beaux-arts de Montréal, *Montréal... plus ou moins* *

1973
Paris, Musée d'art moderne de la ville de Paris, *Canada Trajectoires – '73* *
Milan, *Triennale di Milano*, Section internationale

1975
Montréal, Institut d'art contemporain, mise en tournée par les Musées nationaux du Canada, *Québec 75* *

1976
Montréal, Programme art et culture, Comité organisateur des Jeux de la XXIe Olympiade, *Corridart*

1977
Montréal, Institut d'art contemporain, *03 23 03 : Premières Rencontres internationales d'art contemporain* *

1978
Toronto, A.C.T. Gallery, *Architectural Drawings*

1979
New York, John Weber Gallery, *Invitational IV*
Washington (D.C.), Protech-McIntosh Gallery, *Art and Architecture : Space and Structure*

1980
Paris, Centre national d'art et de culture Georges Pompidou, *11e Biennale de Paris* *
Los Angeles, Los Angeles Institute for Contemporary Art, *Architectural Sculpture* *

Vancouver, Vancouver Art Gallery, *Architectural References* *

1981
Québec, Musée du Québec, *Art–Société/1975–1980* *

1982
Toronto, Visual Arts Ontario et Market Gallery, Archives de la ville de Toronto, *Citysite Sculpture* *
Surrey (Colombie-Britannique), Surrey Art Gallery, *Drawings by Contemporary Sculptors* *
Berlin, Akademie der Künste, *Canada in Berlin* *

1983
Stuttgart (R.F.A.), Württembergischer Kunstverein, *Künstler aus Kanada : Räume und Installationen* *
Québec, Musée du Québec, *Collection du gouvernement*
Montréal, Musée d'art contemporain, *Art et Bâtiment*
Chicago, Chicago International Art Exposition, *Chicago Sculpture International : Mile 2*
Como (Italie), Galleria Il Salotto, *Rendere visibile*
Montréal, Musée des beaux-arts de Montréal, *Les Villas de Pline et l'architecture classique à Montréal*

1984
Chicago, Museum of Contemporary Art, *Ten Years of Collecting*
Düsseldorf, Architektenkammer Nordrhein-Westfalen Akademie, *Festarchitektur* *
Berlin, Internationale Bauausstellung, Martin Gropius Bau, *Idee, Prozess, Ergebnis*
Vancouver, Vancouver Art Gallery, *The Praxis Collection*

1985
Milan, *17ª Triennale di Milano*
Montréal, Musée d'art contemporain, *Vingt Ans de collection*
Québec, Musée du Québec, *La Collection et l'Art du Québec au XX<sup>e</sup> siècle*
Montréal, Centre international d'art contemporain, *Aurora Borealis* *
Chicago, Museum of Contemporary Art, *Projects for Chicago*
Toronto, Evelyn Aimis Fine Art, *Environmental Concerns*

## Écrits choisis sur Melvin Charney


Banham, Reyner, *Megastructures – Urban Futures of the Recent Past*, Oxford University Press, Londres, 1976.

Barber, Bruce, « Architectural Reference : Post-modernism, Primitivism and Parody in the Architectural Image », *Parachute*, vol. 21 (hiver 1980), p. 5–12.

Battisti, Eugenio, « Contro l'International Style », *Casa del Libro* (janvier 1982), p. 24–27.

Bernstein, William, et Ruth Cawker, « Corridart, Montreal », dans *Contemporary Canadian Architecture*, Fitzhenry and Whiteside, Toronto, 1982.

Burkhardt, Lucius, « Melvin Charney », *Werk und Zeit*, vol. 4 (avril 1981), p. 26.

Burns, James T., « A Gallant Try : Canadian National Pavilion Design Competition for 1970 », *Progressive Architecture*, vol. 48, nº 8 (août 1967), p. 164–165.

Charbonneau, François, Marcel St-Pierre et Esther Trépanier, « Pratiques artistiques d'opposition à Montréal », dans *Art–Société/1975–1980* (catalogue d'exposition), Musée du Québec en collaboration avec Les Éditions Interventions, Québec, 1981.

« Corridart : The House of Sherbrooke Street », *Process : Architecture*, vol. 5 (mars 1978), p. 124–127.

Déthier, Jean, « Melvin Charney : Deux Façades, une provocation », dans *11e Biennale de Paris : L'Urbanité* (catalogue d'exposition), Paris, 1980.

Dompierre, Louise, et Melvin Charney, *Melvin Charney 1981–1983* (catalogue d'exposition), Agnes Etherington Art Centre, Kingston (Ontario), 1983.

Forster, Kurt W., « Contradiction of Preservation and Destruction », *Architext* (décembre 1983), p. 3–5.

Freedman, Adele, « Building Metaphors – Literally », *Globe and Mail* de Toronto (13 décembre 1980).

Goldin, Amy, « Report from Toronto and Montreal », *Art in America*, vol. 65, nº 2 (mars–avril 1977), p. 35–47.

Grenville, Bruce, « Melvin Charney », *Parachute*, vol. 32 (novembre 1983), pl. 36–37.

Hatch, Heather, *Citysite Sculpture* (catalogue d'exposition), Visual Arts Ontario et Market Gallery des archives de la ville de Toronto, Toronto, 1982.

Hould, Claudette, « Melvin Charney, ou les traces d'une mémoire collective », *Vie des Arts*, vol. 24, nº 98 (printemps 1980), p. 78–79.

Jacob, Mary Jane, *Melvin Charney : A Chicago Construction* (catalogue d'exposition), Museum of Contemporary Art, Chicago, 1982.

Lamoureux, Johanne, « Melvin Charney, ou l'illusion de la preuve », *Parachute*, vol. 17 (hiver 1979), p. 66–67.

Lippard, Lucy, *Architectural Sculpture* (catalogue d'exposition), Los Angeles Institute for Contemporary Art, Los Angeles, 1980.

McConathy, Dale, « Corridart : Instant Archeology in Montreal », *Artscanada*, vol. 33, nº 206/207 (juillet–août 1976), p. 36–45.

McDougall, Ian, et Kathy Peake, « Melvin Charney », *Transition* de Melbourne, vol. 2, nº 2 (juin 1981), p. 7–10.

Merling, Mitchell, « Truth and Architecture », *The Fifth Column*, vol. 4, nº 1 (automne 1983), p. 5–6.

Needham, Gerald, « Melvin Charney : Constructs and Concepts », *Artscanada*, vol. 37, nº 234–235 (avril–mai 1980), p. 24–26.

Nixon, Virginia, « Melvin Charney – Architectural Sculpture », *The Canadian Forum*, vol. 63, nº 728 (mai 1983), p. 18–19 et 41.

Oechslin, Werner, *Festarchitektur* (catalogue d'exposition), Akademie der Architektenkammer Nordrhein-Westfalen, Verlag Gerd Hatje, Stuttgart, 1984.

Osterwold, Tilman, et Bruce Ferguson, entrevue dans *Künstler aus Kanada : Räume und Installationen* (catalogue d'exposition), Württembergischer Kunstverein, 1983.

Pagé, Suzanne, « Melvin Charney : quelques monuments nationaux », *Canada Trajectoires – '73* (catalogue d'exposition), Musée d'art moderne de la ville de Paris, Paris, 1973.

Patton, Andrew, « Melvin Charney at the Art Gallery of Ontario », *Artists Review* de Toronto, vol. 13 (avril 1978), p. 12–13.

Pontbriand, Chantal, « Melvin Charney : Entretien avec Melvin Charney », *Parachute*, vol. 13 (hiver 1978), p. 26–30.

——, Normand Thériault et Thierry de Duve, *03 23 03 : Premières Rencontres internationales d'art contemporain* (catalogue d'exposition), Institut d'art contemporain, Montréal, 1977.

« Progetto canadese per Osaka '70 », *L'Architettura*, vol. 13, nº 8 (décembre 1967), p. 526–528.

« Self-Constructing Exhibition Pavilion », *Design* de Londres, vol. 231 (mars 1968), p. 54–56.

Shapiro, Babs, *Architectural References* (catalogue d'exposition), Vancouver Art Gallery, Vancouver, 1980.

Thériault, Normand, « Melvin Charney », dans *Québec 75* (catalogue d'exposition), Institut d'art contemporain, Montréal, 1975.

Toupin, Gilles, « Charney : L'Architecture archéologique », *La Presse* de Montréal (10 novembre 1979).

Tzonis, Alexander, « Un monument contre les massacres et la terreur », *Le Carré bleu* (janvier 1972), p. 13–16.

——, et Melvin Charney, *Melvin Charney : Œuvres 1970–1979* (catalogue d'exposition), Musée d'art contemporain, Montréal, 1979.

## Écrits choisis de Melvin Charney

« The Grain Elevators Revisited », *Architectural Design* de Londres, vol. 37, nº 7 (juillet 1967), p. 328–331.

« A Self-Erecting Exhibition System : Project for the Canadian Pavilion, Osaka Expo '70 », *Architecture Canada*, vol. 46, nº 3 (mars 1969), p. 34–36.

« Experimental Strategies : Notes for Environmental Design », *Perspecta : The Yale Architectural Journal*, vol. 12 (mars 1969), p. 21–32. Traduit et reproduit dans *Deutsche Bauzeitung*, vol. 103, nº 8 (août 1969), p. 574–581, et dans *Formalism, Realism, Contextualism*, sous la direction de Hajime Yatsuka, Shokokusha Publishing Co., Tokyo, 1979.

« On the Liberation of Architecture : Memo Series on an Airforce Memorial », *Artforum*, vol. 9 (mai 1971), p. 34–37.

« Pour une définition de l'architecture au Québec », dans *Architecture et urbanisme au Québec*, conférences J.-A. de Sève 13–14, Les Presses de l'Université de Montréal, Montréal, 1971. Extraits traduits et publiés dans « Towards a Definition of Quebec Architecture », *Progressive Architecture*, vol. 53, nº 9 (septembre 1972), p. 104–107.

En collaboration avec Serge Carreau et Colin H. Davidson, *The Adequacy and Production of Low Income Housing in Canada*, Société centrale d'hypothèques et de logement, Ottawa, 1972. Extraits publiés dans « Low Income Housing », *Architectural Design* de Londres, vol. 43, nº 1 (janvier 1972), p. 7–8, et dans *Montréal... plus ou moins* (catalogue d'exposition), Musée des beaux-arts de Montréal, Montréal, 1972.

« Quelques monuments nationaux », *Architectural Design* de Londres, vol. 44, nº 4 (avril 1974), p. 241–243.

« Dead End Choices : Housing in Canada », *Architectural Design* de Londres, vol. 46, nº 4 (avril 1976), p. 202–206.

*Melvin Charney : Other Monuments 1970–1976* (catalogue d'exposition), Université Harvard, 1977. Reproduit dans *Vanguard*, vol. 6, nº 2 (mars 1977), p. 3–8.

« Corridart : Melvin Charney on Art as Urban Activism », *Architectural Design* de Londres, vol. 47, nº 7–8 (juillet–août 1977), p. 545–547.

« Modern Movements in French-Canadian Architecture », *Process : Architecture*, vol. 5 (mars 1978), p. 15–25.

« Monuments Now : On Contemporary Architecture and the Avant-Garde », dans *Avant-Garde : A History of Innovation and Invention in Architecture*, sous la direction de Geert Bekaert, University of Technology, Eindhoven (Pays-Bas), 1978.

*Melvin Charney : Œuvres 1970–1979* (catalogue d'exposition), Musée d'art contemporain, Montréal, 1979.

« The Montrealness of Montreal : Formations and Formalities in Urban Architecture », *Architectural Review*, vol. 167, nº 999 (mai 1980).

« On Architecture : A Statement about Statement », dans *Building with Words*, sous la direction de William Bernstein et Ruth Cawker, Coach House Press, Toronto, 1981.

« À qui le droit : au sujet d'architecture contemporaine au Québec », *Architecture/Québec* (janvier–février 1982), p. 12–24.

« Of Temples and Sheds », *Architecture/Québec* (octobre 1983), p. 11–15.

« Signs of Recognition, Ciphers of Deception », *Parachute*, vol. 36 (septembre–novembre 1984), p. 38–42.

« Aus einem Wörterbuch der Architektur... über 'Clients' und 'Models' », dans *Idee, Prozess, Ergebnis*, Internationale Bauausstellung, Berlin, 1984.

# Krzysztof Wodiczko

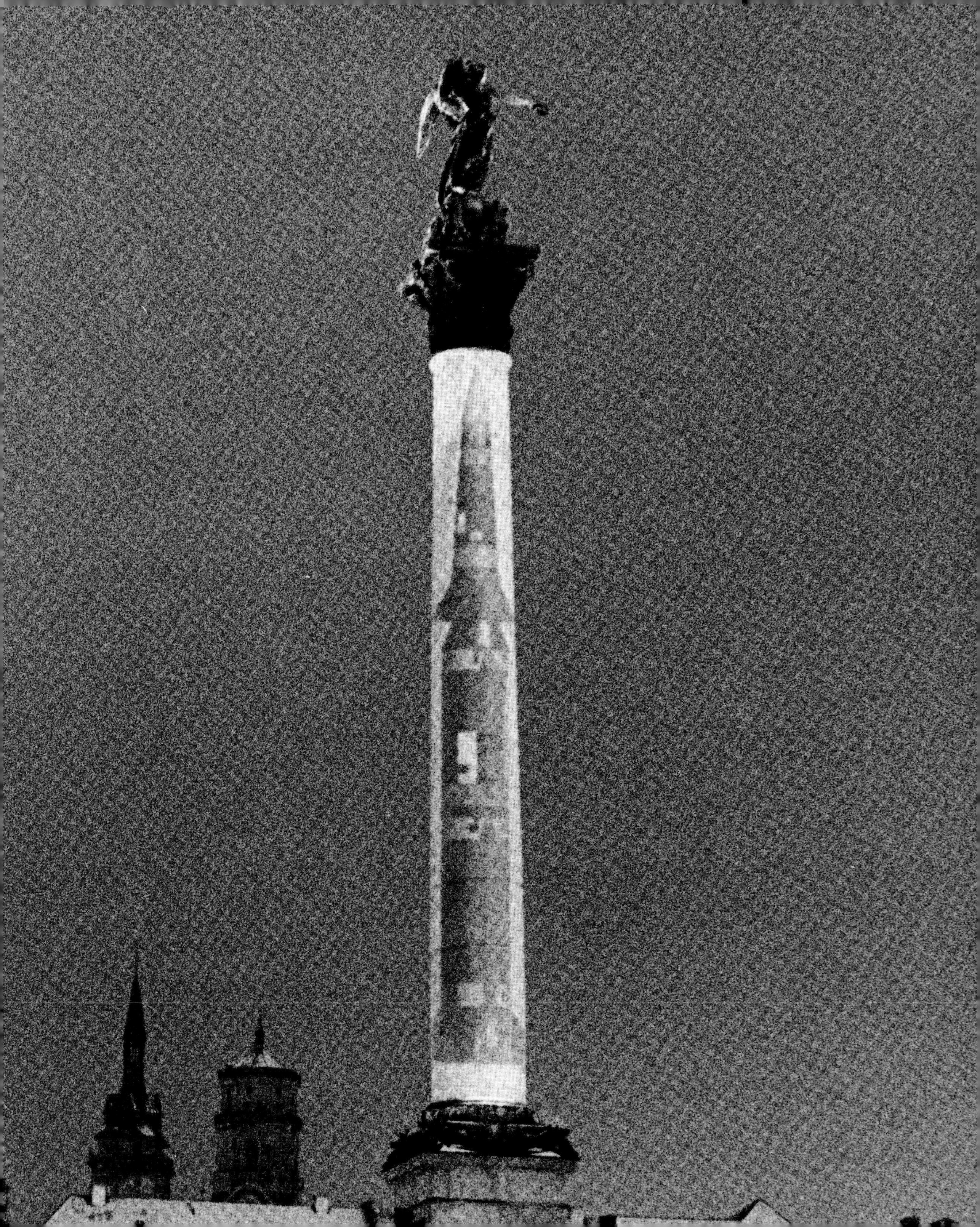

Fig. 3 *Véhicule 1*, Varsovie, 1973

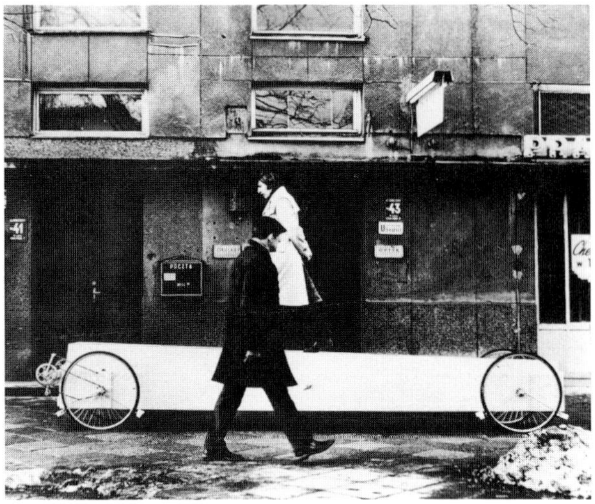

Nous avons sous les yeux trois photographies. Dans la première (fig. 3), nous voyons un jeune homme marcher pensivement de long en large sur la surface légèrement inclinée d'un véhicule étrange. De profil bas et allongé et de fabrication présumée artisanale, le véhicule est équipé de simples roues de bicyclette et d'un système d'engrenages et de poulies qui donnent une idée de son mode de propulsion. Un homme plus âgé, marchant dans la direction opposée, se contente de jeter discrètement un regard oblique au véhicule et à son conducteur et réussit ainsi à contrôler sa curiosité. Tirée d'un journal, la deuxième photographie (fig. 4) est un agrandissement dont certaines parties ont été coupées. Deux hommes vêtus de complets-veston, dont l'un porte des décorations, se serrent la main. La main restée libre de l'un des deux hommes est posée librement sous le bras de l'autre; on aperçoit derrière eux l'aile avant d'une voiture en faction. La séquence, présentée hors contexte, est lourde de signification et suggestive comme si un pacte important était conclu sous notre regard furtif. Dans la troisième photographie (fig. 5), le fronton du Parlement suisse est affublé d'un œil immense qui regarde de côté. Cette image projetée donne un faciès humain étonnant à l'édifice, minant la dignité solennelle de sa façade néo-classique : l'édifice se donne en spectacle.

Bien que figurant des projets conçus à des époques très éloignées (*Véhicule 1* fut réalisé en 1973, alors que Krzysztof Wodiczko vivait encore en Pologne, tandis que la projection sur l'édifice du Parlement de Berne a eu lieu en 1985), ces trois photos démontrent qu'il existe une continuité dans l'œuvre de Wodiczko. Chaque projet implique un éclatement du contexte : l'œuvre est exposée dans un lieu public et provoque la surprise; ou encore une image tirée des médias, à la fois banale et empreinte de signification politique, est révélée en étant exposée dans une galerie. En outre, le corps humain est montré comme le lieu ou l'instrument privilégié de l'inscription du sens. Plus précisément, l'œuvre met l'accent sur l'acte envisagé abstraitement comme geste symbolique. Ces photographies permettent de déduire que les œuvres sont des manifestations éphémères qui sont indissociables de leur réception. Ainsi, la signification et la raison d'être des œuvres sont liées à la présence implicite d'un public, de même qu'à la réaction tout à fait imprévisible de ce dernier.

C'est à l'intérieur de ce cadre que Wodiczko a élaboré une analyse des instances bureaucratiques qui modèlent le pouvoir dans la société contemporaine : l'État, l'armée et les institutions financières et culturelles. L'artiste cherche à démasquer et à démythifier les rapports de forces figurés par ces institutions en exposant brièvement et soudainement leurs édifices, véritables incarnations du mythe, au regard scrutateur du public.

À cette fin, Wodiczko a recours depuis 1980 à des *projections publiques*, montages gigantesques et éphémères d'images et d'architecture, organisés de nuit à l'extérieur, alors que les fonctions quotidiennes de l'édifice sont interrompues. Avec de puissants projecteurs de diapositives à arc au xénon, des images appartenant clairement au langage du pouvoir sont projetées sur la façade endormie d'un édifice dont Wodiczko cherche à libérer le mystère. Délivré de la torpeur que lui confère une vérité statique et éternelle, l'édifice prend vie et révèle les fantasmes inconscients qui se cachent derrière sa façade, comme si un personnage de conte de fée exhibait ses désirs les plus secrets sous l'influence irrésistible de l'habit qu'il aurait revêtu. Cette manifestation se déroule dans la rue devant un auditoire qui, en la circonstance, forme un corps collectif. Cet auditoire disparate aura des réactions diverses, mais, dans la mesure où la projection l'incitera à réagir consciemment et de manière

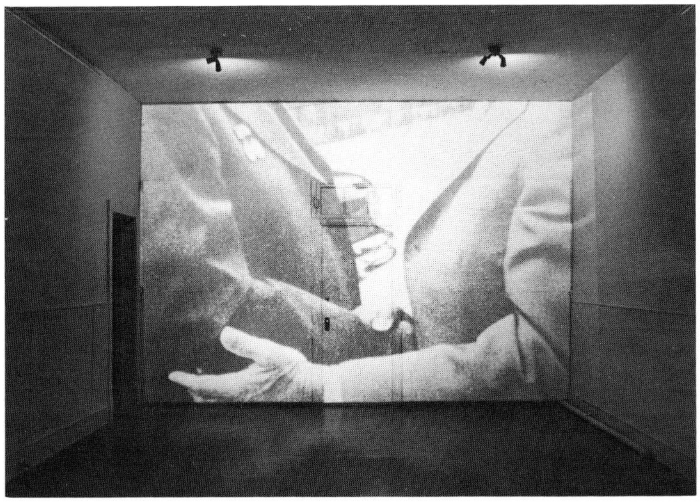

Fig. 4 *Projection* [Léonide Brejnev et Éric Honecker], Eye Level Gallery, Halifax (Nouvelle-Écosse), avril 1979

critique au message architectural, il remettra en question ce que Michel Foucault appelle « la grande fantaisie d'une structure sociale instituée par la volonté universelle[1]. » En s'efforçant de dénoncer les intérêts privés investis dans les édifices qui incarnent ce mythe, Wodiczko adhère à la vision de Foucault pour qui « le phénomène de la structure sociale ne découle pas d'un consensus mais bien de la matérialité d'un pouvoir s'exerçant sur les corps mêmes d'individus[2]. »

L'utilisation stratégique d'images populaires largement répandues dans les médias, l'assujettissement de contextes non artistiques, et la théâtralité sont autant de traits qui apparentent l'œuvre de Wodiczko à plusieurs stratégies critiques du post-modernisme. Cependant, on ne doit pas oublier l'influence de sa vie et de son expérience d'artiste en Pologne jusqu'en 1977. La politique culturelle relativement indépendante de la Pologne en fait l'État le plus libéral des pays de l'Est. Depuis la fin des années 1950, les responsables de la politique culturelle polonaise tolèrent les œuvres les plus complexes du modernisme. Seule la politique est un sujet tabou pour l'art. Toutefois, comme le notaient Andrzej Ostrowski et Karl Beveridge :

> La plupart des artistes polonais mènent une double vie... Dans la vie quotidienne, l'artiste est confronté à la double obligation de dissocier la politique de l'art et de s'engager dans la politique officielle en produisant un art et un design destinés à alimenter le système de propagande de l'État... D'une part, l'État doit développer une propagande efficace pour affermir son pouvoir, mais d'autre part cette même propagande doit donner l'illusion d'un libéralisme culturel[3].

1 Michel Foucault, « Body-Power », dans *Power/Knowledge : Selected Interviews and Other Writings 1972–1977*, Pantheon Books, New York, 1980, p. 55.
2 *Ibid.*
3 Andrzej Ostrowski [alias Krzysztof Wodiczko] et Karl Beveridge, « West/East : The Depoliticization of Art », *Fuse* (mars 1980), p. 141.

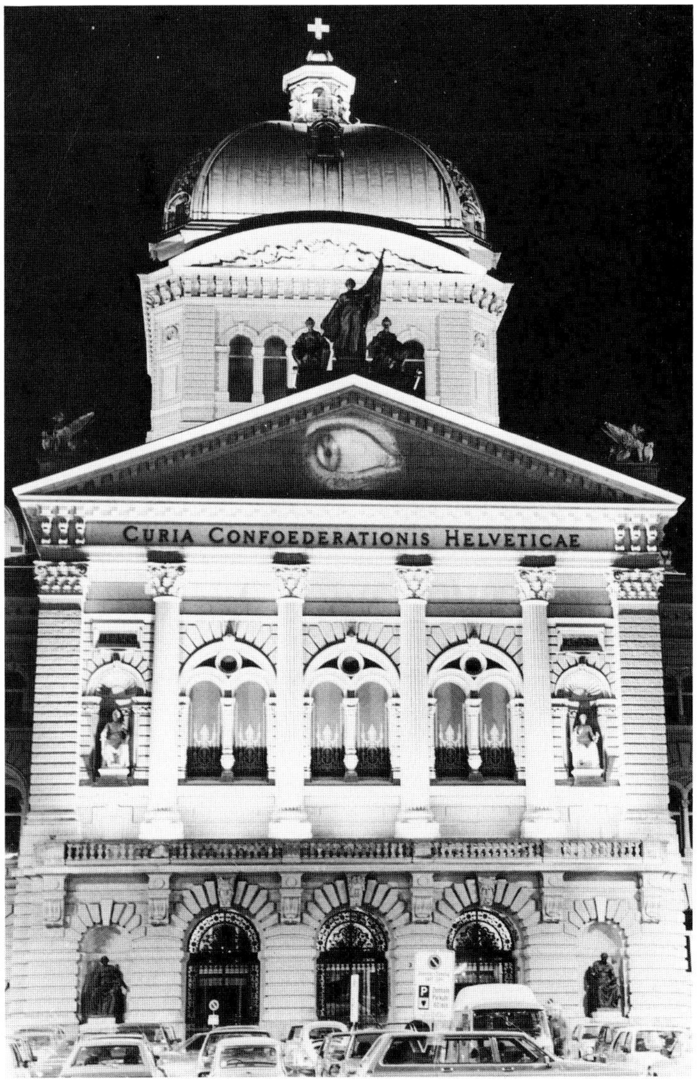


Fig. 5 *Projection de l'édifice du Parlement fédéral de la Suisse*, Berne, du 12 au 14 avril 1985

L'impuissance politique des artistes polonais d'aujourd'hui contraste vivement avec la vision des constructivistes russes et polonais, pour qui l'art était un instrument de changement social. Quoique dans la réalité polonaise il soit impossible même de rêver à ces idéaux héroïques et utopiques, certaines stratégies constructivistes ont été conservées et transmises à Wodiczko et à d'autres au cours de leur formation en design industriel. D'où la nécessité pour eux de penser en fonction de la totalité du milieu environnant, sans toutefois posséder le pouvoir politique qui leur permettrait de créer les conditions nécessaires à l'élaboration d'une critique de la politique mise de l'avant par la bureaucratie culturelle. Mais un état permanent d'opposition théorique, sans la moindre possibilité d'action concrète, rend l'artiste vulnérable à la séduction et à la récupération par la raison bureaucratique (danger d'autant plus grand que l'appareil idéologique de l'État adopte des stratégies qui semblent plus libérales).

Alors qu'il était encore en Pologne, Wodiczko a entrepris de faire face à cette situation en dessinant plusieurs projets de véhicules que l'on pouvait interpréter comme des modèles analytiques des rouages politiques de l'État. *Véhicule 1* (voir fig. 3), de 1973, est le seul pour lequel un prototype fut construit. Plongé dans une attitude de méditation philosophique, l'artiste allait et venait sur la plate-forme à bascule de cette machine élégante dont il avait l'usage exclusif, la faisant avancer du même coup. L'oscillation de la plate-forme permettait à l'énergie produite d'actionner les roues par un système de câbles et d'engrenages. En dépit de tout ce travail, le véhicule ne se déplaçait qu'en ligne droite et toujours dans le même sens. D'autres projets de l'artiste prévoyaient la fabrication de véhicules destinés aux travailleurs, aux assemblées ordinaires de citoyens (sur le modèle d'une place publique) et même aux discoureurs de café. Même si les véhicules offraient différentes possibilités d'action, allant de la répétition évidente et futile à l'absence relative de contrainte, le seul déplacement possible était linéaire et unidirectionnel.

Ces constructions relevaient clairement d'une stratégie allégorique, motivée par la nécessité de « parler publiquement par sous-entendus pour contourner la censure[4]. » Ces œuvres subtiles et d'une ironie mordante nous enseignent que la liberté individuelle se mesure non seulement au degré de mouvement permis, mais également à l'effet de ce mouvement; faute d'un mécanisme de direction pour influer sur les affaires de l'État, l'individu ne possède qu'une capacité théorique de modifier sa condition.

Par la suite, Wodiczko a adopté d'autres stratégies allégoriques dans une série de montages sur le thème de la ligne, réalisés entre 1976 et 1978. Les montages, qui partent d'une présentation analytique des propriétés de la ligne (comme théorie, objet, image et réalité) pour ensuite constituer une étude expérimentale des éléments linéaires comparables dans l'art et la propagande, relèvent d'une nouvelle tentative de lier l'art à la réalité sociale et politique. Ces œuvres transitionnelles sont un point d'interrogation sur le musée. Mettant en jeu les techniques de montage comme la confiscation, la superposition et la fragmentation, répandues tant dans l'allégorie politique que dans la publicité, elles ont surtout le mérite de montrer comment on utilise la structure d'un système pour en structurer ou en traduire un autre, et ainsi en modifier le sens.

La leçon tirée de ces montages a servi aux *Projections publiques*, qui ont marqué la rupture de Wodiczko avec le musée comme support structural de son œuvre. La démarche qui allait conduire Wodiczko à reprendre la stratégie du montage élaborée par ses prédécesseurs au début du XX$^{e}$ siècle impliquait logiquement l'abandon de l'espace muséal au profit du milieu architectural urbain, employé comme écran de projection. Comme le notait Benjamin Buchloh :

> Même si ces activités avaient pris naissance dans l'institution sociale isolée de l'avant-garde et de l'art réservé à une élite, elles eurent dès le début pour caractéristique essentielle d'interroger les instances de la domination idéologique sur le lieu concret de leurs fonctions, c'est-à-dire au cœur même du système de représentation où elles se trouvent et exercent leur pouvoir. Il était également essentiel que les opérations formelles au sein des constructions idéologiques fussent structurées matériellement… de façon à ce que l'œuvre pût s'introduire à nouveau dans le même discours, sa forme de diffusion et son système de distribution[5].

Concordant avec l'opposition de Wodiczko à l'enterrement de l'avant-garde[6], les *Projections publiques* peuvent être envisagées comme le modèle expérimental d'un champ de production public qui demeurerait visible et convaincant sur le plan artistique. La projection provocatrice de ses montages de diapositives sur la surface des édifices publics et des monuments a pour effet de révéler les disparités entre l'expérience concrète et sensuelle de la projection et le langage normal « officiel » de l'architecture, comme *ruptures* dans le tissu mythique du corps social représenté par l'édifice.

4 Benjamin H.D. Buchloh, « Montage and Allegorical Deconstruction », *Vocation/Vacation* (catalogue d'exposition), Walter Phillips Gallery, Banff (Alberta), 1981, n.p.

5 *Ibid.*

6 Krzysztof Wodiczko, « For the De-Incapacitation of the Avant-Garde », *Parallelogramme*, vol. 9, n$^{o}$ 4 (avril–mai 1984), p. 22–26.

Quelle est la nature de ce corps social mythique représenté par l'architecture ? Wodiczko l'envisage comme un « corps discipliné/disciplinant », fondé sur les relations réglées du tout avec les parties, et des parties entre elles. Immuable et universel, son esprit est celui du nom du Père, de la Loi qui séduit « par sa capacité structurale d'incarner... notre désir intime et inexprimé de collaboration disciplinée avec son pouvoir ». L'édifice n'est pas seulement le lieu physique des instances détentrices du pouvoir mais également un « médium spatial où le mythe du pouvoir et le désir universel qu'il suscite ne cessent de se reproduire simultanément et symboliquement[7]. »

Les *Projections publiques* déconstruisent le mythe en visualisant l'idéologie implicite de l'édifice et en superposant ces images sur le corps même du mythe, à savoir le lieu concret de son fonctionnement. L'édifice se trouve soudainement personnifié. Examinons maintenant quelques-unes des projections récentes de Wodiczko. Sur l'immense paroi grise de l'immeuble de l'American Telephone & Telegraph (voir pl. 31), au cœur de Manhattan, une main sortant d'une manchette de chemise fait le geste du serment d'allégeance : allégeance aux idéaux démocratiques des États-Unis d'Amérique... ou à ses propres intérêts multinationaux qui ont contribué à anéantir ces idéaux ailleurs ? Sur la grande base de la tour cruciforme de la place Ville-Marie (voir pl. 34), siège des opérations financières de la Banque Royale du Canada à Montréal (et quartier général du consulat sud-africain), une paire de poings ensanglantés apparaît. La puissance politique des institutions financières internationales et l'apartheid du gouvernement de l'Afrique du Sud sont jumelés au moyen de cette seule scène de violence. La projection interrompt le plat scénario fonctionnel des édifices comme une annonce publicitaire à la télévision. La projection est fragmentaire et brève, mais, tandis que le message séducteur de la publicité cherche à obtenir le consentement, la projection traite de marchandisage, de propriété privée et d'intérêts privés, et vise à provoquer une prise de conscience et un débat.

De même, des images de matériel militaire contemporain sont projetées sur des monuments de style classique perpétuant la gloire de victoires passées. Sur l'arc de triomphe de la Grand Army Plaza à Brooklyn (voir pl. 32), les ogives d'un missile américain et d'un missile soviétique sont enchaînées et retenues par un cadenas. Les idéaux de justice et de liberté, connotés par le langage classique de l'architecture (que chaque nation s'approprie comme sien) reposent en fait sur la lutte mortelle que se livrent les deux puissances pour la supériorité militaire. Des figures de mineurs britanniques en grève défilent au pied de la colonne du Duc d'York (voir pl. 35) à Londres, pendant qu'un char d'assaut en marche est projeté sur le socle de la colonne. Deux mains d'homme se croisent pudiquement au bas de cette éminence phallique comme si le monument sentait le besoin de se protéger de l'agitation en cours et voulait résister à une menace interne. En confrontant le monument rhétorique aux réalités contemporaines, la projection démasque son pseudo-idéalisme humanitaire et met l'accent sur les rapports de forces masqués par cet idéalisme.

Comme les *Projections publiques* ne sont pas de simples messages didactiques cependant, on se doit d'examiner leur effet artistique et particulièrement leur effet théâtral. Elles agissent comme des interruptions spectaculaires du rituel mystificateur de l'architecture : à un moment choisi, les projections sont dirigées vers un édifice ou un monument, qui, hypnotisé, commence son numéro. Chaque interruption, qui vise à étonner les spectateurs par son caractère incongru et inattendu, crée un intervalle, une brèche, qui

7 Wodiczko, « Public Projection », *Revue canadienne de théorie politique et sociale,* vol. 7, nº 1–2 (hiver/printemps 1983), p. 185.

laisse place à une réflexion critique. Ainsi, la projection envisagée comme interruption fonctionne comme un mécanisme aliénant conçu de façon à rendre visibles les fondements idéologiques de l'édifice, troublant du même coup les sentiments du public à son égard.

La façon dont Wodiczko se sert de l'interruption comme d'un mécanisme structural de base nous incite à établir un parallèle avec la théorie brechtienne d'un théâtre épique. Contrairement au drame, dont l'effet repose sur la progression cumulative de l'action, une œuvre épique peut se diviser en fragments ou en interruptions, chaque fragment conservant un dynamisme propre. Walter Benjamin affirmait que ce procédé de l'interruption avait pour effet de privilégier le geste, de sorte que « le théâtre épique est par définition un théâtre gestuel[8]. » Cette observation s'applique avec justesse aux *Projections publiques* : c'est littéralement le geste qui interrompt le « voyage dans la fiction » de l'architecture et qui fait discerner divers degrés d'absorption idéologique masqués par l'autorité physique de l'édifice. Ces montages gestuels humoristiques et incongrus cherchent à révéler des vérités cachées, phénomène semblable au processus d'aliénation (donner au « naturel » le pouvoir d'étonner), que Brecht considérait comme essentiel à toute compréhension.

Comme dernier parallèle, la projection publique est une performance qui met en scène son appareil de production. Les projecteurs et les câbles électriques sont laissés à la vue du public, et Wodiczko lui-même est présent, travaillant avec les appareils et prêt à discuter avec les gens. Cette attitude décontractée est aussi celle des spectateurs, libres de discuter et d'aller et venir comme bon leur semble. À l'opposé du récit dramatique (dont on trouve l'expression la plus achevée de nos jours dans le cinéma de divertissement), le récit épique de Wodiczko remplace la représentation réaliste par la réalité de la production. Dans une telle interaction, non seulement le rôle de l'artiste est démythifié, mais l'œuvre d'art est redéfinie comme lieu d'échange dialectique plutôt qu'économique. Ainsi, le récit projeté se fond avec sa réception pour former un modèle critique visant la réinsertion de l'art dans la vie sociale.

*D.N.*

8 Walter Benjamin, « What is Epic Theater ? » dans *Illuminations*, Schocken Books, New York, 1969, p. 151.

# Biographie / Projections / Expositions / Bibliographie

## Biographie

Krzysztof Wodiczko est né à Varsovie, en Pologne, en 1943. Il a étudié l'art et le design industriel à l'Académie des beaux-arts de cette ville et obtenu une maîtrise en beaux-arts en 1968. De 1968 à 1977, il a travaillé comme concepteur industriel et a enseigné à la Polytechnique de Varsovie. En 1975, il a été invité à l'Université de l'Illinois à titre d'artiste en résidence, et a reçu en 1976 une invitation semblable de la part de la galerie alternative A Space, à Toronto. Wodiczko a immigré au Canada en 1977, enseignant d'abord en Ontario, à l'Université de Guelph et à l'Ontario College of Art, à Toronto, puis au Nova Scotia College of Art and Design, à Halifax (Nouvelle-Écosse), et à l'Université Trent, à Peterborough (Ontario). Depuis 1983, Wodiczko fait la navette entre New York, où il enseigne au New York Institute of Technology, et Halifax, où il continue d'enseigner au Nova Scotia College of Art and Design. Il est devenu citoyen canadien en 1984. Wodiczko est représenté par The Ydessa Gallery, de Toronto, et par la Hal Bromm Gallery, de New York.

## Projections publiques

1980
Toronto, Université de Toronto, installations électriques
Toronto, Métro de Toronto

1981
Boston, Massachusetts Institute of Technology
Halifax (Nouvelle-Écosse), Université Dalhousie, école d'architecture
Halifax (Nouvelle-Écosse), Nova Scotia Power Corporation Plant
Halifax (Nouvelle-Écosse), immeuble de Scotia Square
Peterborough (Ontario), hôtel de ville
Toronto, Musée des beaux-arts de l'Ontario

1982
Adélaïde (Australie), monument commémoratif de la guerre
Adélaïde (Australie), Festival Centre Complex
Sydney (Australie), Art Gallery of New South Wales
Sydney (Australie), MLC (Mutual Life and Citizens Assurance Company) Centre Tower
Sydney (Australie), Qantas International Centre
Sydney (Australie), immeuble d'American Express, dans le cadre de la *Biennale* de Sydney

1983
Banff (Alberta), projection des chutes de la rivière Bow
Dayton (Ohio), Memorial Hall
Dayton (Ohio), Old Courthouse
Dayton (Ohio), Community College Complex
Regina, Museum of Natural History
Stuttgart (République fédérale d'Allemagne), gare centrale
Stuttgart (République fédérale d'Allemagne), colonne de la Victoire
Toronto, monument commémoratif de la guerre d'Afrique du Sud, conjointement à l'exposition à l'Ydessa Gallery

1984
Columbus (Ohio), conférence internationale des humanités sur *1984*, par George Orwell
London (Ontario), Palais de justice fédéral
New York, *Completing Façades*, projections sur l'arc de triomphe de Washington Square et sur l'immeuble de la société American Telephone and Telegraph
New York, Tower Gallery, conjointement à l'exposition *Body Politic*
New York, immeuble Astor/New Museum, dans le cadre d'une exposition tenue au New Museum of Contemporary Art, New York
Seattle (Washington), Seattle Art Museum

1985
Brooklyn (New York), arc de triomphe de la Grand Army Plaza
Berne, édifice du Parlement fédéral
Montréal, place Ville-Marie, Banque Royale du Canada, conjointement à l'exposition *Aurora Borealis*
Purchase (New York), Université d'État de New York, Performing Arts Center
Halifax (Nouvelle-Écosse), monument commémoratif Grand Parade
Londres, Trafalgar Square, colonne de Nelson
Londres, place Waterloo, colonne du Duc d'York
Derry (Irlande du Nord), Guildhall

## Expositions solo

* publication d'un catalogue d'exposition

1970, 1972
Varsovie, Galerie Wspolczesna

1973, 1975, 1976
Varsovie, Galerie Akumulatory 2

1973, 1974, 1975, 1976, 1977
Varsovie, Galerie Foksal

1975
Chicago (Illinois), NAME Gallery
Urbana (Illinois), Université de l'Illinois

1976
Lund (Suède), Galerie St Petri
Montréal, Véhicule

1976, 1977
Toronto, A Space

1977
New York, P.S. 1
Toronto, université York

1977, 1979, 1981
Halifax (Nouvelle-Écosse), Eye Level Gallery

1977, 1978, 1980, 1984
New York, Hal Bromm Gallery

1978
New York, Artists Space

1979
Montréal, Optica
Toronto, Gallery 76

1981
Charlottetown (Île-du-Prince-Édouard), Great George Street Gallery
New York, Franklin Furnace
Peterborough (Ontario), Artspace

1982
Adélaïde (Australie), galerie du South Australian College of Advanced Education *

1983, 1985
Toronto, The Ydessa Gallery

1985
Purchase (New York), Université d'État de New York, Neuberger Museum
Londres, Maison du Canada
Oshawa (Ontario), Robert McLaughlin Gallery
Derry (Irlande du Nord), Orchard Gallery
Halifax (Nouvelle-Écosse), Nova Scotia College of Art and Design, Anna Leonowens Gallery *

## Principales expositions collectives

1969, 1975
Paris, *Biennale de Paris*

1977
Kassel (République fédérale d'Allemagne), *Documenta 6*

1979
Lisbonne, *Biennale du dessin*
Rome, Musée de Rome, *Avant-garde polonaise*

1979, 1982
Sydney (Australie), *Biennale* de Sydney

1981
Vienne, Erweiterte Fotografie, *5 Biennial*

1983
Paris, Centre national d'art et de culture Georges Pompidou, *Présence polonaise*
Stuttgart (République fédérale d'Allemagne), Württembergischer Kunstverein, *Künstler aus Kanada : Räume und Installationen* *
Banff (Alberta), Walter Phillips Gallery, *Social Space*

1984
New York, Tower Gallery, *Body Politic*
Seattle (Washington), COCA (Center on Contemporary Art), *Public Comments*
New York, 49e Parallèle / Centre d'art contemporain canadien, *New York/ Canada*

1985
New York, *Eastern Europeans in New York*
Montréal, *Aurora Borealis* *
São Paulo (Brésil), *Biennale de São Paulo*
Berne, Kunstmuseum, *Alles und Noch Viel Mehr* *

## Écrits choisis sur Krzysztof Wodiczko


*Alles und Noch Viel Mehr : das poetische ABC* (catalogue d'exposition), Benteli, Berne, 1985.

Borsa, Joan, « Krzysztof Wodiczko : Power and Ideology », *Vanguard*, vol. 12 (novembre 1983), p. 14–17.

Coutts-Smith, Kenneth, « Vehicles : Krzysztof Wodiczko at Optica, Montreal and Eye Level, Halifax », *Artists Review* de Toronto, vol. 2 (avril 1979), p. 2–4.

Fleming, Martha, « Künstler aus Kanada », *Artforum*, vol. 22 (automne 1983), p. 81–82.

Horne, Stephen, « Krzysztof Wodiczko : Grand Parade Memorial Projection », *Vanguard*, vol. 14 (novembre 1985), p. 30.

Hume, Christopher, « Not Your Average Slide Show », *Toronto Star*, 16 avril 1983.

Maxwell, Ailsa, *Poetics of Authority : Krzysztof Wodiczko* (catalogue d'exposition), South Australian College of Advanced Education, Adélaïde (Australie), 1982.

Monk, Philip, « Künstler aus Kanada », *Parachute*, vol. 31 (juin–août 1983), p. 46–47.

——, « Krzysztof Wodiczko », *Parachute*, vol. 32 (septembre–novembre 1983), p. 45–46.

Nemiroff, Diana, « Identity and Difference : Canadians at Stuttgart », *Vanguard*, vol. 12 (été 1983), p. 18–21.

Osterwald, Tilman, et Bruce Ferguson, interview dans *Künstler aus Kanada : Räume und Installationen* (catalogue d'exposition), Württembergischer Kunstverein, Stuttgart (République fédérale d'Allemagne), 1983.

« Unmasking Monuments : Krzysztof Wodiczko », *Section a*, vol. 2 (février–mars 1984), p. 2.


## Écrits choisis de Krzysztof Wodiczko


Ostrowski, Andrzej [alias Krzysztof Wodiczko], et Karl Beveridge, « West/East : The Depoliticization of Art », *Fuse* (mars 1980), p. 140–143.

« Public Projection », *Revue canadienne de théorie politique et sociale/Canadian Journal of Political and Social Theory*, vol. 7, nº 1–2 (hiver/printemps 1983), p. 185–187.

« For the De-Incapacitation of the Avant-Garde », *Parallelogramme* de Toronto, vol. 9, nº 4 (avril–mai 1984), p. 22–26.

« The Wall », *Krzysztof Wodiczko Public Projection* (dépliant d'exposition), Anna Leonowens Gallery, Nova Scotia College of Art and Design, Halifax (Nouvelle-Écosse), 1985.

# Prefazione

La Galleria Nazionale del Canadà ha il piacere di partecipare, per la diciassettesima volta, alla *Biennale di Venezia*. Quest'anno Diana Nemiroff, conservatore aggiunto per l'arte contemporanea, ha scelto due artisti legati uno all'altro dall'architettura a rappresentare alla Biennale un aspetto importante dell'arte canadese. Uno è Melvin Charney, l'altro è Krzysztof Wodiczko.

Tutti e due cercano di collocare l'architettura nello spazio. Charney tenta di farlo nello spazio sociale e Wodiczko nel contesto burocratico e politico. Nei due casi, la critica della « costruzione » tenta di rivelare la vita degli esseri umani nel paesaggio urbano.

La Galleria Nazionale del Canadà ci tiene a ringraziare i due artisti per aver consacrato il loro tempo e per aver contribuito alla organizzazione della mostra, e per aver concepito la presentazione dei loro lavori in modo da accomodarli nello spazio e nel luogo che erano stati loro offerti. Ringraziamo anche il Centre Canadien d'Architecture/Canadian Centre for Architecture, Montréal, e la Galleria Ydessa, di Toronto, per averci fornito fotografie della opere. Vogliamo poi dire ancora a Marietta Stern-Guetta, il nostro angelo custode, che la sua presenza a Venezia ci è preziosa. Esprimiamo infine la nostra viva gratitudine a Guy Plamondon, direttore della Divisione Affari Culturali del Ministero per gli Affari Esteri, ed a Yves Pépin, direttore per le arti visuale, per aver contribuito con generosità all'organizzazione di questa esposizione con un aiuto finanziario che ha reso possible la partecipazione attiva degli artisti e la pubblicazione del catalogo. Gli sforzi dei nostri colleghi ed amici al Ministero per gli Affari Esteri rendono ancora una volta possibile la presenza all'estero dell'arte canadese contemporanea.

*Joseph Martin*
Direttore, Galleria Nazionale del Canadà
e Commissario per il Canadà

# Introduzione

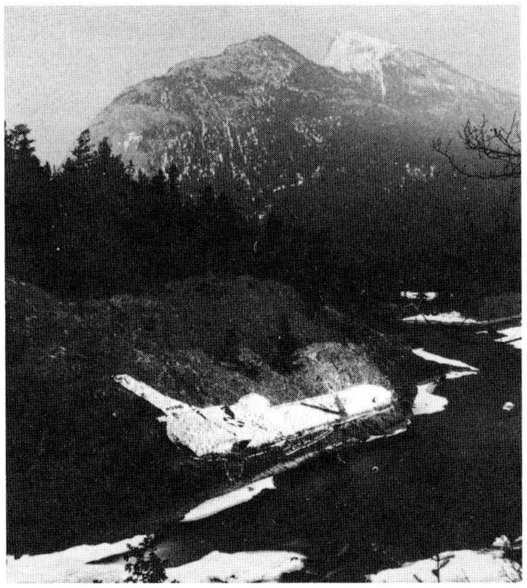

Fig. 1 Krzysztof Wodiczko
*La proiezione di Bow Falls*,
Banff, Alberta, 1983
L'immagine di un missile viene proiettata sulla scogliera di Bow Falls

Il dibattito a riguardo del ruolo dell'arte pubblica (cioè, di qualsiasi lavoro d'arte situato fuori delle mura di un museo, sia se inteso a commemorare qualcosa che a scopo decorativo) si è riacceso recentemente in seguito alla controversia sull'opera *Tilted Arc* [Arco inclinato] di Richard Serra, controversia che è culminata l'estate scorsa nella decisione di togliere l'opera dalla piazza di fronte al Complesso Federale di edifici nella Manhattan bassa. Le implicazioni più profonde del dibattito vanno ben al di là della questione puramente procedurale a riguardo di quale è la consultazione necessaria ed appropriata da avere con il pubblico sulla scelta di punti esterni e sulla posizione di opere d'arte. Esse sollevano la questione se sia possibile o no ora aspirare ad una arte che sia largamente significativa per il pubblico e che nello stesso tempo sia artisticamente viabile. Il dibattito verte sulla mancanza del modernismo di saper indirizzare il problema del posto dell'arte nel forum del discorso pubblico.

Eppure, se opere come *Tilted Arc*, austeramente senza compromessi nel loro ideale formalista, sono state tolte o sono state forzate a sparire dalle strade, i monumenti classici iconograficamente dogmatici che occupano le piazze pubbliche delle nostre città non possono essere riesumati. La loro morte è stata forse simbolizzata nel diciannovesimo secolo dalla distruzione di Haussmann dei caseggiati popolari parigini al fine di creare gli ampi *boulevards* che servono da lunghi tracciati portanti ai monumenti napoleonici tipo Arco di Trionfo. Haussmann ha considerato la città come un vuoto, una superficie deserta su cui tracciare le linee goemetriche dei suoi *boulevards*; egli ha tagliato fuori i monumenti dalla vitalità organica della città, facendoli diventare dei segni eterni di remembranza invece che dei momenti viventi del passato.

L'arte pubblica che è accettabile al giorno d'oggi è quella che sfida il monumento mentre nello stesso tempo cerca di riconoscere l'intersezione di discorsi che compone la realtà del dominio pubblico. Forse è inevitabile e persino necessario, data la natura frammentaria della società contemporanea, che tale arte critica e antimonumentale debba essere marginale e non duratura.

Sia Melvin Charney che Krzysztof Wodiczko contestano il monumento, Charney in uno sforzo di ricuperare quello che è stato escluso dalla rappresentazione e Wodiczko per rivelare quello che è stato nascosto. L'architettura è il legame comune dei due artisti: ciascuno indaga sul significato del linguaggio architettonico, sia quello chiaro e simbolico che quello coperto e ideologico. E così pure, ciascuno usa degli edifici o dei monumenti già esistenti come punti focali dei loro effimeri lavori specificamente concepiti per quei siti.

Molto probabilmente non è accidentale il fatto che sia Charney che Wodiczko abbiano avuto il loro apprendistato in campi al di fuori dell'arte (arte definita nel suo senso più ristretto): Charney in architettura, Wodiczko in disegno industriale. Il tirocinio dei due artisti, necessariamente attaccato alla realtà materiale, non poteva permettersi di essere così coscientemente idealista come lo sono le belle arti; eppure, un idealismo utopistico e tecnologicamente ispirato sta alla base dell'opera di tutti e due gli artisti. Essi, pur essendo scettici su questo idealismo utopistico ed essendo coscienti delle sue limitazioni sociali e politiche, nondimeno portano nella loro arte forme mentali acquisite in discipline con una forte componente sociale.

Charney è « saltato » dall'architettura all'arte agli inizi degli anni Settanta. L'artista è maggiormente conosciuto per i suoi disegni e le sue costruzioni frammentarie, spettrali che esaminano in che modo l'architettura occupa e definisce lo spazio sociale. La sua arte, così come quella di Wodiczko, è anacorata su certe idee fondamentali a riguardo delle esperienze collettive. Ciò ha condotto ad una certa contestazione contro il pregiudizio astorico del movimento moderno nell'architettura. Dalla posizione di cultura di minoranza in Nord-America (quella dei Franco-Canadesi) egli ha criticato quelle premesse antilocali e internazionaliste, il cui solo successo è stato quello di le tracce di memorie collettive immerse nelle strutture urbane.

Wodiczko lasciò la sua nativa Polonia nel 1977. Il suo lavoro aveva già cominciato a trattare con i sistemi, partendo dalla galleria vera e propria per finire alla ampia burocrazia culturale sulla quale la galleria si fonda. Da allora, l'artista è divenuto noto per le sue « Proiezioni pubbliche ». Questi eventi transitori, che hanno luogo di notte, consistono di immagini proiettate su monumenti architettonici scelti, immagini studiate per smascherare il significato nascosto degli edifici e per dare forma al corpo invisibile dell'autorità che essi rappresentano. Wodiczko ha cercato di difendere l'interesse pubblico come interesse collettivo contro quello pubblico come interesse privato mettendo in evidenza la subordinazione dell'architettura agli interessi privati. Se l'architettura è l'incarnazione della macchina burocratica, le proiezioni sono, al contrario, « un controrituale estetico, comunale... un festival urbano notturno[1] ».

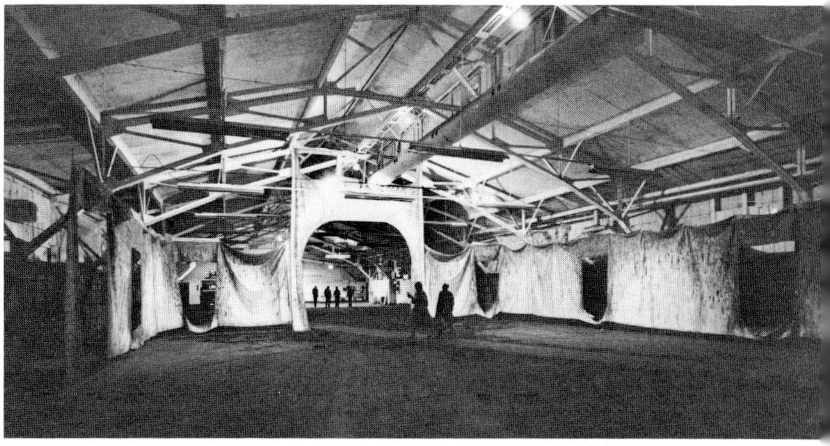

Fig. 2 Melvin Charney
*Una facciata di Stoccarda*, 1983
Costruzione in tela, parzialmente pitturata
7,6 × 39,4 × 0,40 cm
Installata al Navy Pier, Chicago, per l'Esposizione *Chicago Sculpture International: Mile 2*, 1983 (Esposizione internazionale d'arte di Chicago)
Collezione dell'artista, Montreal

Tutti e due, Charney e Wodiczko, pongono i loro lavori in relazione allo spazio sociale delle strade, affermando così i suoi rituali collettivi contro una ipnotica volontà di dimenticare, volontà che è manifesta nella blanda architettura delle città moderne.

Laddove Wodiczko usa un certo senso di umorismo nelle sue proiezioni per fermare lo spettatore e farlo impegnare in un riconoscimento profondo del significato nascosto dietro le facciate, i disegni e le costruzioni rovinate di Charney evocano la storia che gli edifici oscurano, storia dei margini dimenticati della società. Ciascuno dei due artisti cerca a suo modo di scoprire un aspetto vitale della struttura inconscia dell'architettura e, così facendo, rivela la dimensione metaforica dell'ambiente di ogni giorno.

*Diana Nemiroff*
Commissario per l'esposizione

1 Krzysztof Wodiczko, « Public Projection, » *Canadian Journal of Political and Social Theory* 7, No. 1–2 (inverno/primavera 1983): 186–87.

# Melvin Charney

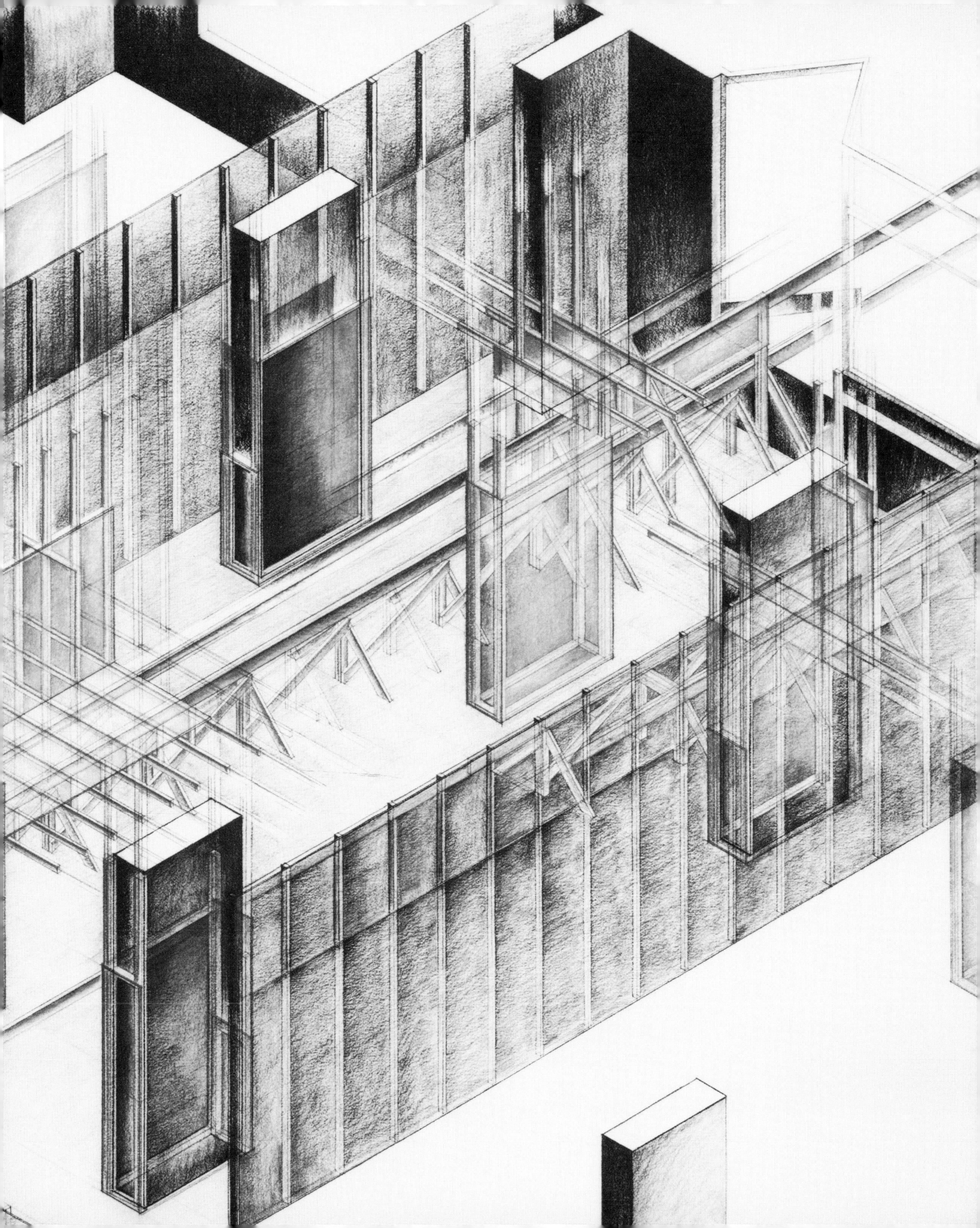

Nella *Civilization and Its Discontents*, Freud usa un'analogia per illustrare la conclusione che « nella vita mentale nulla di quello che è formato puo morire – tutto in un certo qual modo viene conservato[1] ». L'immagine che egli porta è quella di Roma, la Città Eterna, nel cui presente si trovano le tracce del passato. « Ora, con un volo di immaginazione », egli ci dice, « supponiamo che Roma non sia un abitato umano ma un'entità psichica con uno stesso passato lungo e pieno – un'entità, cioè, in cui nulla di quello che un tempo è venuto ad esistere possa essere cancellato e tutte le fasi di sviluppo precedenti continuino ad esistere a fianco di quelle più recenti[2]. » Freud rinuncia successivamente a questa sua metafora, trovandola disadatta. Infatti, una città, a differenza della mente, è normalmente soggetta ad influenze distruttive, come quelle date da lavori di demolizione oppure di rimpiazzo di edifici, ed in questo modo le tracce del suo passato diventano incomplete e frammentarie.

Eppure, se è la città che cerchiamo di conoscere, come avviene nelle costruzioni architettoniche e nei disegni di Melvin Charney, la metafora di Freud della città come psiche, con i suoi strati consci e semi-inconsci, in cui il passato primitivo ed il presente razionale coesistono, è straordinariamente suggestiva. Le costruzioni di Charney possono essere vedute come una specie di scavo nell'inconscio della città. Esse provocano intenzionalmente un ricupero di strati dimenticati di riferimenti, corrispondenze ed allusioni figurative da quel terreno d'amnesia. Le costruzioni costituiscono una serie di spaccature diagrammatiche del paesaggio. Fatte di materiale rozzo che ricordano le impalcature e le strutture di legno dei cantieri edilizi, esse sono incomplete e deliberatamente frammentarie nell'apparenza. Più spesso, esse sono sovrapposte su un edificio già esistente o su un luogo al fine di riportarne in vita la storia fornendo così, attraverso associazioni ed allusioni, un campo di energia simbolica.

In un lavoro precedente, *Les Maisons de la rue Sherbrooke* [Le case della via Sherbrooke], 1976 (vedi ill. 2), viene rivelata la ricchezza di questi riferimenti. Charney scelse per quest'opera un'area urbana in rovina come se ne trovano tante nelle città nordamericane, uno spiazzo vuoto nel centro città di Montreal, che faceva parte di un ampio tratto di terreno lasciato abbandonato inattesa di essere riattivato per l'edilizia. Questa area si trova, e ciò è significativo, all'incrocio di due strade principali, una delle quali era l'arteria principale e passaggio processionale quando Montreal divenne un importante centro metropolitano, mentre l'altra conduce alla parte più vecchia della città, terminando in una piazza davanti alla cattedrale. In questo incrocio egli eresse due facciate fatte di legno compensato con finestre e porte tagliate rozzamente, che specchiavano le case di pietra grigia del diciannovesimo secolo proprio di fronte. Con questo doppione egli creò una configurazione a cancello, che serviva a formalizzare il punto di incontro delle due strade e per richiamare la figura di una piazza cittadina. Eppure, come immagini speculari, le facciate vanno al di là della ricostruzione storica diventando una ricostruzione rituale, quella della ripetizione simmetrica delle loro forme connotanti il piacere dei gesti mimetici.

Abbracciata da impalcature tubolari come un frammento di falsa facciata di casa in un set di Hollywood, questa struttura ricordava, appropriatamente, gli allestimenti creati per gli atti collettivi di una parata stradale. Ed infatti la struttura era parte di un percorso a composto di opere

1 Sigmund Freud, *Civilization and Its Discontents*, trans. Joan Riviere, ed. James Strachey (Londra: The Hogarth Press e the Institute of Psychoanalysis, 1930; ed. riv. 1963; ristampa 1969), 6.

2 Ibid., 7.

d'arte, di bandiere, e di opere fotografiche che si sviluppava per tutti gli otto chilometri della via Sherbrooke, parata che celebrava storicamente e poeticamente la vita di quella via. L'esposizione *Corridart* era stata creata per le XXI Olimpiadi, tenute quell'estate a Montreal. Ma, quattro giorni prima che i Giochi fossero aperti, del personale municipale venne di notte con ordini di demolire questo museo stradale. Ben presto, le tracce di quella espressione monumentale di « libido » comunitario, comprese *Les Maisons de la rue Sherbrooke*, sparivano del tutto.

L'aspetto elegiaco della facciata di Charney si rivelò nella scia di questa distruzione. Ma questa lettura non è da considerarsi più conclusiva di una qualsiasi altra lettura. Costruita in uno strappo del tessuto cittadino, la costruzione era un segno ambiguo. Questa era infatti nello stesso tempo una struttura in costruzione ed una struttura in rovina, un testo di rinnovamento e di distruzione cittadina, ed un'opera d'arte esistente puramente per piacere.

Altri lavori più recenti, come *A Toronto Construction* [Una costruzione in Toronto], 1982 (vedi ill. 8 e 9), e *A Kingston Construction* [Una costruzione in Kingston], 1983 (vedi ill. 10 e 11), sono apparsi analogamente su aree cittadine vuote o aperte, fornendo così una riflessione in relativa tranquillità sul tema della memoria collettiva rappresentata nel tessuto urbano da forme architettoniche archetipe inflesse localmente. In queste costruzioni successive, tuttavia, Charney ha scelto di penetrare il luogo attraverso strati di riferimento proiettati dagli edifici circostanti verso il suo interno, in modo di riproiettare il luogo di nuovo verso la strada, come aveva fatto in precedenza con *Les Maisons*. Ciascun lavoro era unificato a mezzo di un asse processionale che permetteva allo spettatore di attraversare gli strati ricostruiti del luogo. Sebbene entrambe queste costruzioni fossero più dense e strutturalmente più complesse di *Les Maisons* (particolarmente in *A Toronto Construction*), la loro configurazione era radicalmente più astratta dai loro dintorni. In ciascuna, la forma archetipa di una piccola casa con timpano (derivata dagli edifici domestici indigeni) serviva per collegare fra di loro i limiti fisici del posto e le forme più monumentali di una rete rettilinea o di una torre riflettenti le dimensioni secolari/commerciali e sacro/ecclesiastiche della città.

Il vocabolario astratto ed il carattere volumetrico delle costruzioni di Toronto e di Kingston possono essere rintracciati in un gruppo di lavori che aveva tenuto occupato Charney nei sei anni successivi a *Les Maisons*, e che comportava la costruzione di strutture direttamente entro edifici esistenti o fuori da essi. In queste costruzioni, egli si impegnò a decifrare il contenuto figurativo di parecchi edifici tardomoderni (tentando così di restituire a questi pallidi e burocratici esempi di quello stile la memoria del loro eroico periodo d'origine).

Nella prima di queste costruzioni, *Streetwork*, 1978 (vedi ill. 3), commissionata dalla Galleria d'arte dell'Ontario, egli costruì un muro che passava attraverso uno esistente in un edificio e che conduceva dall'interno, dove funzionava da partizione, all'esterno, dove diventava un porticato. La costruzione dava forma concreta alla figura di intersezione di due piani, elemento fondamentale nella sintassi dell'edilizia, che veniva ad essere così richiamata alla mente attraverso l'intermediario di una composizione suprematistica di Malevich (vedi ill. 4). *Streetwork* rendeva concrete fisicamente le origini architettoniche dell'astrazione idealizzata di Malevich, la quale derivava dalla risposta al dinamismo delle forme costruite, ed aveva così un significato metaforico e strutturale nello stesso tempo. Inoltre, apriva una breccia nell'involucro dell'edificio, negandogli il desiderio di esistere come entità separata dal suo ambiente, e spingendo il suo contenuto (e ciò perchè la costruzione era stata fatta per un museo, anche se si rifiutava di essere contenuta in esso) nello spazio della strada.

Dopo *Edifice* [Edificio], 1979 (vedi ill. 5), fatto in Montreal per il Museo d'arte contemporanea, e *Room 202* [Stanza 202], 1979, creato per il P.S. 1 di New York (entrambi questi lavori si ponevano sulla scia delle idee di *Streetwork*), Charney cominciò *A Chicago Construction* [Una costruzione in Chicago], 1981–82 (vedi ill. 6 e 7). Qui egli propose un'analisi molto più elaborata di una struttura che prendeva origine nel suo ambiente e nei precedenti storici locali, ed integrò queste tracce con la rappresentazione di una rete ideale ed astratta simboleggiante un paesaggio industriale. La costruzione si spingeva fuori dalla facciata del Museo d'arte contemporanea di Chicago, creando così un effetto stratificato di palinsesto collegantesi morfologicamente alle costruzioni di Toronto e di Kingston. Le allusioni di Charney alla storia architettonica di Chicago erano quindi molteplici: una stava nella torre mai costruita schematizzata nelle massicce forme della facciata a due piani; un'altra stava nella forma strutturale di tali torri (il disegno muro-schermo del grattacielo stile Chicago) e nella sua rappresentazione idealizzata nel reticolato a quadretti; un'altra ancora era nelle file di case a timpano dai tetti intervallati, tipiche delle case di operai negli anni Venti e le cui forme apparivano, mezze nascoste e ornamentali, nella capriata della facciata; un'altra allusione ancora stava nelle necessità strutturali della costruzione in legno così come si rifletteva in quelle forme; ed infine nella funzione simbolica della facciata stessa come luogo di passaggio dall'edificio alla strada. La costruzione era un assemblaggio di frammenti volti a ricordare la storia sedimentaria degli edifici, tangibilmente materiale eppure semitrasparente come nella metafora di Freud, ed a permettere la lettura simultanea di strati multipli.

La struttura più recente di Charney, costruita come parte di un gruppo di istallazioni specifiche per un porticato semifinito di negozi in un nuovo palazzo in Montreal, continuava il suo esame delle origini dell'architettura moderna. *From Laugier to Popova: A Construction in Parts* [Da Laugier a Popova: una costruzione in parti], 1985 (vedi ill. 21 e 22), dà origine a delle riflessioni sulle costruzioni a trabeazione fatte con lastre di cemento e colonne degli edifici contemporanei, considerandole come della versioni moderne della « capanna primitiva » immaginata da Laugier e da quegli altri che cercavano un modello generativo dell'ordine architettonico. Charney delineò gli elementi base del linguaggio riduttivo della costruzione – mura, colonne, e lastre – racchiudendole parzialmente entro del legno compensato con lo scopo di evocare la loro struttura originale. Alcuni di questi elementi venivavo posti su binari e mossi su di essi, in modo da assumere così un significato di movimento aereo libero, frammenti di un linguaggio da essere manipolato a volontà in qualsiasi configurazione. Il risultato di questa « de-costruzione » richiamava alla mente l'architettura scheletrica delle « macchine » teatrali di Popova e, per associazione, Le Corbusier, la cui teoria della casa come « macchina per vivere » lo pone nella tradizione del razionalismo utopistico i cui tempi vanno indietro fino ai *philosophes* francesi del diciottesimo secolo.

In punti differenti della sua carriera Charney ha costruito strutture relativamente indipendenti tra loro di un posto specifico. Queste costruzioni sono più vicine ai confini tra la scultura e l'architettura di quanto lo siano normalmente altri suoi lavori. Due di queste, *Le Trésor de Trois-Rivières* [Il tesoro di Trois-Rivières], 1975 (vedi ill. 1), e *Pliny on My Mind No. 1 and No. 2* [Pensando al Plinio No. 1 e No. 2], 1983 (vedi ill. 14 e 15), furono entrambe fatte come parte di alcune esposizioni di gruppo e sistemate entro un museo. Ciascuno di questi lavori tratta la relazione fra il linguaggio classico e quello comune nell'architettura e nell'edilizia, un tema che è servito a Charney come veicolo per un'esplorazione delle figure architettoniche archetipe e dei processi a mezzo dei quali il significato dell'ambiente costruito viene comunicato senza riguardo delle distinzioni di scala e di materiali.

Oggetti ritrovati ai margini della società, quelle cose che usualmente vengono considerate rozze, inferiori e rimpiazzabili sono spesso servite a Charney come fonte di ispirazione. Un tale oggetto è stato una fotografia di una casupola di un operaio in una cittadina industriale del Quebec – Trois-Rivières – che lui scoprì nel corso di una sua ricerca sugli inizi della industrializzazione del Quebec. In questa casuccia, costruita di materiale scadente, egli scoprì un aspetto eroico trasmesso attraverso i dispositivi figurativi nascosti nel progetto. Ironicamente, considerata la sua umile costruzione, la forma della casa faceva invece venire alla mente un tesoreria greca. *Le Trésor de Trois-Rivières* si riferisce alla fondamentale ambivalenza della struttura originale la quale era nello stesso tempo un monumento ed una baracca, un tempio ed una tomba. La costruzione di Charney non era una idealizzazione, tuttavia, perchè essa chiaramente commemorava attraverso il suo materiale costruttivo rudimentale la particolare congiunzione delle circostanze economiche e sociali che avevano prodotto questo modesto posto per abitare.

Nel *Pliny on My Mind* Charney si rivolge la questione delle origini, da un punto di vista filosofico piuttosto che storicistico. Nel contesto di una esposizione che celebrava il classicismo architettonico in generale e la villa antica in particolare, egli mise su due costruzioni. La prima, un tempietto classico composto di pilastri e architrave, si trovava in alto su una larga scalinata all'entrata dell'esposizione, il che faceva ricordare il cerimoniale ingresso dalla strada al museo stesso. La seconda, collegata alla prima dal suo assemblaggio e dal materiale rozzo, aveva più del capannone che del tempio, sebbene, come *Le Trésor*, contenesse chiari riferimenti a quest'ultimo. Qui Charney si riferì alla struttura dell'edificio come parte di un caseggiato della città, costrutto questo apparentemente in antitesi con il tema rustico dell'esposizione.

La scala delle due costruzioni e la loro audace ma allo stesso tempo elegante materialità esprimevano la natura concettuale del progetto di Charney. Il classicismo che esse evocavano era reperibile nella logica della struttura espressa razionalmente. Inoltre, estraendo la similarità archetipa delle due strutture, egli metteva in risalto la loro origine comune come bisogno di riparo, bisogno questo la cui elaborazione rituale nell'architettura riflette lo stato materiale del tessuto sociale.

Testimoni permanenti di costruzioni altrimenti transitorie, i disegni di Charney hanno occupato un posto nel corso dei suoi lavori eguale in importanza a quello delle costruzioni. Frequentemente essi sono basati su immagini che egli aveva raccolto dall'ambiente edilizio circostante, oppure immagini prese dai giornali, da cartoline postali, libri e riprese di film. Qui le cose costruite sono rappresentate come avvenimenti della vita quotidiana che compongono le tracce di una memoria collettiva. Questa scorta di immagini gioca, nel lavoro di Charney, più che un ruolo di documentario. Essa include uno strato mitico dal quale egli costruisce proposizioni che si collocano come contromiti, critiche, e commentari sull'architettura come sistema culturale.

La relazione fra i disegni e le costruzioni è fluida. Alcuni disegni precedono una costruzione, altri la seguono, mentre altri infine si collocano come costrutti di per sè stessi. Tale è la serie di disegni sul quale Charney ha lavorato sin dal 1982, a cominciare dalle due proposte per facciate da essere costruite a Kassel, nella Germania occidentale, per la sezione, poi non realizzata, Documenta-Urbana della *Documenta 7*. Intitolata « *Better if they think they are going to a farm* ... » [E' meglio se pensano che stanno andando verso una tenuta agricola...], 1982 (vedi ill. 12 e 13), la proposta intendeva far erigere una facciata ideale di una azienda agricola nella Bahnhofplatz opposta alla stazione ferroviaria oppure passante attraverso i binari del tranvai su una delle strade principali di Kassel.

Nel corso del suo lavoro, Charney è stato cosciente della doppia natura della facciata in parte una struttura, e in parte una messinscena. L'immagine idealizzata della azienda agricola esumava dalla storia recente della Germania l'inganno sinistro degli architetti delle SS, i quali avevano costruito un simile passaggio come bucolico camuffamento dell'ingresso ferroviario al campo di sterminio di Auschwitz-Birkenau: « E' meglio se pensano che stanno andando verso una tenuta agricola... ». Questo portale collega il presente con il passato; è un monumento per piangere e per ricordare, da essere appropriatamente eretto in un luogo di arrivo e di partenza.

Dopo i riferimenti specificamente storici dei disegni di Kassel, Charney si mosse metaforicamente attraverso il passaggio per trovare nei campi di sterminio la figura di una città spettrale: una necropoli disegnata in colori rosso e violetto, una visione di una schiacciante volontà di ordine (vedi ill. 16–19). « Immagina per un momento » dice con percezione improvvisa l'innocente Generale Stumm ne *The Man without Qualities* di Robert Musil « un ordine universale completo che abbracci tutta l'umanità, in una parola, uno stato di ordine civile perfetto. Credimi, è pura entropia, *rigor mortis*, un paesaggio sulla luna, una piaga geometrica[3]! » La città, nei disegni visionari di Charney, è costruita sul modello delle baracche del campo di concentramento, impostata in file intersecantesi di edifici stretti, le cui porte sono aperte per rivelare file di ripiani: spazi crudeli destinati a vite umane. Come ne *Le Trésor*, Charney ha ridotto in una la figura della casa e quella del mausoleo, il che richiama la dichiarazione solenne di Adolf Loos che il lavoro ideale dell'architettura è la tomba dove il « libido » viene finalmente seppellito.

Questi disegni portano all'estremo la logica che governa tutte le asserzioni di Charney. Nella sua opera l'architettura è considerata una « iscrizione dell'uomo nello spazio », un testo da leggere e da interpretare. I disegni e le costruzioni scovano le tracce della volontà umana impresse negli oggetti costruiti, proponendo letture mutevoli, allusive e plurali. Dove i traumi della storia hanno creato blocchi mentali, come nel caso dell'Olocausto, Charney impiega l'architettura come una chiave per schiudere la memoria. Espiato in questo modo il passato, alla città (come alla psiche) è permesso un nuovo inizio. Le sue opere rievocano dunque il passato non per malinconia o per nostalgia, ma col desiderio di basare l'esperienza del presente in un senso pienamente storico, nell'ordine umano così come si trova espresso nelle forme architettoniche. Charney è fondamentalmente un allegorista che, mediante l'uso di costruzioni material mente rozze e frammentarie, abbozza opere dai contenuti monumentali.

*D.N.*

3 Robert Musil, *The Man without Qualities*, vol. 2 (Londra: Picador 1954; ristampa, 1979), 198.

# Biografia / Mostre / Bibliografia

## Biografia

Melvin Charney è nato a Montreal, nella Provincia del Quebec, nel 1935. Dopo aver studiato arte alla School of Art and Design del Musée des beaux-arts de Montréal, egli si iscrive ad architettura presso l'Università McGill di Montreal e continua gli studi presso l'Università di Yale. Nel 1959 si laurea in Architettura a Yale. Dal 1961 al 1964 lavora a New York e Parigi. Nel 1964 ritorna a Montreal, dove ora insegna architettura presso l'Università di Montreal. Oltre all'insegnamento e all'esposizione dei propri lavori, Charney ha anche organizzato due mostre trattanti l'aspetto sociale e architetturale del paesaggio della città di Montreal: *Montréal... plus ou moins* (1972), e *Corridart* (1976), mostra prodotta nel contesto dei Giochi Olimpici di Montreal.

## Mostre personali

* indica il catalogo dell'esposizione

1977
Cambridge, Massachusetts, Università di Harvard*

1978
Toronto, Art Gallery of Ontario

1979
Montreal, Musée d'art contemporain*
Long Island City, New York, Institute for Art and Urban Resources, P.S. 1

1980
Parigi e Bruxelles, Centri Culturali Canadesi

1982
Chicago, Museum of Contemporary Art*
Chicago, Galleria Richard Gray
New York, 49th Parallel, Centre for Contemporary Canadian Art

1983
Kingston, Ontario, Agnes Etherington Art Centre*

1985
Lethbridge, Alberta, Southern Alberta Art Gallery

## Mostre collettive maggiori

1972
Montreal, Musée des beaux-arts de Montréal, *Montréal... plus ou moins**

1973
Parigi, Musée d'art moderne de la ville de Paris, *Canada Trajectoires – '73**
Milano, *Triennale di Milano*, Sezione internazionale

1975
Montreal, Institut d'art contemporain, fatta circolare dai Musei Nazionali del Canadà, *Québec 75**

1976
Montreal, Programma arte e cultura, Comitato organizzatore delle XXI Olympiadi, *Corridart*

1977
Montreal, Institut d'art contemporain, *03 23 03: Premières Rencontres internationales d'art contemporain**

1978
Toronto, Galleria A.C.T., *Architectural Drawings*

1979
New York, Galleria John Weber, *Invitational IV*
Washington, D.C., Galleria Protech-McIntosh, *Art and Architecture: Space and Structure*

1980
Parigi, Centre national d'art et de culture Georges Pompidou, *II^e Biennale de Paris**
Los Angeles, Los Angeles Institute for Contemporary Art, *Architectural Sculpture**
Vancouver, Vancouver Art Gallery, *Architectural References**

1981
Quebec, Musée du Québec, *Art–Société/ 1975–1980**

1982
Toronto, Visual Arts Ontario e la Market Gallery degli Archivi della città di Toronto, *Citysite Sculpture**
Surrey, Columbia Britannica, Surrey Art Gallery, *Drawings by Contemporary Sculptors**
Berlino, Akademie der Künste, *Canada in Berlin*

1983
Stoccarda, Württembergischer Kunstverein, *Künstler aus Kanada: Räume und Installationen**
Quebec, Musée du Québec, *Collection du gouvernement*
Montreal, Musée d'art contemporain, *Art et Bâtiment*
Chicago, Esposizione internazionale d'arte, *Chicago Sculpture International: Mile 2*
Como, Italia, Galleria Il Salotto, *Rendere visibile*
Montreal, Musée des beaux-arts de Montréal, *Les Villas de Pline et l'architecture classique à Montréal*

1984
Chicago, Museum of Contemporary Art, *Ten Years of Collecting*
Düsseldorf, Architektenkammer Nordrhein-Westfalen Akademie, *Festarchitektur**
Berlino, Internationale Bauausstellung, Martin Gropius Bau, *Idee, Prozess, Ergebnis*
Vancouver, Vancouver Art Gallery, *The Praxis Collection*

1985
Milan, *17ª Triennale di Milano*
Montreal, Musée d'art contemporain, *Vingt Ans de collection*
Quebec, Musée du Québec, *La Collection et l'Art du Québec au XXᵉ siècle*
Montreal, Centre international d'art contemporain, *Aurora Borealis**
Chicago, Museum of Contemporary Art, *Projects for Chicago*
Toronto, Evelyn Aimis Fine Art, *Environmental Concerns*

## Scritti scelti su Melvin Charney


Banham, Reyner. *Megastructures – Urban Futures of the Recent Past*. Londra: Oxford University Press, 1976.

Barber, Bruce. « Architectural Reference: Post-modernism, Primitivism and Parody in the Architectural Image ». *Parachute* 21 (inverno 1980): 5–12.

Battisti, Eugenio. « Contro l'International Style ». *Casa del Libro* (gennaio 1982): 24–27.

Bernstein, William e Ruth Cawker. « Corridart, Montreal ». In *Contemporary Canadian Architecture*. Toronto: Fitzhenry e Whiteside, 1982.

Burkhardt, Lucius. « Melvin Charney ». *Werk und Zeit* 4 (aprile 1981): 26.

Burns, James T. « A Gallant Try: Canadian National Pavilion Design Competition for 1970 ». *Progressive Architecture* 48, No. 8 (agosto 1967): 164–65.

Charbonneau, François, Marcel St-Pierre, e Esther Trépanier. « Pratiques artistiques d'opposition à Montréal ». In *Art–Société/ 1975–1980*. Catalogo dell'esposizione. Quebec: Musée du Québec in collaborazione con Les Éditions Interventions, 1981.

« Corridart: The House of Sherbrooke Street ». *Process: Architecture* 5 (marzo 1978): 124–27.

Déthier, Jean. « Melvin Charney: Deux Façades, une provocation ». In *11ᵉ Biennale de Paris: L'Urbanité*. Catalogo dell'esposizione. Parigi, 1980.

Dompierre, Louise e Melvin Charney. *Melvin Charney 1981–1983*. Catalogo dell'esposizione. Kingston, Ontario: Agnes Etherington Art Centre, 1983.

Forster, Kurt W. « Contradiction of Preservation and Destruction ». *Architext* (dicembre 1983): 3–5.

Freedman, Adele. « Building Metaphors – Literally ». *The Globe and Mail* (Toronto) 13 dicembre 1980.

Goldin, Amy. « Report from Toronto and Montreal ». *Art in America* 65, No. 2 (marzo–aprile 1977): 35–47.

Grenville, Bruce. « Melvin Charney ». *Parachute* 32 (novembre 1983): 36–37.

Hatch, Heather. *Citysite Sculpture*. Catalogo dell'esposizione. Toronto: Visual Arts Ontario e la Market Gallery degli Archivi della città di Toronto, 1982.

Hould, Claudette. « Melvin Charney, ou les traces d'une mémoire collective ». *Vie des Arts* 24, No. 98 (primavera 1980): 78–79.

Jacob, Mary Jane. *Melvin Charney: A Chicago Construction*. Catalogo dell'esposizione. Chicago: Museum of Contemporary Art, 1982.

Lamoureux, Johanne. « Melvin Charney, ou l'illusion de la preuve ». *Parachute* 17 (inverno 1979): 66–67.

Lippard, Lucy. *Architectural Sculpture*. Catalogo dell'esposizione. Los Angeles: Los Angeles Institute for Contemporary Art, 1980.

McConathy, Dale. « Corridart: Instant Archeology in Montreal ». *Artscanada* 33, No. 206/207 (luglio–agosto 1976): 36–45.

McDougall, Ian e Kathy Peake. « Melvin Charney ». *Transition* (Melbourne) 2, No. 2 (giugno 1981): 7–10.

Merling, Mitchell. « Truth and Architecture ». *The Fifth Column* 4, No. 1 (autunno 1983): 5–6.

Needham, Gerald. « Melvin Charney: Constructs and Concepts ». *Artscanada* 37, No. 234/235 (aprile–maggio 1980): 24–26.

Nixon, Virginia. « Melvin Charney – Architectural Sculpture ». *The Canadian Forum* 63, No. 728 (maggio 1983): 18–19, 41.

Oechslin, Werner. *Festarchitektur*. Catalogo dell'esposizione. Akademie der Architektenkammer Nordrhein-Westfalen. Stoccarda: Verlag Gerd Hatje, 1984.

Osterwold, Tilman e Bruce Ferguson. Intervista. In *Künstler aus Kanada: Räume und Installationen*. Catalogo dell'esposizione. Stoccarda: Württembergischer Kunstverein, 1983.

Pagé, Suzanne. « Melvin Charney: quelques monuments nationaux ». *Canada Trajectoires – '73*. Catalogo dell'esposizione. Parigi: Musée d'art moderne de la ville de Paris, 1973.

Patton, Andrew. « Melvin Charney at the Art Gallery of Ontario ». *Artists Review* (Toronto) 13 (aprile 1978): 12–13.

Pontbriand, Chantal. « Melvin Charney: Entretien avec Melvin Charney ». *Parachute* 13 (inverno 1978): 26–30.

____, Normand Thériault, e Thierry de Duve. *03 23 03: Premières Rencontres internationales d'art contemporain*. Catalogo dell'esposizione. Montreal: Institut d'art contemporain, 1977.

« Progetto canadese per Osaka '70 ». *L'Architettura* 13, No. 8 (dicembre 1967): 526–28.

« Self-Constructing Exhibition Pavilion ». *Design* (Londra) 231 (marzo 1968): 54–56.

Shapiro, Babs. *Architectural References*. Catalogo dell'esposizione. Vancouver: Vancouver Art Gallery, 1980.

Thériault, Normand. « Melvin Charney ». In *Québec 75*. Catalogo dell'esposizione. Montreal: Institut d'art contemporain, 1975.

Toupin, Gilles. « Charney: L'Architecture archéologique ». *La Presse* (Montreal) 10 novembre 1979.

Tzonis, Alexander. « Un monument contre les massacres et la terreur ». *Le Carré bleu* (gennaio 1972): 13–16.

____ e Melvin Charney. *Melvin Charney: Œuvres 1970–1979*. Catalogo dell'esposizione. Montreal: Musée d'art contemporain, 1979.

## Scritti scelti di Melvin Charney

« The Grain Elevators Revisited ». *Architectural Design* (Londra) 37, No.7 (luglio 1967): 328–31

« A Self-Erecting Exhibition System: Project for the Canadian Pavilion, Osaka Expo '70 ». *Architecture Canada* 46, No.3 (marzo 1969): 34–36.

« Experimental Strategies: Notes for Environmental Design ». *Perspecta: The Yale Architectural Journal* 12 (marzo 1969): 21–32. Traduzione e ristampa in *Deutsche Bauzeitung* 103, No.8 (agosto 1969): 574–81, e in *Formalism, Realism, Contextualism*, curato da Hajime Yatsuka. Tokyo: Shokokusha Publishing Co., 1979.

« On the Liberation of Architecture: Memo Series on an Airforce Memorial ». *Artforum* 9 (maggio 1971): 34–37.

« Pour une définition de l'architecture au Québec ». In *Architecture et urbanisme au Québec*, conférences J.-A. de Sève 13–14. Montreal: Les Presses de l'Université de Montréal, 1971. Traduzione e ristampa in parte in « Towards a Definition of Quebec Architecture ». *Progressive Architecture* 53, No. 9 (settembre 1972): 104–07.

Con Serge Carreau and Colin H. Davidson. *The Adequacy and Production of Low Income Housing in Canada*. Ottawa: Canada Mortgage and Housing Corporation, 1972. Brani scelti in « Low Income Housing ». *Architectural Design* (Londra) 43, No. 1 (gennaio 1972): 7–8, e in *Montréal... plus ou moins*. Catalogo dell'esposizione. Montreal: Musée des beaux-arts de Montréal, 1972.

« Quelques monuments nationaux ». *Architectural Design* (Londra) 44, No.4 (aprile 1974): 241–43.

« Dead End Choices: Housing in Canada ». *Architectural Design* (Londra) 46, No.4 (aprile 1976): 202–06.

*Melvin Charney: Other Monuments 1970–1976*. Catalogo dell'esposizione. Università di Harvard, 1977. Ristampa in *Vanguard* 6, No.2 (marzo 1977): 3–8.

« Corridart: Melvin Charney on Art as Urban Activism ». *Architectural Design* (Londra) 47, No. 7–8 (luglio–agosto 1977): 545–47.

« Modern Movements in French-Canadian Architecture ». *Process: Architecture* 5 (marzo 1978): 15–25.

« Monuments Now: On Contemporary Architecture and the Avant-Garde ». In *Avant-Garde: A History of Innovation and Invention in Architecture*, curato da Geert Bekaert. Eindhoven, Olanda: Università della Tecnologia, 1978.

*Melvin Charney: Œuvres 1970–1979*. Catalogo dell'esposizione. Montreal: Musée d'art contemporain, 1979.

« The Montrealness of Montreal: Formations and Formalities in Urban Architecture ». *Architectural Review* 167, No. 999 (maggio 1980).

« On Architecture: A Statement about Statement ». In *Building with Words*, curato da William Bernstein e Ruth Cawker. Toronto: Coach House Press, 1981.

« À qui le droit: au sujet d'architecture contemporaine au Québec ». *Architecture/Québec* (gennaio–febbraio 1982): 12–24.

« Of Temples and Sheds ». *Architecture/Québec* (ottobre 1983): 11–15.

« Signs of Recognition, Ciphers of Deception ». *Parachute* 36 (settembre–novembre 1984): 38–42.

« Aus einem Wörterbuch der Architektur... über 'Clients' und 'Models' ». In *Idee, Prozess, Ergebnis*. Berlino: Internationale Bauausstellung, 1984.

# Krzysztof Wodiczko

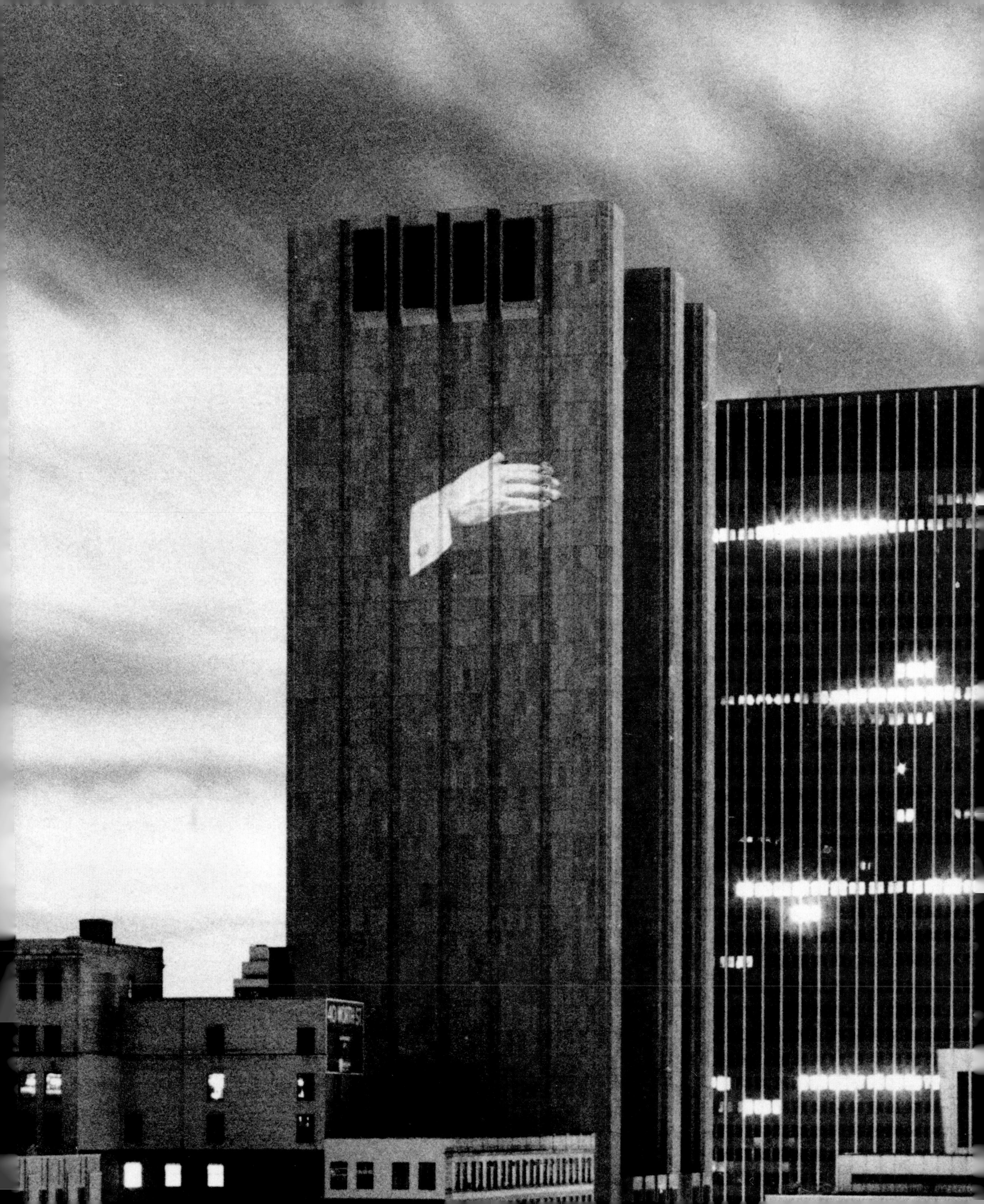

Fig. 3 *Veicolo 1*, Varsavia, 1973

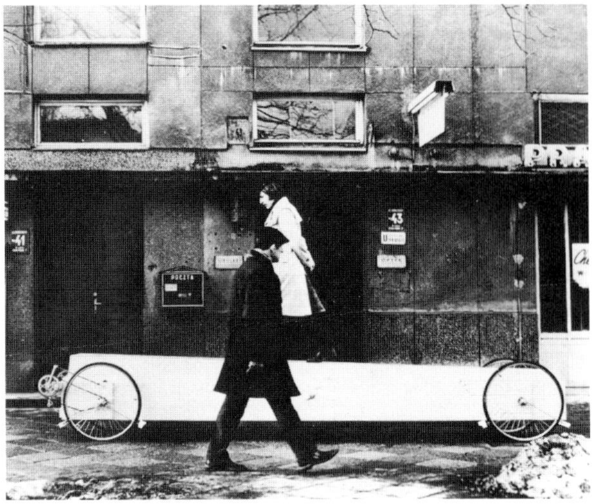

Di fronte a noi vi sono tre fotografie. La prima (fig. 3) mostra un giovane uomo che cammina pensieroso sulla superficie leggermente inclinata di un mezzo insolito di trasporto. Questo veicolo è lungo, basso, e forse è stato costruito con mezzi primitivi: esili ruote di biciclette attaccate alle estremità del veicolo, ed un sistema di ingranaggi e di puleggie, danno un'idea di quale sia il suo mezzo di propulsione. Un uomo più anziano che passeggia nella direzione opposta, pur dando un'occhiata al veicolo ed al suo guidatore, sembra tenere la sua curiosità sotto controllo. La seconda fotografia (fig. 4) è un'immagine presa da un giornale, fortemente ingrandita e drasticamente spuntata. Vi sono due uomini in abito elegante, uno decorato con medaglie, le mani giunte. Con la mano libera, l'altro uomo sostiene leggermente il braccio del primo. Dietro a loro si vede chiaramente il parafango anteriore di una macchina in attesa. Il gesto, separato dall'ambiente circostante, acquista valore e suggestività, come se stessimo intravvedendo in questo frammento il segno di un patto importante. Nella terza fotografia (fig. 5) un grande occhio staccato dal corpo continua a guardare fissamente di sbieco dal frontone del Palazzo del Parlamento svizzero. Questa immagine proiettata dà all'edificio un aspetto sorprendentemente umano che sminuisce la solenne dignità della sua facciata neoclassica. Il Palazzo dà spettacolo di sè.

Le tre fotografie, sebbene rappresentino situazioni ampiamente separate nel tempo (*Vehicle 1* [Veicolo 1] fu scattata nel 1973, quando Krzysztof Wodiczko abitava ancora in Polonia, mentre quella in Berna fu fatta nel 1985), indicano dei filoni comuni del lavoro di Wodiczko. In ciascun caso vi è una rottura di contesto. Un confronto sorprendente con l'opera avviene in un ambiente pubblico, cittadino; oppure un frammento, un'immagine presa dai mezzi di comunicazione, banale e nello stesso tempo politicamente significativo, viene esposto con l'inserzione nella galleria.

E così pure, il corpo viene designato come il sito privilegiato o lo strumento per l'iscrizione del significato. In particolare, l'attenzione viene messa a fuoco nell'atto mentre questo viene trasformato in un gesto simbolico. Dalle fotografie si può dedurre che i lavori sono eventi transitori, contigui alla loro ricezione. Così, il significato e lo scopo dei lavori sono collegati al loro indirizzarsi verso un pubblico e con la risposta di questo fattore largamente imprevedibile.

Entro questa struttura Wodiczko ha elaborato un'analisi delle istituzioni burocratiche a mezzo delle quali il potere viene formalizzato nella società contemporanea: lo stato, l'apparato militare, le istituzioni finanziarie e culturali. Il suo scopo è quello di smascherare e di smitizzare l'autorità ed il potere resi concreti da queste istituzioni, e ciò assoggettando i loro edifici – il corpo fisico, letterale del mito – ad un breve ed improvviso riverbero di scrutinio pubblico.

Sin dal 1980 egli ha usato delle proiezioni composte di montaggi evanescenti in grande scala di immagini e di elementi architettonici, proiezioni pubbliche fatte di notte all'esterno quando tutte le funzioni dell'edificio in cui si svolgono sono interrotte. Con l'aiuto di potenti proiettori alimentati con lampade ad arco di xenon, le immagini dalle diapositive che parlano il linguaggio inconfondibile del potere vengono dirette sul corpo addormentato di un edificio il cui significato ideologico Wodiczko cerca di spogliare dal mistero. Stimolato nel torpore della sua autorità statica ed eterna, l'edificio comincia a gesticolare ed a rivelare le fantasie inconsce nascoste dietro la sua facciata, come quel personaggio di fiaba il cui vestito lo obbliga ad esprimere la pura verità sui suoi desideri. Questo spettacolo ha luogo nelle strade, davanti ad un pubblico che diviene, per tutta la durata dello spettacolo stesso, un unico corpo. Tale pubblico, raccolto a caso, darà una risposta eterogenea, ma esso, come un corpo unico, per quanto venga stimolato dalla proiezione a rispondere coscientemente e criticamente al

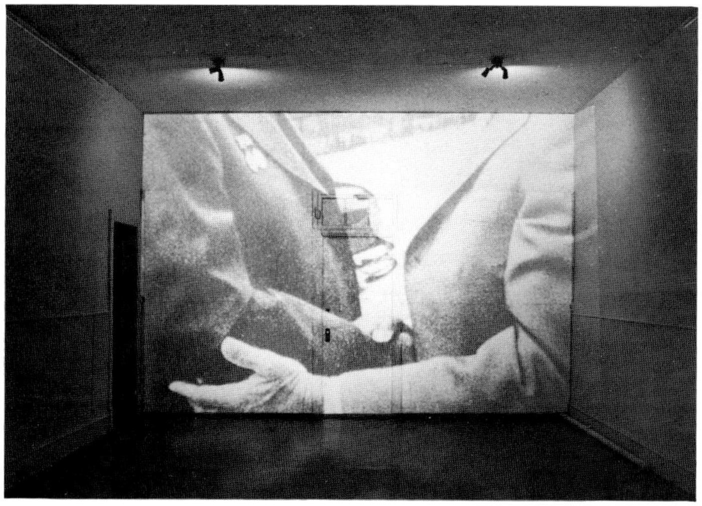

Fig. 4 *Proiezione* (Leonid Brezhnev e Erich Honecker), Galleria Eye Level, Halifax, Nuova Scozia, aprile 1979

messaggio velato dell'architettura, sfida quello che Michel Foucault chiama « la grande fantasia... di un corpo sociale costituito dalla universalità delle volontà[1]. » Il desiderio di Wodiczko di smascherare questo mito, così come è intrinsicamente incorporato negli edifici pubblici, mettendo in mostra gli interessi privati investiti in essi, segue da quanto dice Foucault: « Il fenomeno del corpo sociale è il risultato non di un consenso ma della materialità del potere che opera nei corpi stessi degli individui[2]. »

Nel suo uso di immagini popolari facilmente riconoscibili ed associate con i mezzi di comunicazione, nella sua appropriazione di contesti non artistici, e nella sua teatralità, il lavoro di Wodiczko può essere associato con parecchie delle strategie critiche del post-modernismo. In ogni caso, può trascurare quanto Wodiczko sia stato influenzato, come cittadino e come artista, dalla sua vita in Polonia, dove rimase fino al 1977. La relativa indipendenza della politica culturale dello Stato polacco ha reso quel paese il più liberale di tutti i paesi d'oltre cortina. Sin dalla fine degli anni Cinquanta la burocrazia culturale polacca tollera senza difficoltà le più astruse espressioni di modernismo; il solo tabù è quello di non fare entrare la politica nell'arte. Eppure, come hanno osservato Andrzej Ostrowski e Karl Beveridge:

> La maggior parte degli artisti in Polonia conduce una doppia vita... Il bisogno di disimpegnare l'arte dalla politica è contrapposto alla vita quotidiana dell'artista ed alla necessità di essere coinvolto nella politica ufficiale attraverso la produzione di arte e disegno utili al sistema propagandistico dello Stato... Da una parte, lo Stato ha bisogno di sviluppare dei mezzi di propaganda efficaci per consolidare il suo potere, e dall'altra

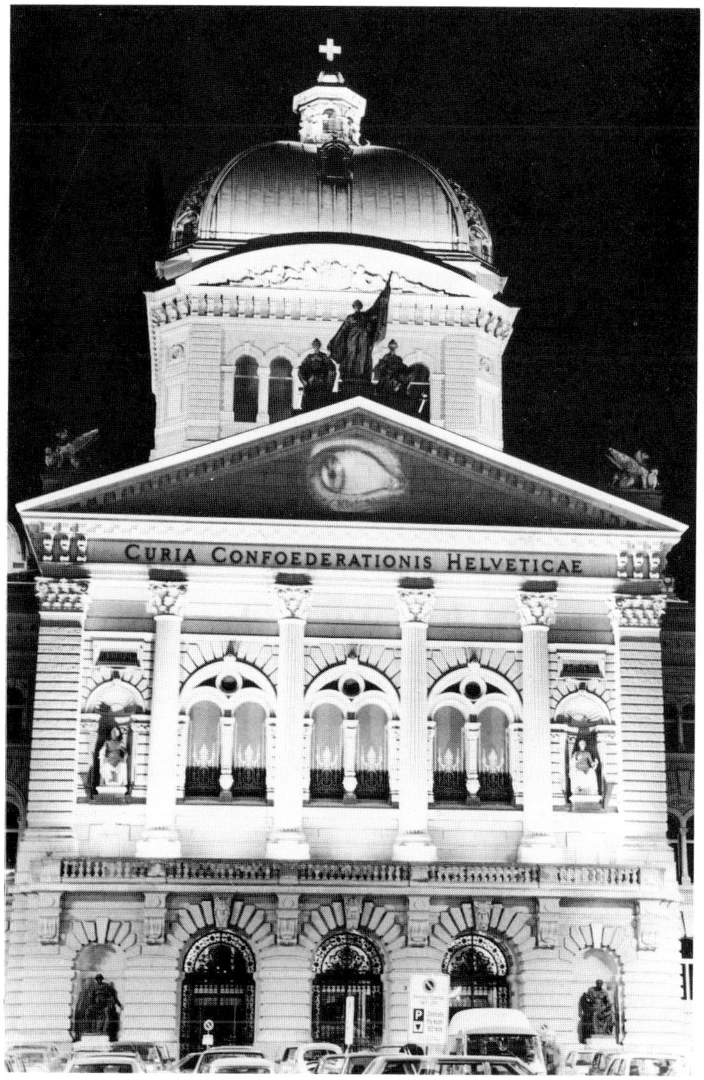


Fig. 5 *La proiezione del Palazzo del Parlamento nazionale svizzero*, Berna, Svizzera, 12–14 aprile 1985

1 Michel Foucault, « Body/Power », in *Power/Knowledge: Selected Interviews and Other Writings 1972–1977* (New York: Pantheon Books, 1980), 55.
2 Ibid.

parte ha anche bisogno di coltivare l'illusione di libertà culturale come una componente della stessa propaganda[3].

In stridente contrasto con la politica di neutralizzazione degli artisti nella Polonia d'oggi sta il ricordo delle aspirazioni dell'arte come strumento di mutamenti sociali da parte dei Costruttivisti Russi e Polacchi. Sebbene nella realtà polacca sia impossibile persino il sogno di questi ideali eroici ed utopistici, alcune strategie del Costruttivismo furono ritenute e trasmesse a Wodiczko e ad altri attraverso il loro apprendistato in disegno. E così, la necessità di pensare in termini dell'ambiente globale in combinazione con l'attuale impotenza politica crearono le premesse per una potente spinta ad elaborare una critica delle politiche della burocrazia culturale.

Eppure, il pericolo di uno stato incessante di opposizione teorica nell'assenza di una qualsiasi azione concreta immaginabile (pericolo questo tanto più grande quanto più l'apparato ideologico dello Stato adotta una politica apparentemente sempre più liberale) viene a realizzarsi nella vulnerabilità dell'artista alla seduzione e al suo assorbimento alla ragione burocratica.

Mentre era ancora in Polonia, Wodiczko cominciò a dare delle risposte a questa situazione problematica con dei disegni che proponevano dei veicoli i quali potevano essere interpretati come dei modelli analitici dei meccanismi politici dello Stato. *Vehicle 1*, 1973, fu il solo per il quale un prototipo fu costruito. Questa elegante macchina, costruita per uso esclusivo dell'artista, veniva mossa dall'azione dell'artista che camminava in atteggiamento di contemplazione filosofica avanti e indietro lungo una piattaforma inclinata. Il movimento ad altalena che ne risultava permetteva che l'energia liberata venisse trasmessa alle ruote a mezzo di un sistema di cavi e di ingranaggi. Tutto il lavoro veniva però convertito in un movimento del veicolo in una direzione sola su una linea retta. Fra le altre proposte di Wodiczko vi fu quella di un veicoloper i lavoratori, di un veicolo per un gruppo occasionalmente formato di cittadini (allineati su una piazza), e persino per della gente che discuteva in un caffè. Sebbene i veicoli variassero nel tipo di moto permesso – dall'ovvia e futile ripetizione alla relativa assenza di costrizioni – tutti erano limitati ad un moto lineare e unidirezionale.

La strategia di queste costruzioni è chiaramente allegorica, dettata dal bisogno di « parlare pubblicamente con mezzi nascosti, per rispondere alla proibizione di parlare liberamente in pubblico[4]. » Esse ci informano obliquamente e con un senso vivo di ironia che la misura della libertà individuale non sta solo nel grado di movimento permesso, ma anche nell'effetto di quel movimento; in assenza di un meccanismo di guida che possa influenzare la direzione verso cui va lo Stato, la capacità dell'individuo di cambiare questa direzione è minima.

Wodiczko, in seguito, estese il suo uso della strategia allegorica quando introdusse il montaggio in un gruppo di lavori prodotti fra il 1976 ed il 1978. Questi lavori, che hanno inizio con una presentazione analitica delle proprietà delle linee (linee come teoria, oggetto, immagine, e realtà) e proseguono fino al tentativo d'esplorazione degli elementi lineari analoghi ai gesti nell'arte e nella propaganda, rappresentano un ulteriore tentativo di associare l'arte con la realtà sociale e politica. Come opere di transizione, esse costituiscono un punto di interrogazione della galleria. A seconda della tecnica di montaggio usata (confisca, sovrapposizione, oppure frammentazione), comune sia alla allegoria politica che alla pubblicità, questi lavori sono di interesse principalmente per la loro dimostrazione di come la struttura di un sistema possa essere usata per dare struttura ad un'altra costruzione o per trasferire tale struttura ad un'altra, eseguendo così un trasferimento di significato.

La lezione appresa da questo lavoro fu trasferita nelle *Public Projections*, che segnarono la rottura definitiva di Wodiczko con il museo come supporto strutturale del suo lavoro. La logica del movimento dallo spazio del museo allo spazio pubblico offerto dall'ambiente architettonico urbano che agiva come schermo per le sue proiezioni era insita nella sua applicazione della strategia del montaggio appresa dai suoi predecessori d'avanguardia degli inizi del ventesimo secolo. Benjamin Buchloh fa notare:

> Anche se queste attività hanno avuto origine nell'istituzione socialmente isolata dell' « avanguardia » e nella pratica di arte, una caratteristica essenziale di queste attività sin dal loro inizio fu di considerare le questioni di dominazione ideologica nel posto materiale della loro funzione, e cioè proprio nel sistema di rappresentazione dove si verificano ed esercitano il loro potere. E fu ugualmente essenziale che l'operazione formale nei costrutti ideologici dovesse essere strutturata materialmente... in un modo che garantisse la capacità dell'opera di rientrare proprio nello stesso discorso, nella sua forma di circolazione e sistema di distribuzione[5].

Consone con l'opposizione di Wodiczko alla sepoltura dell'avanguardia[6], le *Public Projections* possono essere vedute come un tentativo di modello di una sfera pubblica di

3 Andrzej Ostrowski (conosciuto anche come Krzysztof Wodiczko) e Karl Beveridge, « *West/East: The Depoliticization of Art* », *Fuse* (marzo 1980), 141.

4 Benjamin H.D. Buchloh, « Montage and Allegorical Deconstruction », in *Vocation/Vacation*, catalogo dell'esposizione, Galleria Walter Phillips (Banff, Alberta, 1981), senza numerazione delle pagine.

5 Ibid.

6 Krzysztof Wodiczko, « For the De-Incapacitation of the Avant-Garde », *Parallelogram* 9, No. 4 (aprile–maggio 1984), 22–26.

produzione che rimane tuttora visibile e persuasiva come arte. L'effetto di questo montaggio provocante di immagini da diapositive sul corpo degli edifici pubblici e dei monumenti è quello di mettere in risalto la differenza che esiste fra l'esperienza sensuale, materiale della proiezione ed il linguaggio normale, « ufficiale », dell'architettura come *rottura* nel tessuto mitico del corpo sociale rappresentato dall'edificio.

Quale'è la natura di questo corpo sociale rappresentato dall'architettura? Secondo Wodiczko, è un « corpo disciplinato e disciplinante » basato sulla relazione regolamentata fra il tutto e le parti e fra ciascuna parte e le altre parti. Immutevole ed universale, il suo spirito è lo spirito del nome del padre, la Legge che seduce « per la sua capacità strutturale di assorbire... la nostra spinta nascosta, intima, che ci invita ad una collaborazione disciplinata con il suo potere ». L'edificio non è solo il sito fisico degli istituti del potere, ma è anche un « mezzo spaziale per la reproduzione simbolica continua e simultanea sia del mito generale del potere che del desiderio universale di potere[7]. »

Le *Public Projections* distruggono il mito rendendo visualmente concreta l'ideologia implicita dell'edificio e poi sovrapponendo queste immagini al corpo stesso del mito, cioè, nel luogo materiale della sua funzione. Improvvisamente l'edificio viene impersonificato. Consideriamo ora brevemente alcune delle proiezioni più recenti. Sulla facciata grigia dell'alto edificio della AT & T nel cuore di Manhattan (vedi ill. 31) una mano in un polsino inamidato invita all'impegno americano di fedeltà: agli ideali democratici degli Stati Uniti d'America, oppure ai suoi interessi multinazionali che hanno aiutato ad abbattere altrove quegli stessi ideali? Sull'ampia base della torre cruciforme di Place Ville-Marie di Montreal, sede delle operazioni finanziarie della Royal Bank of Canada (ed anche sede del consolato del Sudafrica, che affitta locali nell'edificio), appaiono un paio di pugni minacciosi (vedi ill. 34). Il potere politico della comunità bancaria internazionale e la politica dell'apartheid del governo sudafricano sono così congiunte in quest'unica immagine della violenza. La proiezione interrompe la funzionalità blanda degli edifici, così come avviene quando si ha un annuncio commerciale pagato da chi l'ha voluto. La forma della proiezione è allo stesso modo frammentaria e la sua durata è breve ma, là dove il linguaggio seducente dell'annuncio commerciale invita al consenso, la proiezione parla di proprietà privata e di interessi privati al fine di sollecitare una presa di coscienza ed una discussione.

Analogamente, su dei monumenti classici che commemorano la gloria eterna delle vittorie passate, egli proietta immagini di strumentazione militare moderna. Sull'arco commemorativo della Grand Army Plaza di Brooklyn due testate di missili, una americana e l'altra russa, sono unite con una catena e con un catenaccio (vedi ill. 32). La realtà degli ideali di giustizia e di libertà identificati dal linguaggio classico dell'architettura (fatto proprio da ogni nazione) contrasta con la battaglia acerrima che è in corso fra le due superpotenze per la superiorità militare. Ai piedi della Colonna del Duca di York in Londra vengono proiettate delle figure marcianti di minatori di carbone inglesi in sciopero, mentre sopra di loro la base del monumento viene temporaneamente mobilitata dalla struttura di un carro armato in moto (vedi ill. 35). Due mani d'uomo sono incrociate come per difendere il fondo di questa sporgenza fallica, come se il monumento avvertisse il bisogno di protezione dai tumulti d'oggigiorno e volesse indirizzare le sue forze verso campi d'azione domestici. Mettendo a confronto il monumento

7 Wodiczko, « Public Projection », *Canadian Journal of Political and Social Theory* 7, No. 1–2 (inverno/primavera 1983), 185.

retorico con l'evidenza offerta dalla realtà contemporanea, la proiezione mette in risalto l'inganno del suo idealismo umanistico e rimette a fuoco le relazioni di potere che tale idealismo maschera.

Siccome le *Public Projections* non sono puramente didattiche, è necessario domandarsi qual'è il loro effetto in termini di arte, in particolare il loro effetto teatrale. Esse operano come interruzioni spettacolari nel rituale mistificatore dell'architettura: in un momento scelto lo sguardo dei proiettori viene girato verso un edificio o un monumento, ed il palazzo ipnotizzato comincia il suo spettacolo. Ciascuna interruzione, essendo stata studiata per sorprendere gli spettatori a causa della sua incongruenza e imprevedibilità, crea un intervallo, un'apertura per una riflessione critica. Quindi, la proiezione-come-interruzione funziona come meccanismo alienante studiato al fine di disturbare la disposizione che il pubblico ha verso la sua unione con l'edificio, e ciò perchè vengono rese improvvisamente visibili le sue fondamenta ideologiche.

L'uso da parte di Wodiczko dell'interruzione come dispositivo fondamentale di strutturazione invita ad una considerazione su alcuni paralleli fra le *Public Projections* e la teoria di Brecht del teatro epico. Sebbene l'effetto di ciascuna proiezione sia calcolato in relazione a ciascun lavoro specifico di architettura, le proiezioni collettivamente assumono il carattere di narrazione epica. A differenza del teatro drammatico, il cui effetto dipende dal progresso cumulativo dell'azione, un'opera epica può essere rotta o interrotta, pur conservando in ciascun segmento una vita completa. Walter Benjamin ha osservato che il risultato di questo processo di interruzione è di privilegiare il gesto, e quindi: « Il teatro epico è per definizione un teatro di gesti[8]. » La appropriatezza di questa osservazione nel caso di *Public Projections* è ovvia: è letteralmente attraverso gesti che il discorso fittizio dell'architettura viene interrotto e le condizioni per l'assorbimento ideologico mascherate dalla sua autorità fisica vengono rese riconoscibili. Lo smascheramento che Wodiczko cerca attraverso l'incongruenza comica del gesto montato può essere considerato come analogo al processo di alienazione (cioè dare al « naturale » la forza di ciò che è sorprendente) che Brecht ritenne necessario per una comprensione completa.

Un parallelo finale dovrebbe essere messo in evidenza. La proiezione pubblica è uno spettacolo che mette in mostra l'apparato della sua produzione. Non solo sono chiaramente in vista i proiettori e tutti i fili elettrici di collegamento, ma Wodiczko stesso appare mentre lavora sull'apparato ed è disponibile al dibattito. Questa atmosfera rilassata si allarga agli spettatori che sono liberi di discutere gli eventi e di andare e venire a loro piacere. In contrasto con la narrazione drammatica (evidente nel film d'intrattenimento d'oggigiorni), la narrazione epica di Wodiczko sostituisce realismo di produzione a realismo di rappresentazione. Non solo viene reso chiaro il ruolo dell'artista attraverso tale interazione, ma il lavoro d'arte viene ridefinito come il luogo dove avviene uno scambio che è dialettico in natura, invece che economico. E così la narrativa proiettata si fonde con la sua recezione, creando un modello critico per la reintegrazione dell'arte nella vita sociale.

*D.N.*

8 Walter Benjamin, « What is Epic Theater? », in *Illuminations* (New York: Shocken Books, 1969), 151.

# Biografia / Proiezioni / Mostre / Bibliografia

## Biografia

Krzysztof Wodiczko è nato a Varsavia, in Polonia, nel 1943. Ha studiato arte e disegno all'Accademia delle Belle Arti di Varsavia, dove si è laureato in Disegno Industriale nel 1968. Dal 1968 al 1977 egli lavora come « industrial designer »; nello stesso tempo, insegna al Politecnico di Varsavia. Nel 1975 viene invitato dall'Università dell'Illinois e, contemporaneamente, dalla galleria A Space di Toronto ad occupare il posto di « artista interno ». Wodiczko si trasferisce in Canadà nel 1977, dove insegna dapprima all'Università di Guelph, nell'Ontario e, successivamente, nel Ontario College of Art in Toronto, nel Nova Scotia College of Art and Design in Halifax, e nell'Università di Trent a Peterborough in Ontario. Sin dal 1983 Wodiczko vive e lavora per parte dell'anno in New York, dove insegna nel New York Institute of Technology, e parte in Canadà, dove continua ad insegnare al Nova Scotia College of Art and Design. Wodiczko ha assunto la cittadinanza canadese nel 1984. I suoi lavori sono rappresentati alla Galleria Ydessa di Toronto, ed alla Galleria Hal Bromm di New York.

## Proiezioni pubbliche

1980
Toronto, Università di Toronto, Edificio della centrale elettrica
Toronto, Sotterranea di Toronto

1981
Boston, Massachusetts Institute of Technology
Halifax, Nuova Scozia, Università di Dalhousie, Scuola di Architettura
Halifax, Nuova Scozia, Stabilimento della Nova Scotia Power Corporation
Halifax, Nuova Scozia, Palazzi della Scotia Square
Peterborough, Ontario, Municipio
Toronto, Art Gallery of Ontario

1982
Adelaide, Australia, Monumento commemorativo ai caduti di guerra
Adelaide, Australia, Complesso centrale per i festivali
Sydney, Art Gallery of New South Wales
Sydney, Palazzo centrale della MLC (Mutual Life and Citizens Assurance Company)
Sydney, Centro internazionale della Qantas
Sydney, Edificio della American Express (in concomitanza con la *Sydney Biennale*)

1983
Banff, Alberta, Cascate di Bow, proiezioni sulla scogliera
Dayton, Ohio, Memorial Hall
Dayton, Ohio, Old Courthouse
Dayton, Ohio, Community College Complex
Regina, Museum of Natural History
Stoccarda, Stazione ferroviaria principale
Stoccarda, Colonna della Vittoria
Toronto, Monumento commemorativo ai caduti della guerra sudafricana (in concomitanza con l'esposizione della Galleria Ydessa)

1984
Columbus, Ohio, Conferanza Internazionale sull'Umanità nel *1984* di George Orwell
London, Ontario, Tribunale Federale
New York, *Completing Façades*, proiezioni sull'Arco commemorativo di Washington, Washington Square, e sul Palazzo della AT & T
New York, Galleria Tower (in concomitanza con l'esposizione *Body Politic*)
New York, Edificio Astor/New Museum (in concomitanza con le esposizioni *On View* e *Difference: Representation and Sexuality*)
Seattle, Washington, Seattle Art Museum

1985
Brooklyn, Grand Army Plaza, Arco commemorativo
Berna, Svizzera, Palazzo del Parlemento
Montreal, Place Ville-Marie, Edificio della Royal Bank of Canada (in concomitanza con l'esposizione *Aurora Borealis*)
Purchase, New York, Università di Stato di New York, Performing Arts Center
Halifax, Nuova Scozia, Monumento commemorativo della Grand Parade
Londra, Trafalgar Square, Monumento a Nelson
Londra, Waterloo Place, Monumento al Duca di York
Derry, Irlanda del Nord, Guildhall

## Mostre personali

* indica il catalogo dell'esposizione

1970, 1972
Varsavia, Galleria Wspolczesna

1973, 1975, 1976
Varsavia, Galleria Akumulatory 2

1973, 1974, 1975, 1976, 1977
Varsavia, Galleria Foksal

1975
Chicago, Galleria NAME
Urbana, Illinois, Università dell'Illinois

1976
Lund, Svezia, Galleria St. Petri
Montreal, Véhicule

1976, 1977
Toronto, A Space

1977
New York, P.S. 1
Toronto, Università di York

1977, 1979, 1981
Halifax, Nuova Scozia, Galleria Eye Level

1977, 1978, 1980, 1984
New York, Galleria Hal Bromm

1978
New York, Artists Space

1979
Montreal, Optica
Toronto, Galleria 76

1981
Charlottetown, Isola del Principe Edoardo, Galleria di Great George Street
New York, Franklin Furnace
Peterborough, Ontario, Artspace

1982
Adelaide, Australia, Galleria della South Australian College of Advanced Education*

1983, 1985
Toronto, Galleria Ydessa

1985
Purchase, New York, Università di Stato di New York, Neuberger Museum
London, Canada House
Oshawa, Ontario, Galleria Robert McLaughlin
Derry, Irlanda del Nord, Galleria Orchard
Halifax, Nuova Scozia, Nova Scotia College of Art and Design, Galleria Anna Leonowens*

## Mostre collettive maggiori

1969, 1975
Parigi, *Biennale de Paris*

1977
Kassel, Repubblica Federale della Germania, *Documenta* 6

1979
Lisbona, *Drawing Biennal*
Roma, Museo di Roma, *Avanguardia polacca*

1979, 1982
Sydney, *Sydney Biennale*

1981
Vienna, Erweiterte Fotografie, *5 Biennial*

1983
Parigi, Centre national d'art et de culture Georges Pompidou, *Présence polonaise*
Stoccarda, Württembergischer Kunstverein, *Künstler aus Kanada: Räume und Installationen**
Banff, Alberta, Galleria Walter Phillips, *Social Space*

1984
New York, Galleria Tower, *Body Politic*
Seattle, Washington, COCA (Center on Contemporary Art), *Public Comments*
New York, 49th Parallel, Centre for Contemporary Canadian Art, *New York/ Canada*

1985
New York, *Eastern Europeans in New York*
Montreal, *Aurora Borealis**
San Paolo, Brasile, *São Paulo Biennal*
Berna, Svizzera, Kunstmuseum, *Alles und Noch Viel Mehr* *

## Scritti scelti su Krzysztof Wodiczko


*Alles und Noch Viel Mehr: das poetische ABC*. Catalogo dell'esposizione. Berna, Svizzera: Benteli, 1985.

Borsa, Joan. « Krzysztof Wodiczko: Power and Ideology ». *Vanguard* 12 (novembre 1983): 14–17.

Coutts-Smith, Kenneth. « Vehicles: Krzysztof Wodiczko at Optica, Montreal, and Eye Level, Halifax ». *Artists Review* (Toronto) 2 (aprile 1979): 2–4.

Fleming, Martha. « Künstler aus Kanada ». *Artforum* 22 (autunno 1983): 81–82.

Horne, Stephen. « Krzysztof Wodiczko: Grand Parade Memorial Projection ». *Vanguard* 14 (novembre 1985): 30.

Hume, Christopher. « Not Your Average Slide Show ». *Toronto Star*, 16 aprile 1983.

Maxwell, Ailsa. *Poetics of Authority: Krzysztof Wodiczko*. Catalogo dell'esposizione. Adelaide, Australia: South Australian College of Advanced Education, 1982.

Monk, Philip. « Künstler aus Kanada ». *Parachute* 31 (guigno, luglio, agosto 1983): 46–47.

____. « Krzysztof Wodiczko ». *Parachute* 32 (settembre, ottobre, novembre 1983): 45–46.

Nemiroff, Diana. « Identity and Difference: Canadians at Stuttgart ». *Vanguard* 12 (estate 1983): 18–21.

Osterwold, Tilman e Bruce Ferguson. Intervista. In *Künstler aus Kanada: Räume und Installationen*. Catalogo dell'esposizione. Stoccarda: Württembergischer Kunstverein, 1983.

« Unmasking Monuments: Krzysztof Wodiczko ». *Section a* 2 (febbraio–marzo 1984): 2.


## Scritti scelti di Krzysztof Wodiczko


Ostrowski, Andrzej (conosciuto anche come Krzysztof Wodiczko) e Karl Beveridge. « West/East: The Depoliticization of Art ». *Fuse* (marzo 1980): 140–43.

« Public Projection ». *Canadian Journal of Political and Social Theory/Revue canadienne de théorie politique et sociale* 7, No. 1–2 (inverno/primavera 1983): 185–87.

« For the De-Incapacitation of the Avant-Garde ». *Parallelogramme* (Toronto) 9, No. 4 (aprile–maggio 1984): 22–26.

« The Wall ». *Krzysztof Wodiczko Public Projection*. Foglietto dell'esposizione. Halifax, Nuova Scozia: Nova Scotia College of Art and Design, Galleria Anna Leonowens, 1985.

# Plates
# Planches
# Illustrazioni

# Melvin Charney

1 *The Treasury of Three Rivers*, 1975
*Le Trésor de Trois-Rivières*, 1975
*Il tesoro di Trois-Rivières*, 1975

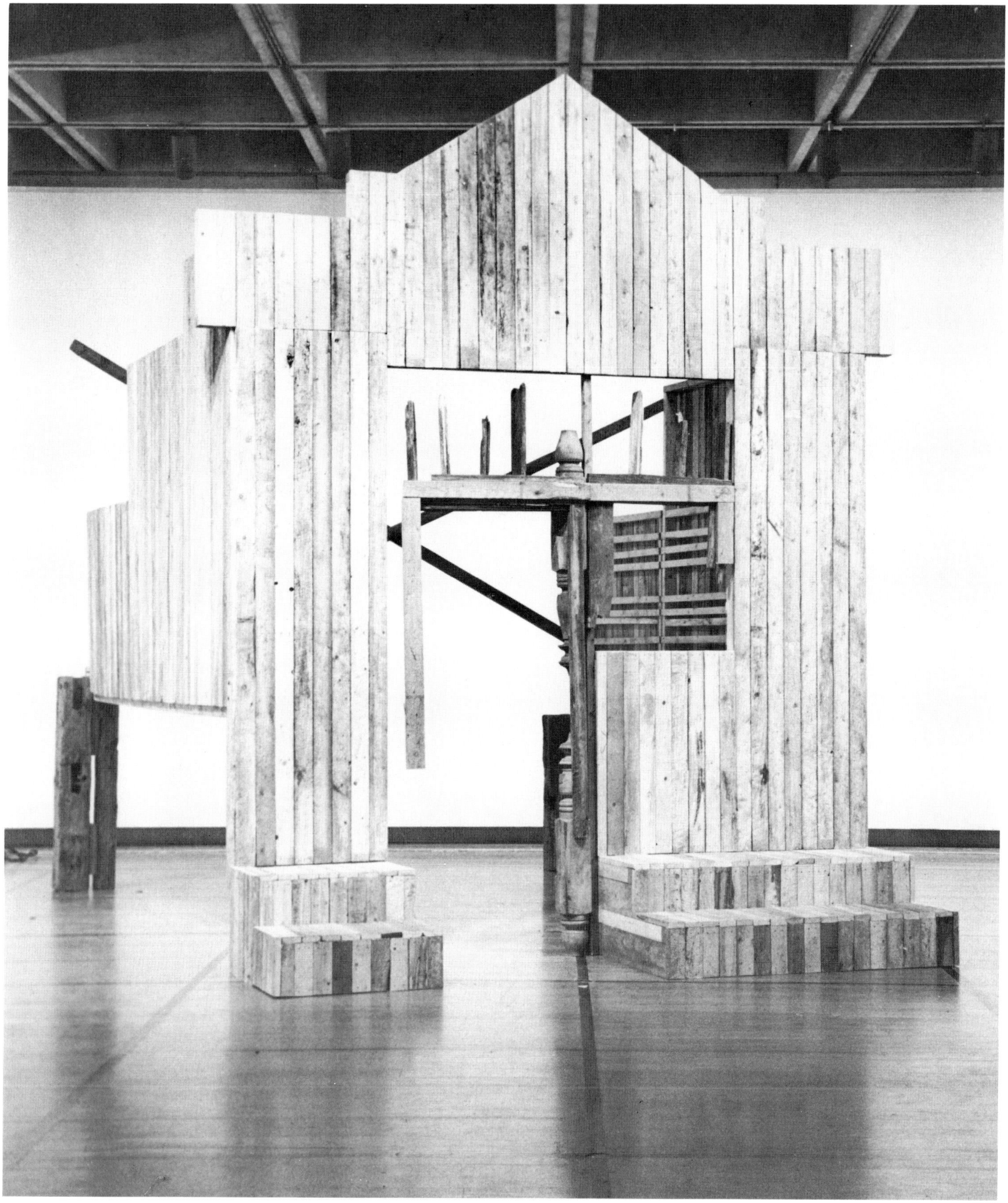

2 *The Houses of Sherbrooke Street*, 1976
*Les Maisons de la rue Sherbrooke*, 1976
*Le case de la via Sherbrooke*, 1976

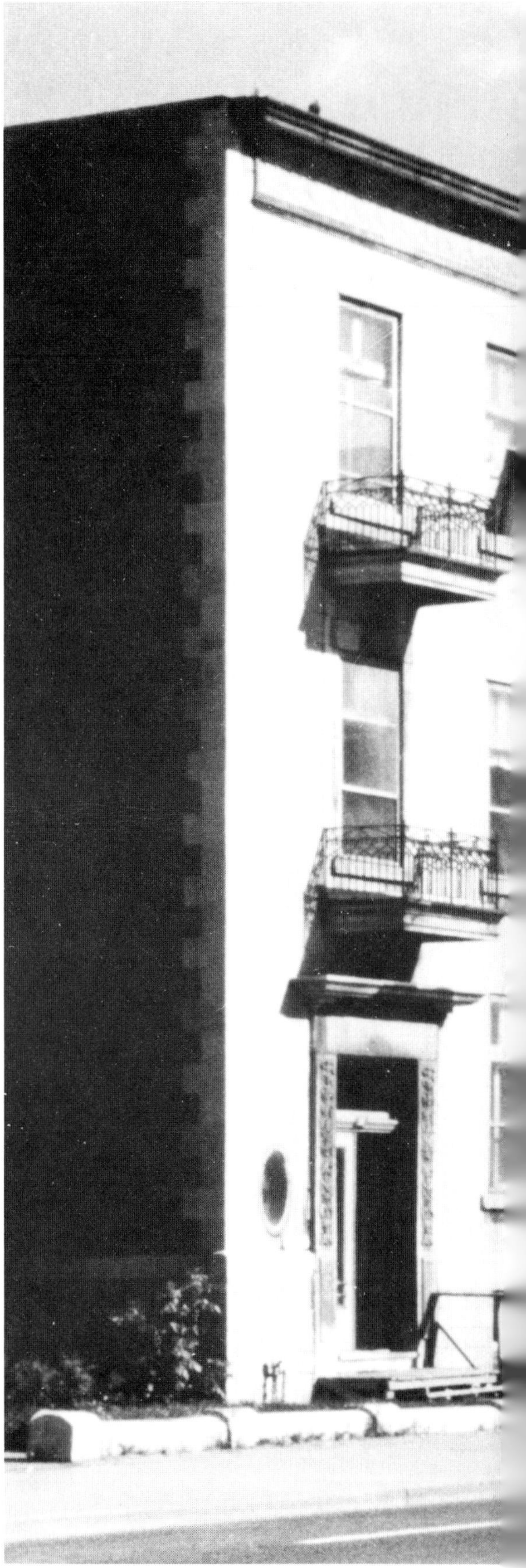

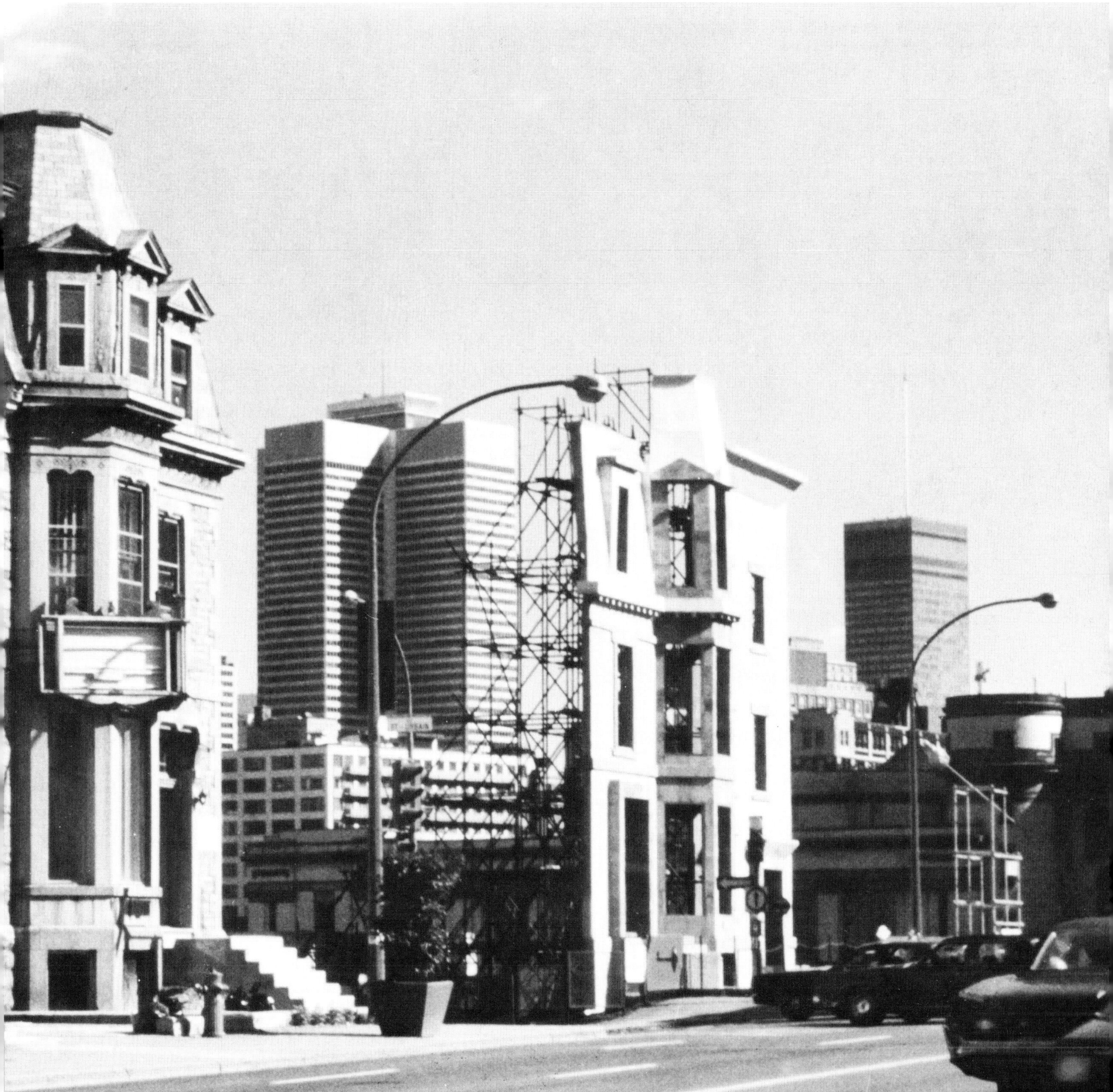

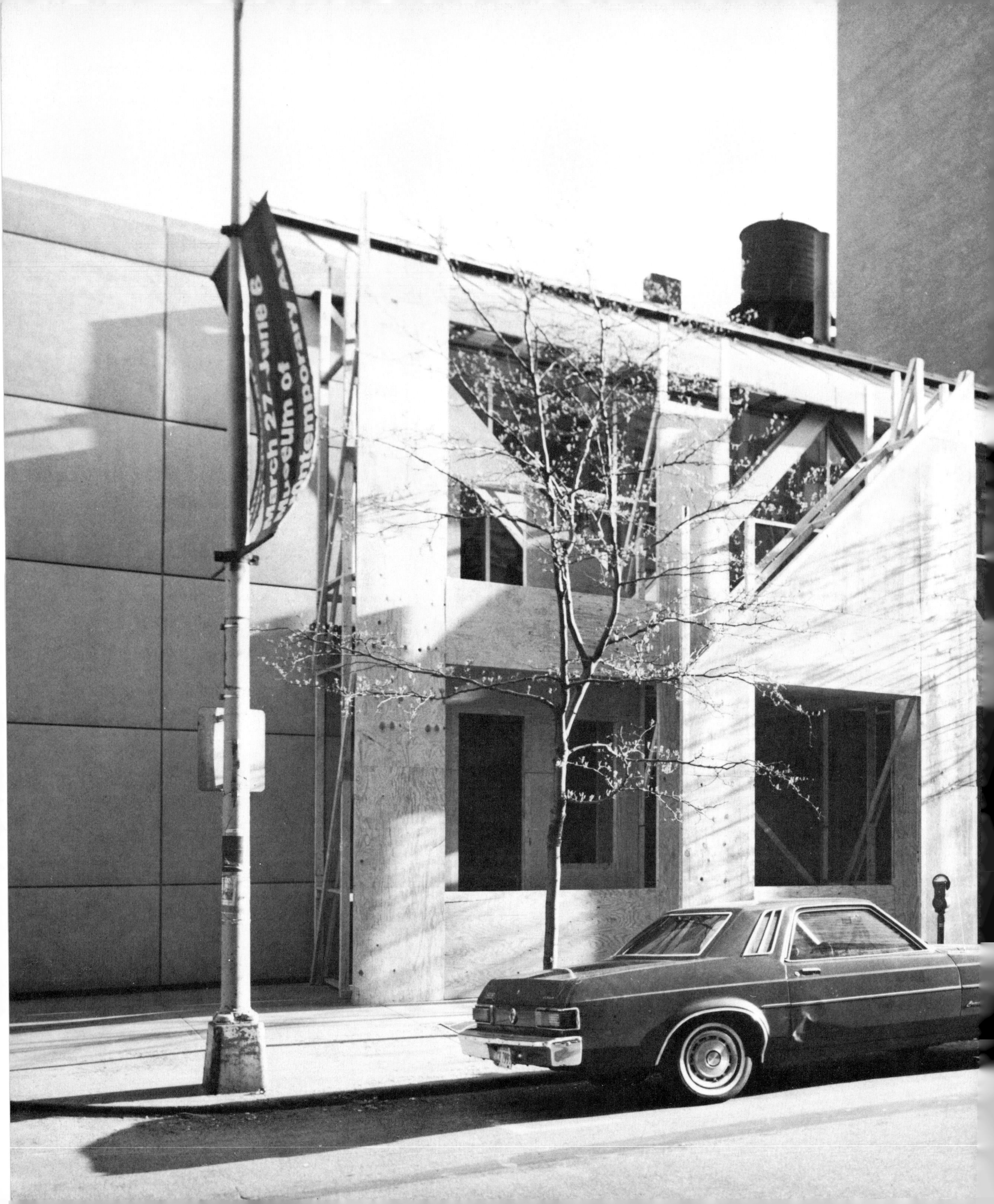
March 27-June 6
Museum of

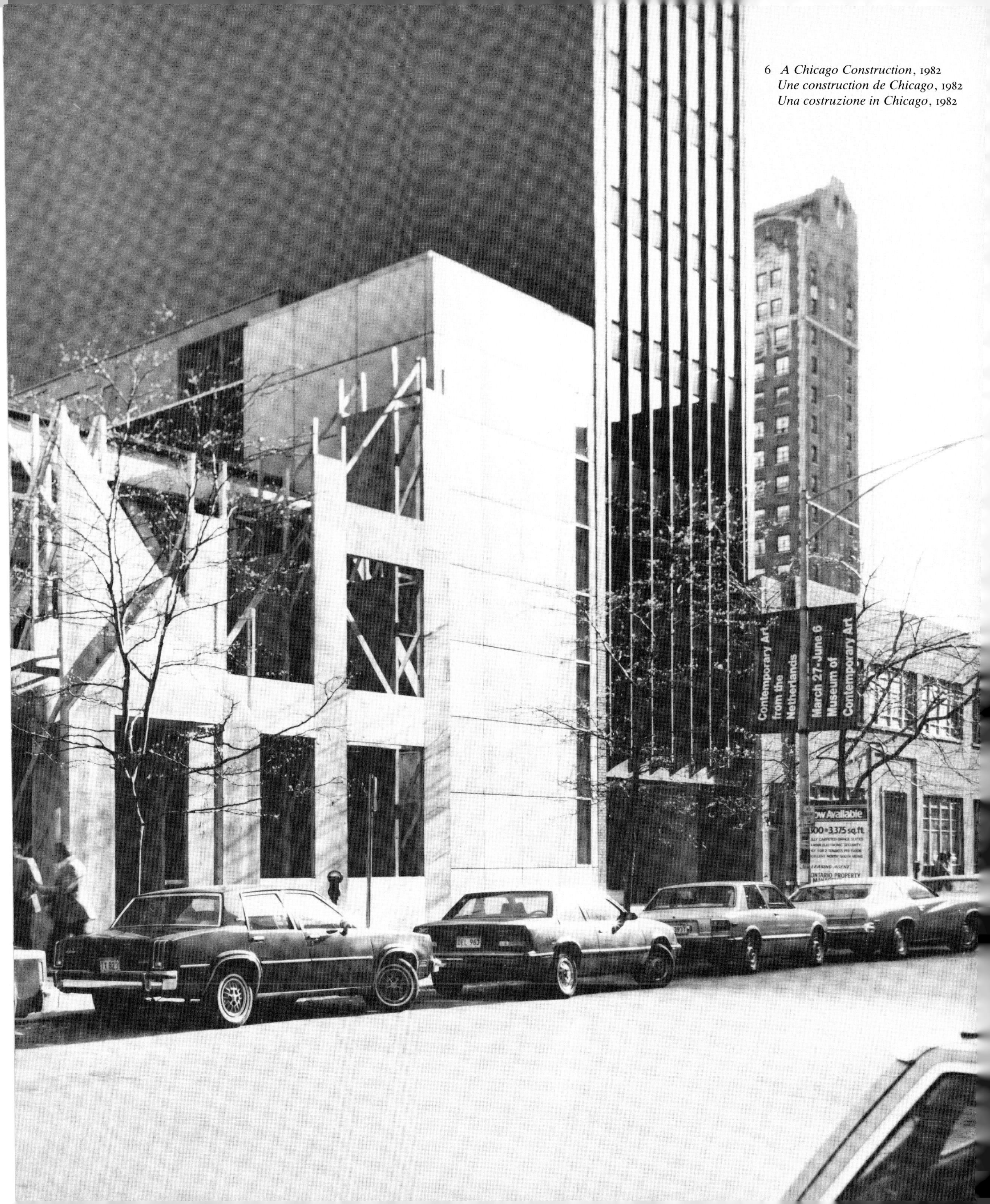


6 *A Chicago Construction*, 1982
*Une construction de Chicago*, 1982
*Una costruzione in Chicago*, 1982

9 *A Toronto Construction*, 1982
*Une construction de Toronto*, 1982
*Una costruzione in Toronto*, 1982

V View from the street
Vue depuis la rue
Vista dalla strada

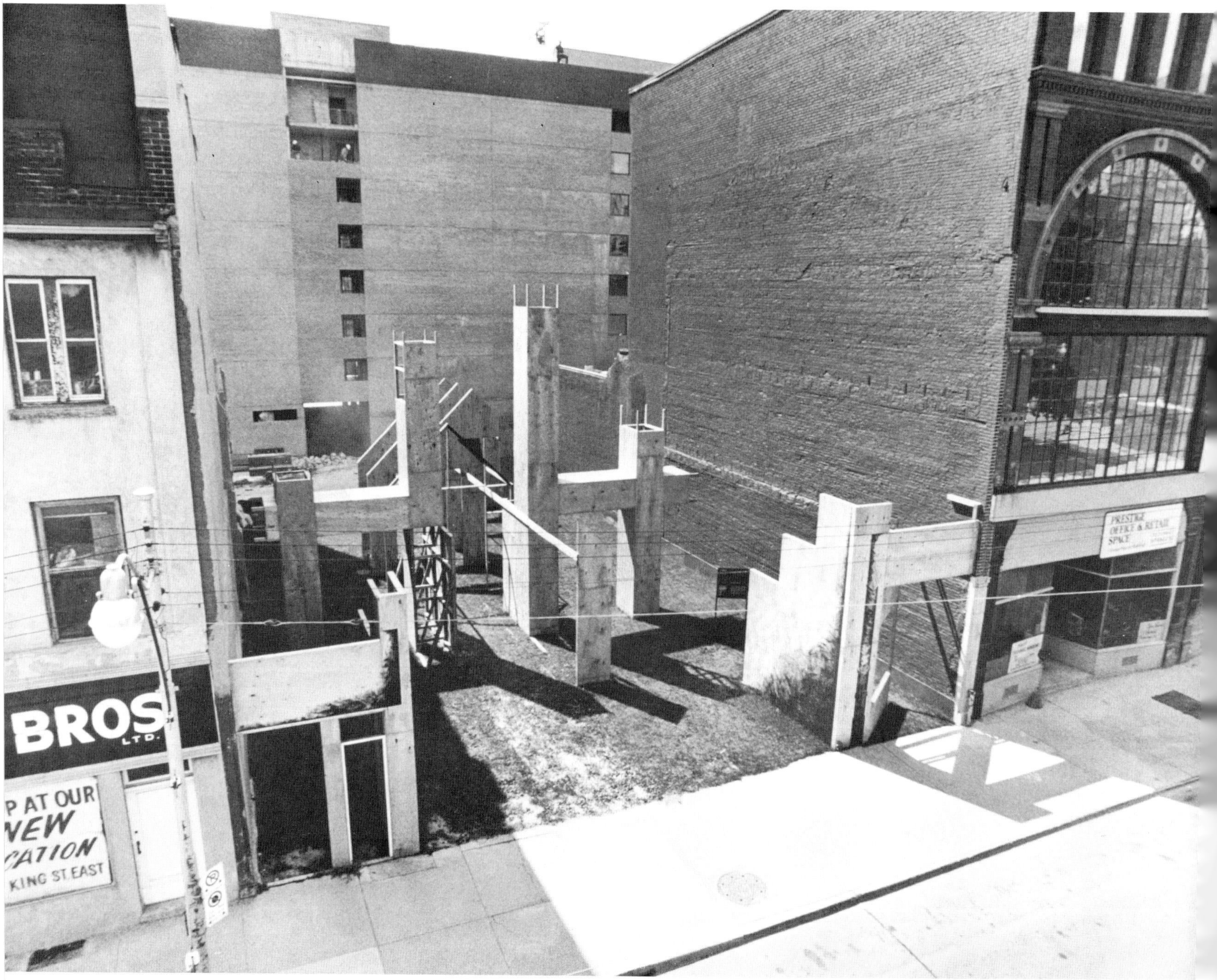

∨ View from the back
Vue depuis l'arrière
Vista dal di dietró

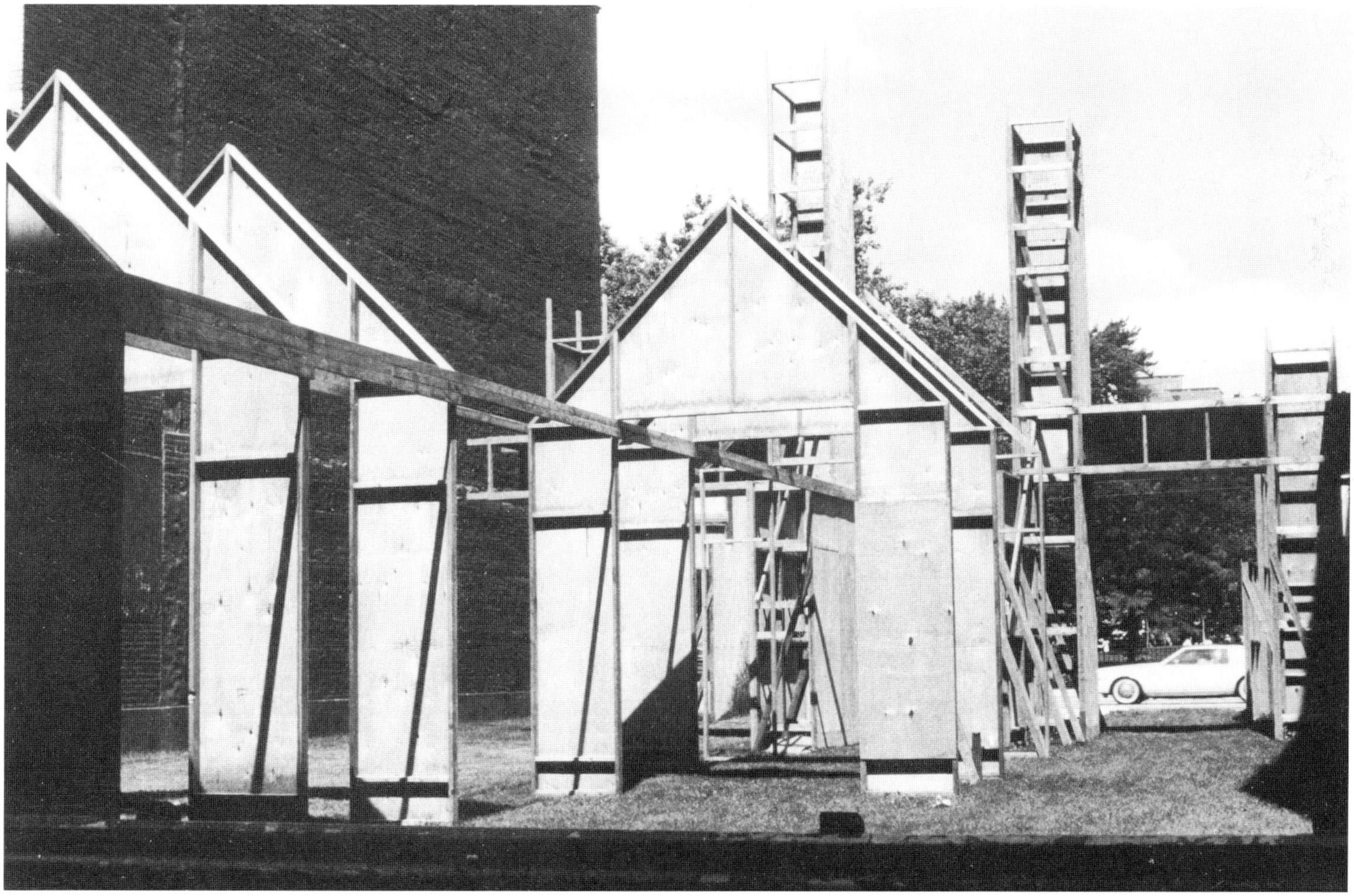

10 *Kingston Construction*, 1982
> *Construction de Kingston*, 1982
*Costruzione in Kingston*, 1982

11 *A Kingston Construction*, 1983
∨ *Une construction de Kingston*, 1983
*Una costruzione in Kingston*, 1983

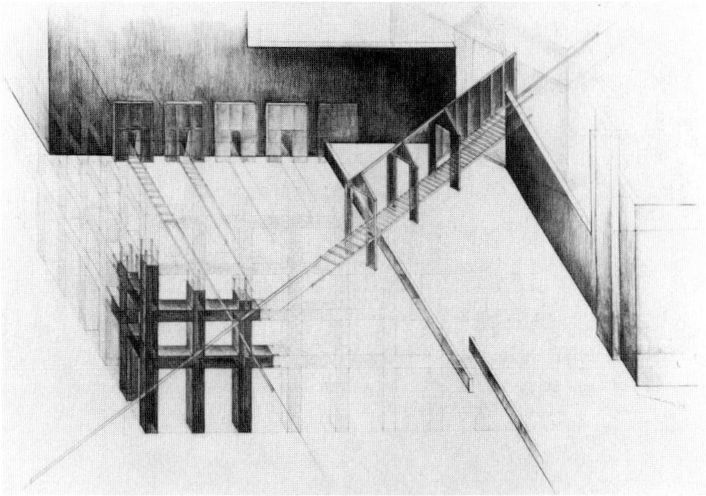

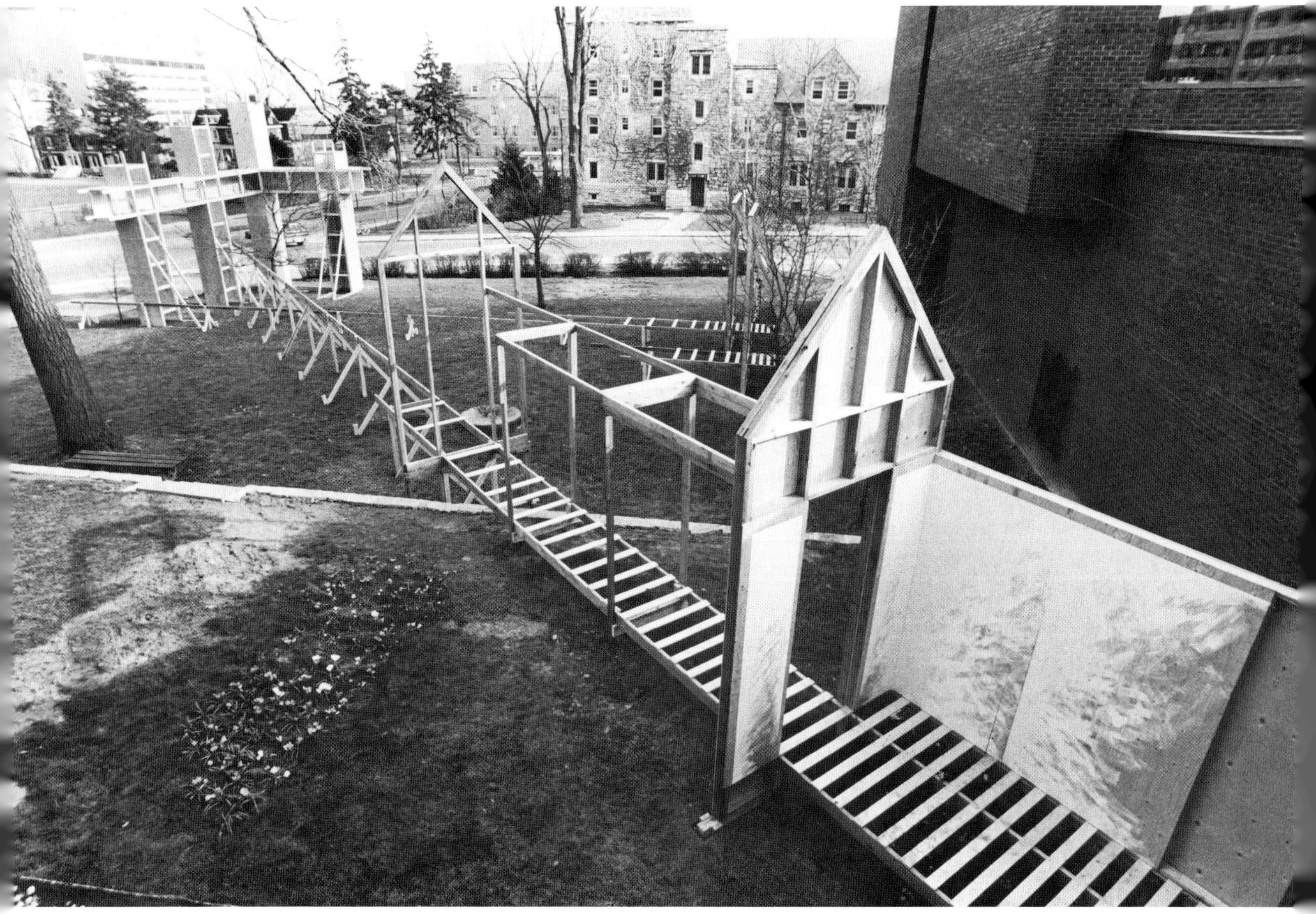

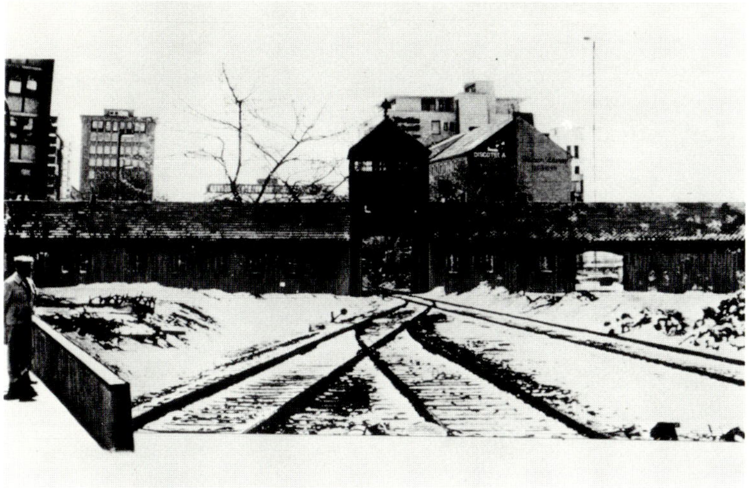

12 *"Better if they think they are going to a farm ...,"* 1982
< *« Il vaut mieux qu'ils croient aller à la ferme... »*, 1982
*« E' meglio se pensano che stanno andando verso una tenuta agricola... »*, 1982

13 *"Better if they think they are going to a farm ..." No.* 2, 1982
∨ *« Il vaut mieux qu'ils croient aller à la ferme... » n*[o] 2, 1982
*« E' meglio se pensano che stanno andando verso una tenuta agricola... » No.* 2, 1982

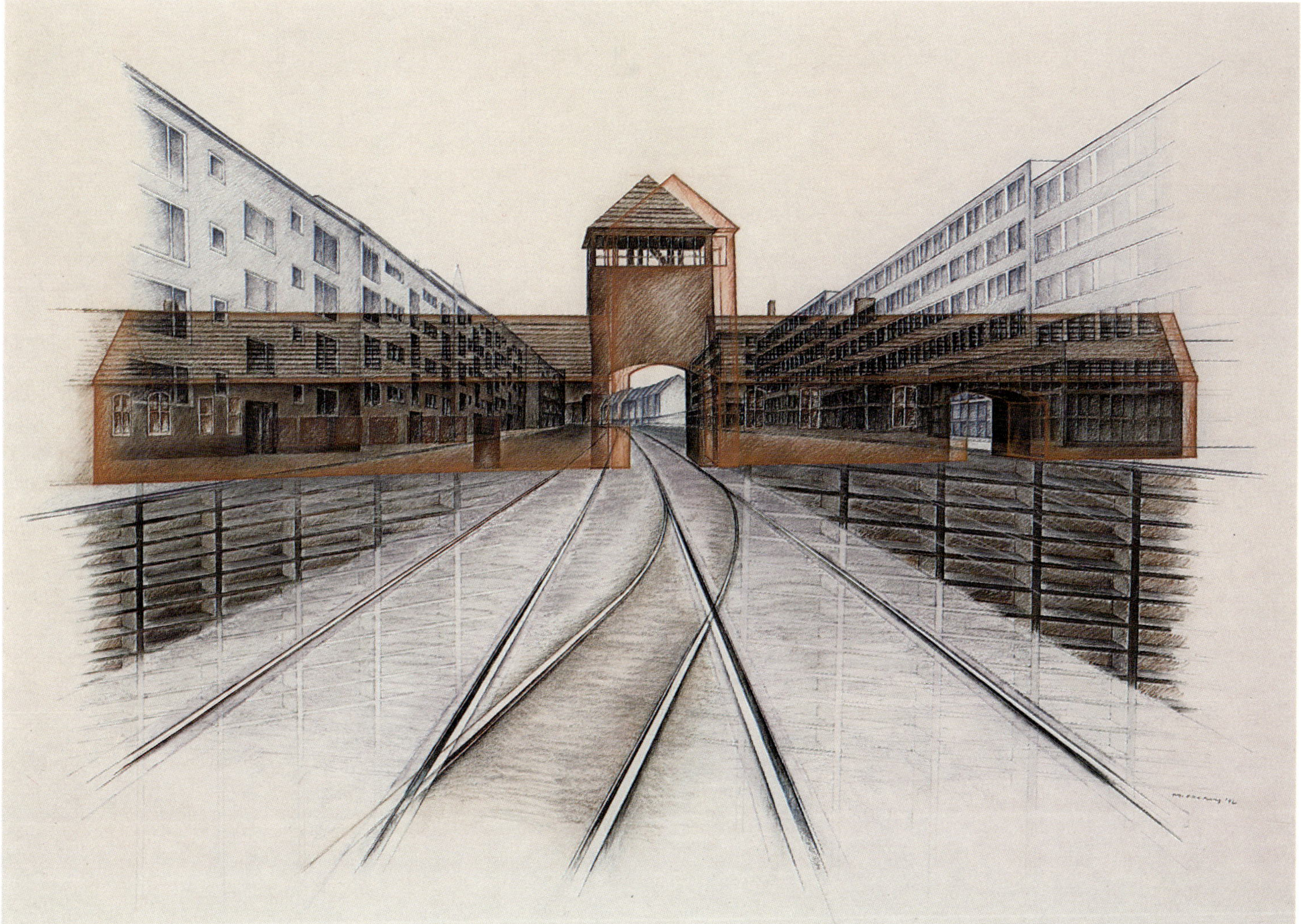

14 *Pliny on My Mind No. 1 and No. 2*, 1983
*Pline en tête n° 1 et n° 2*, 1983
*Pensando al Plinio No. 1 e No. 2*, 1983

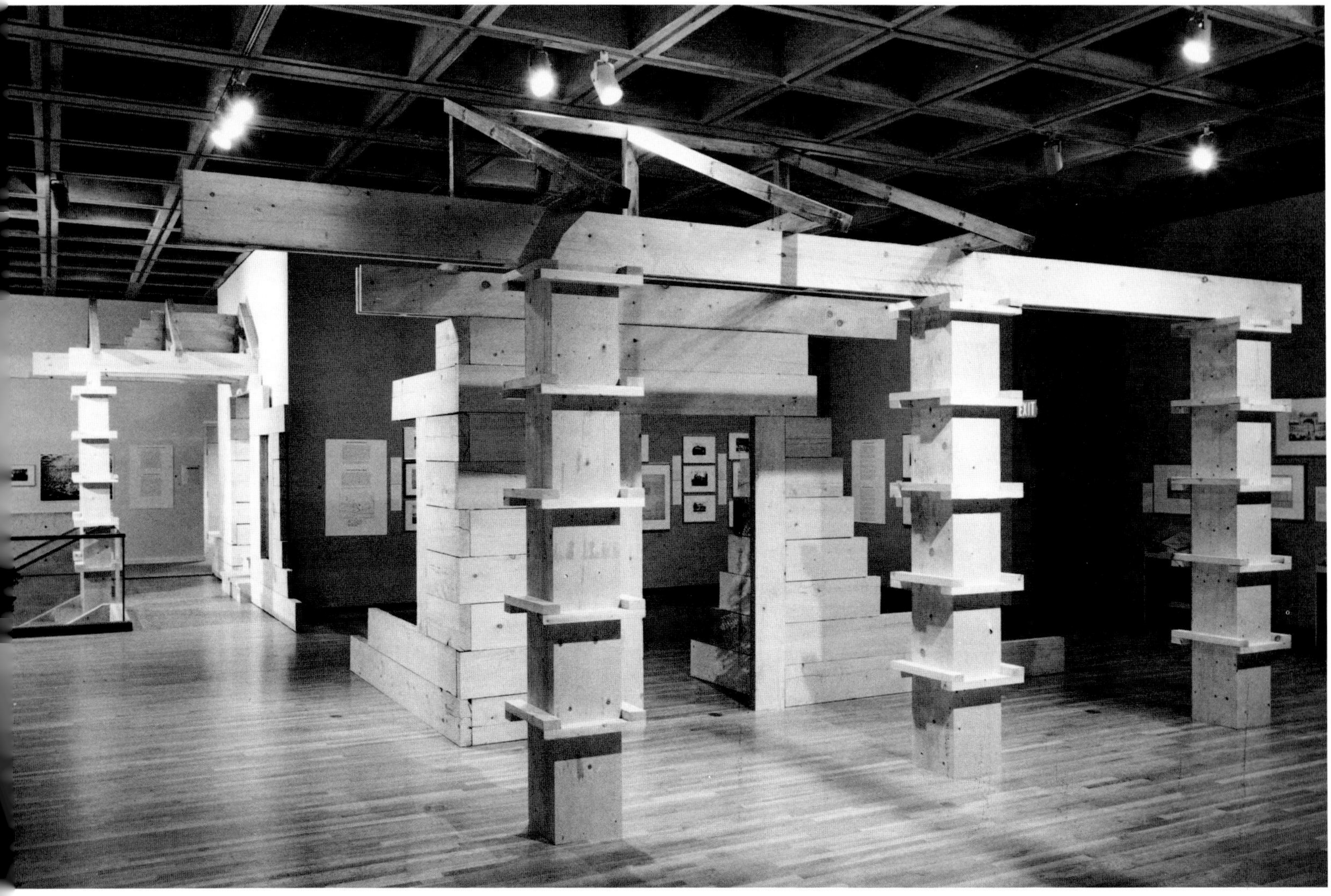

15 *Pliny on My Mind No. 1 and No. 2*, 1983
*Pline en tête nº 1 et nº 2*, 1983
*Pensando al Plinio No. 1 e No. 2*, 1983

16 *Pliny's Other Villa*, 1984
*L'Autre Villa de Pline*, 1984
*L'altra villa di Plinio*, 1984

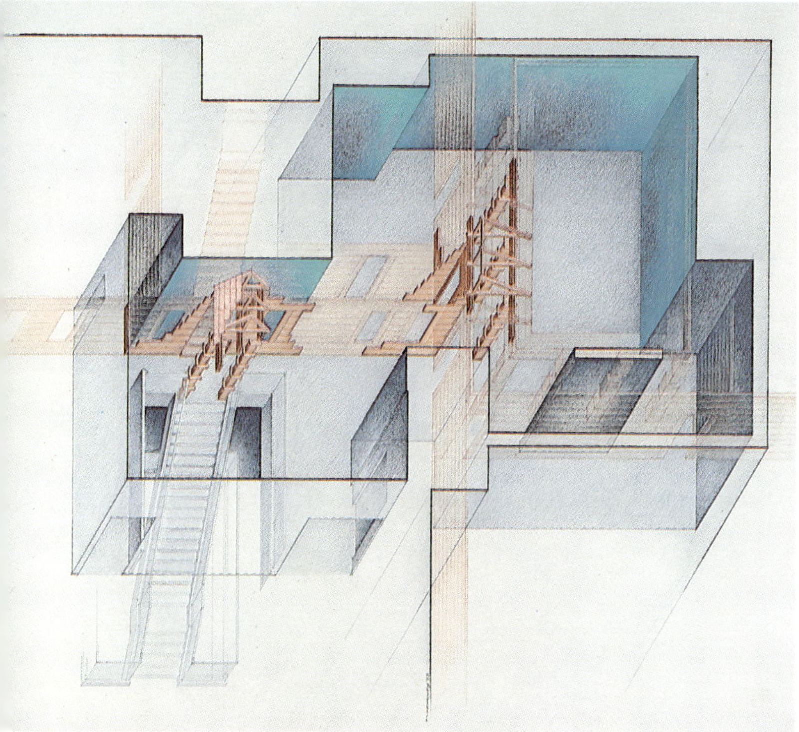

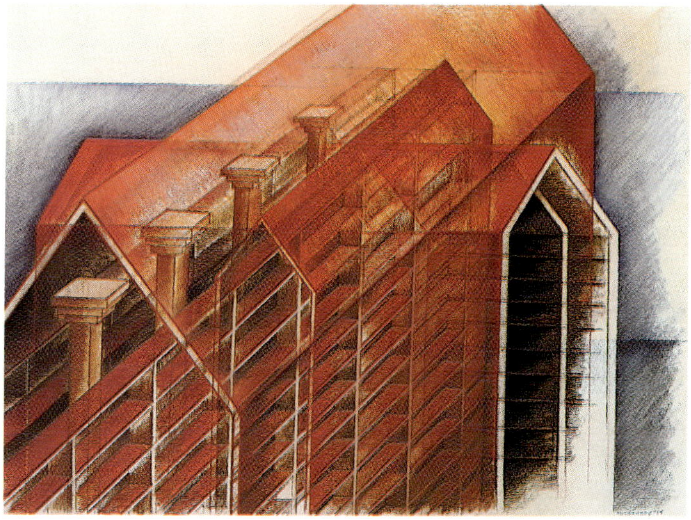

17 *Fragments of the Forgotten City No. 6*, 1984
*Fragments de la Cité oubliée nº 6*, 1984
*Frammenti della città dimenticata No. 6*, 1984

18 *Fragments of the Forgotten City No. 14*, 1985
*Fragments de la Cité oubliée nº 14*, 1985
*Frammenti della città dimenticata No. 14*, 1985

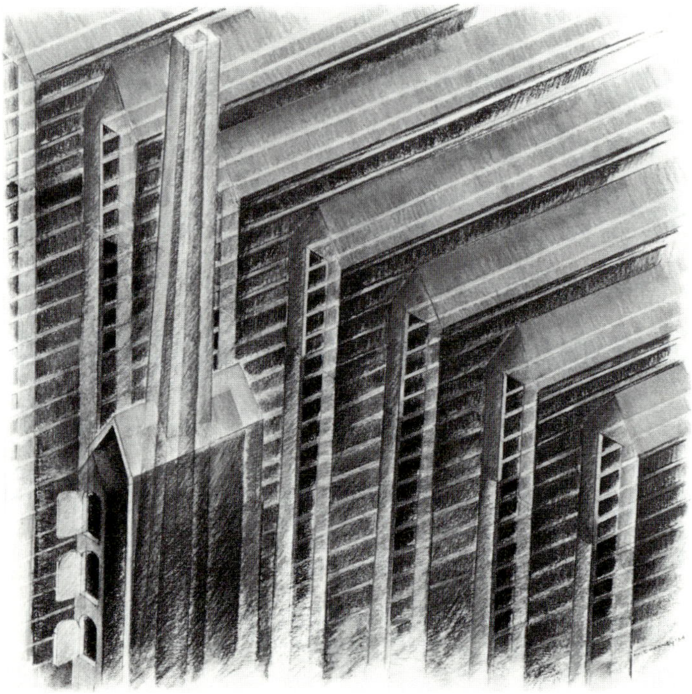

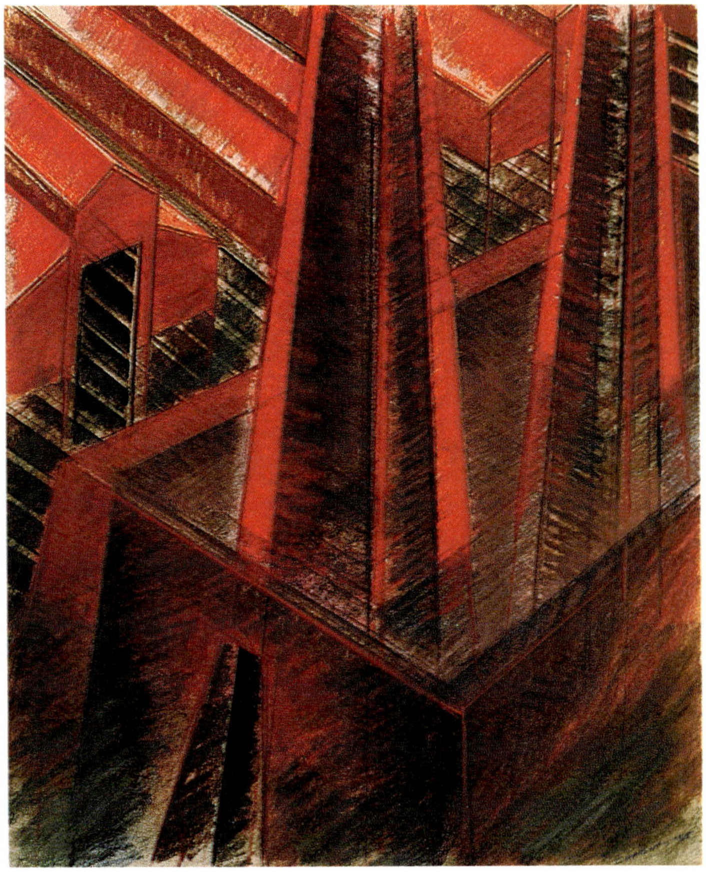

19 *Way Station No. 6*, 1985
*Chemin de la station nº 6*, 1985
*Stazione secondaria No. 6*, 1985

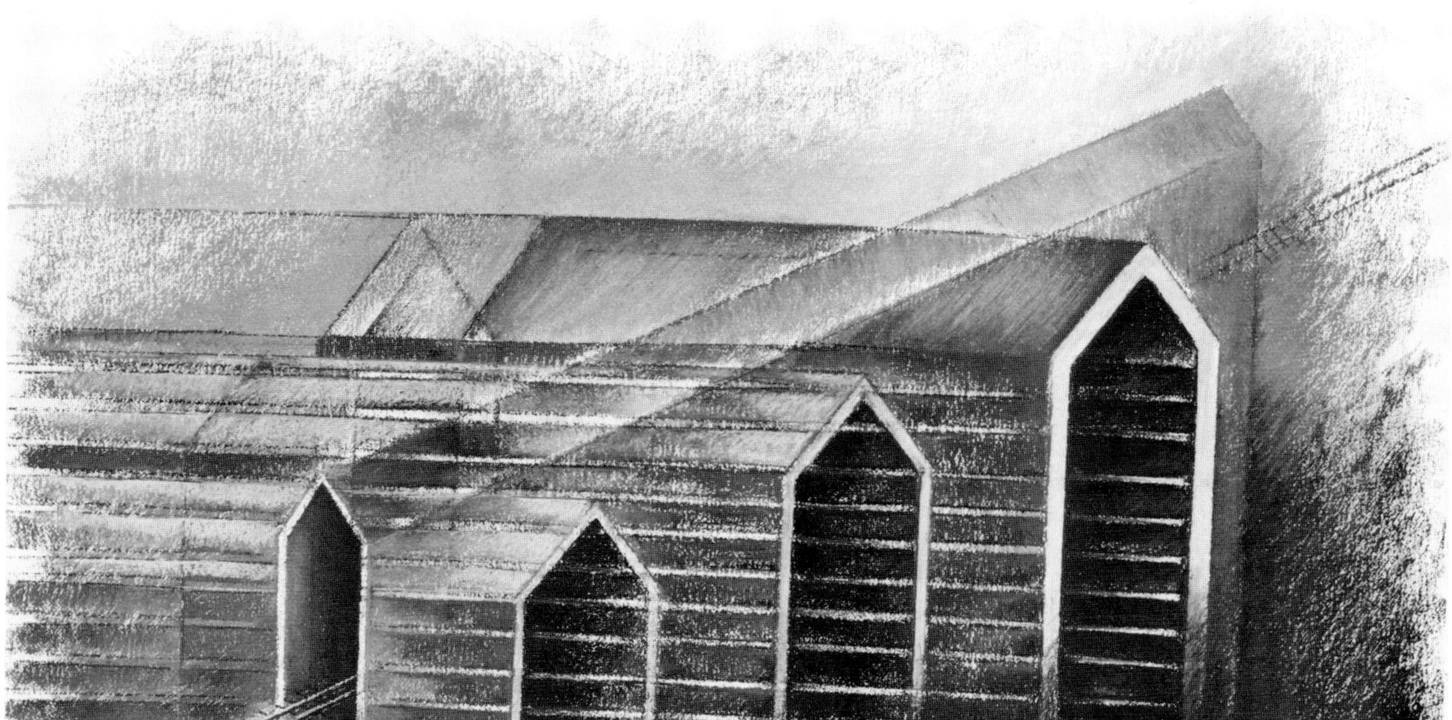

20 *Building Displacements, No. 2... Study for a Construction at La Cité*, 1985
*Déplacements d'édifice nº 2... Étude pour une construction à la Cité*, 1985
*Spostamenti edilizi No. 2... Studio per una costruzione a La Cité*, 1985

21 *From Laugier to Popova: Construction in Parts*, 1985
*De Laugier à Popova : Construction en parties*, 1985
*Da Laugier a Popova: costruzione in parti*, 1985

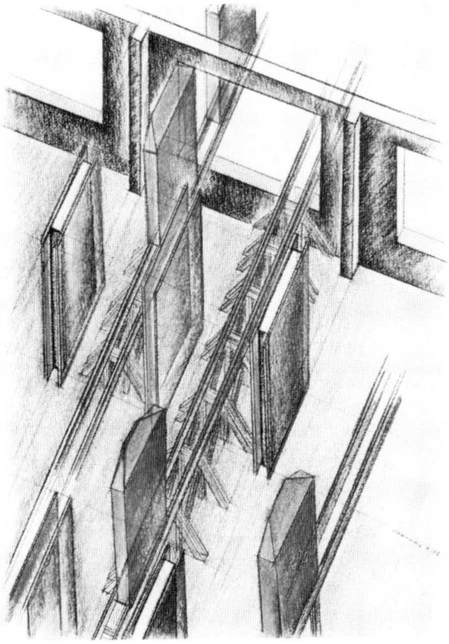

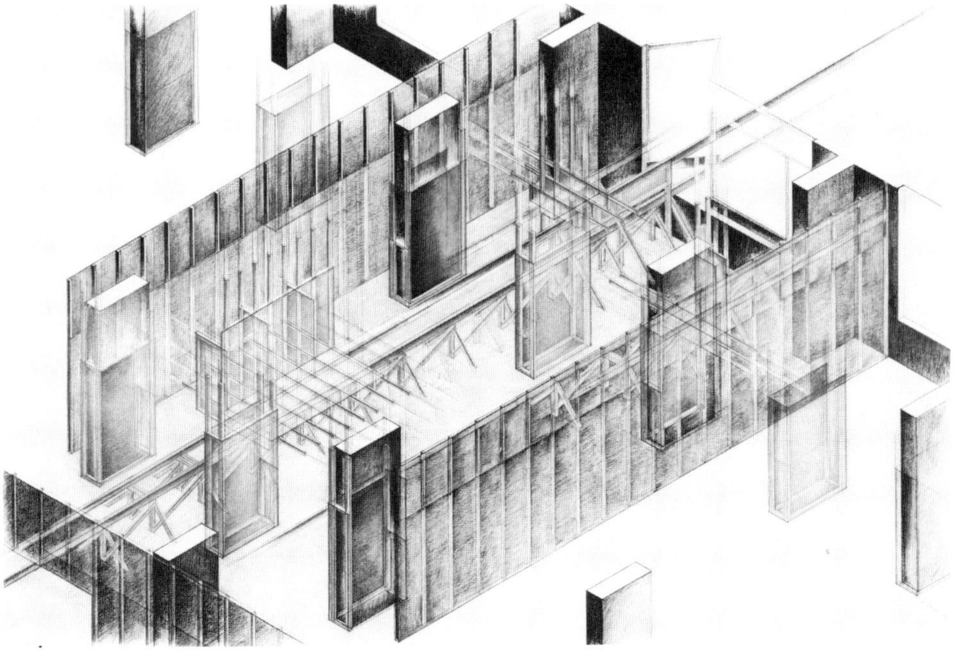

22 *From Laugier to Popova: A Construction in Parts*, 1985
*De Laugier à Popova : Une construction en parties*, 1985
*Da Laugier a Popova: una costruzione in parti*, 1985

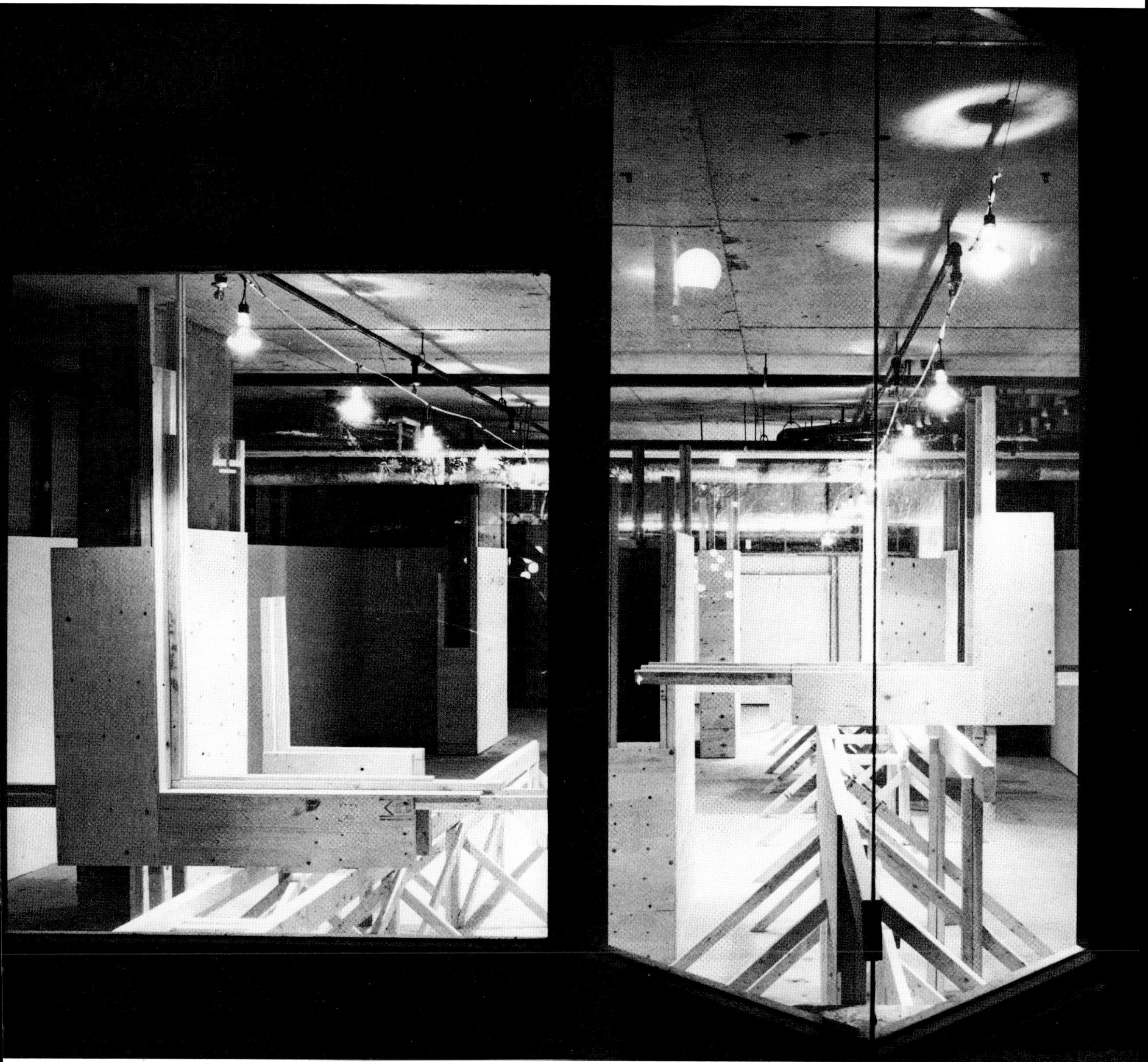

# Krzysztof Wodiczko

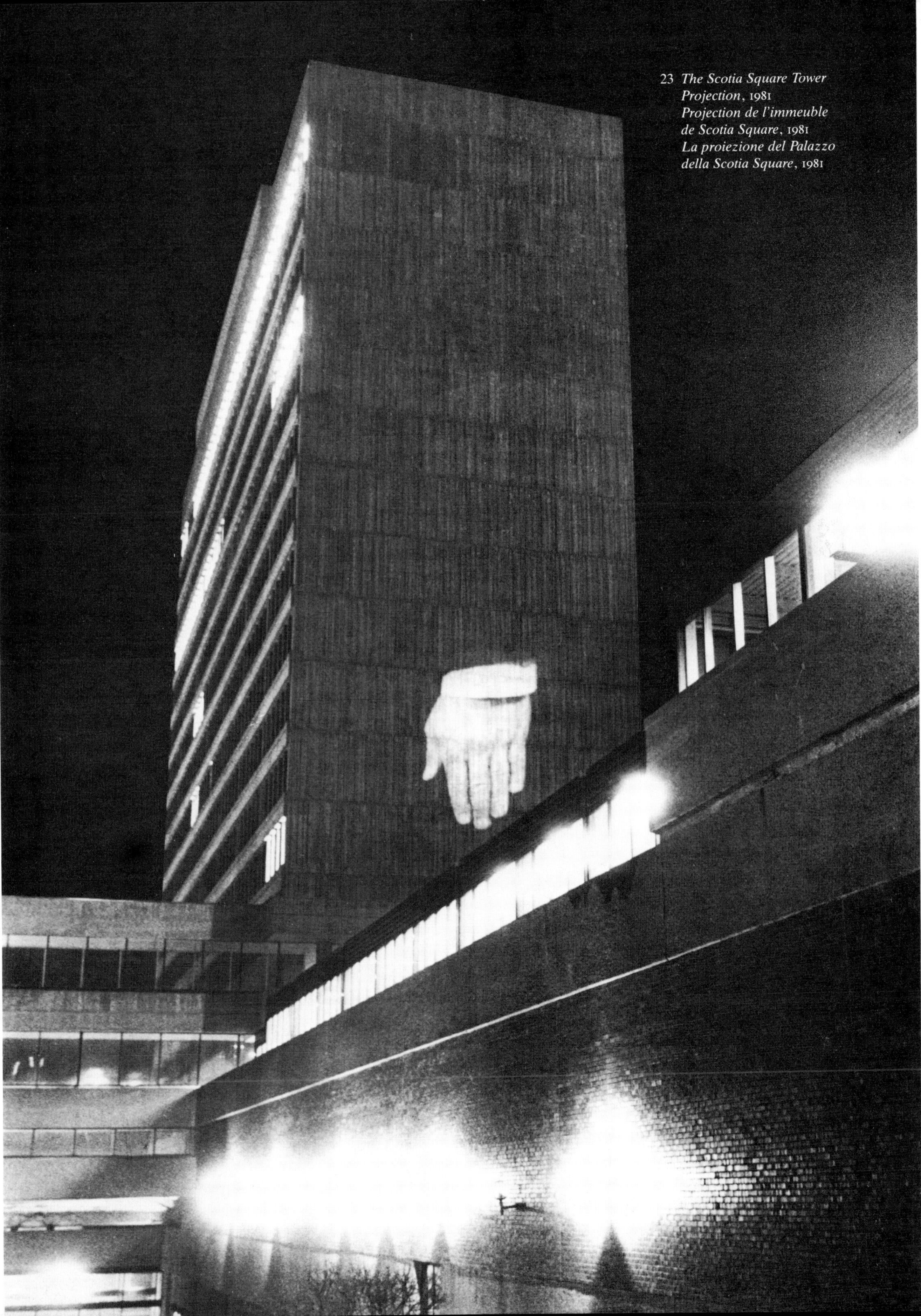

23 *The Scotia Square Tower Projection*, 1981
*Projection de l'immeuble de Scotia Square*, 1981
*La proiezione del Palazzo della Scotia Square*, 1981

24 *The Art Gallery of New South Wales Projection*, 1982
*Projection de l'Art Gallery of New South Wales*, 1982
*La proiezione della Art Gallery of New South Wales*, 1982

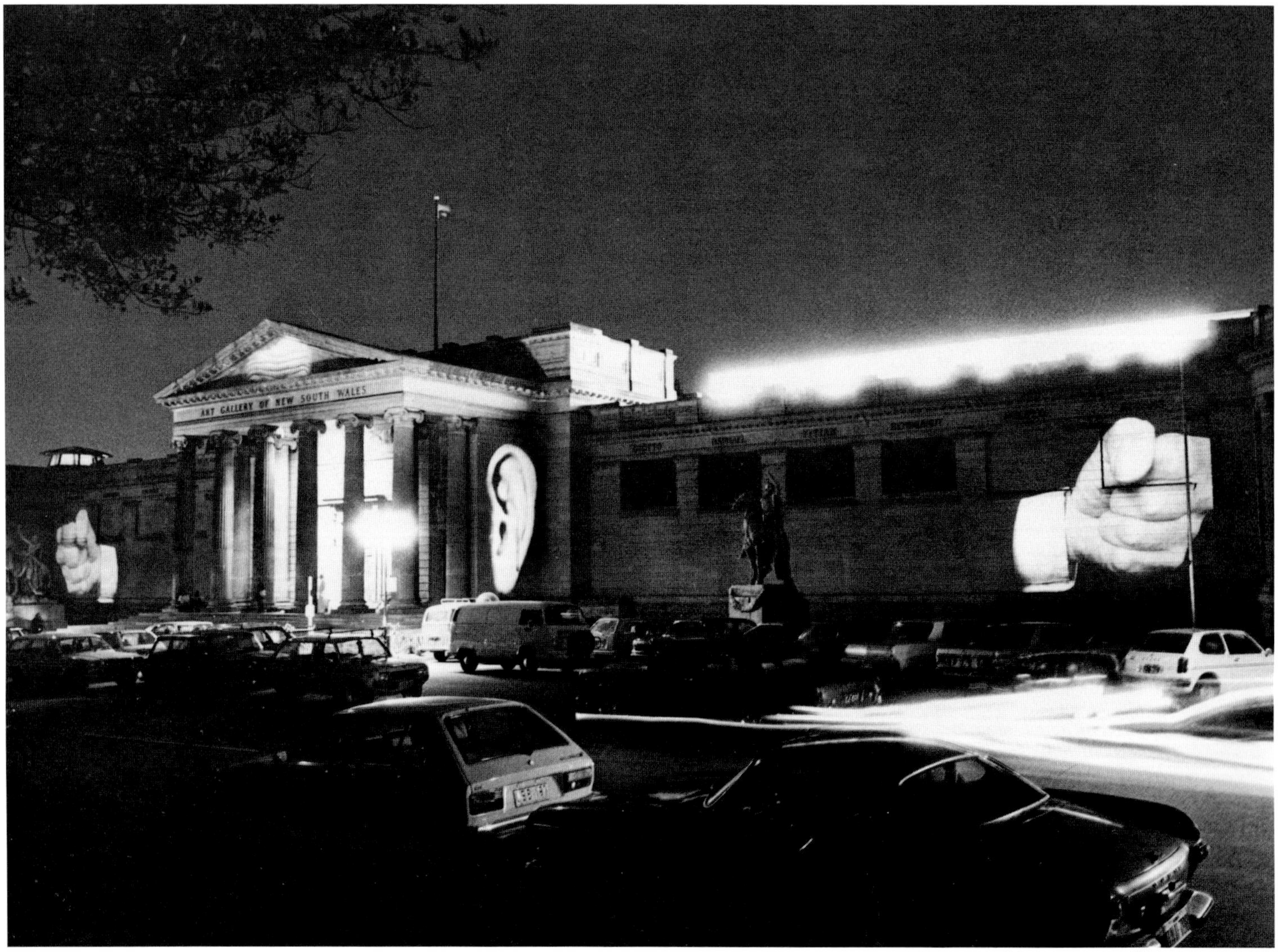

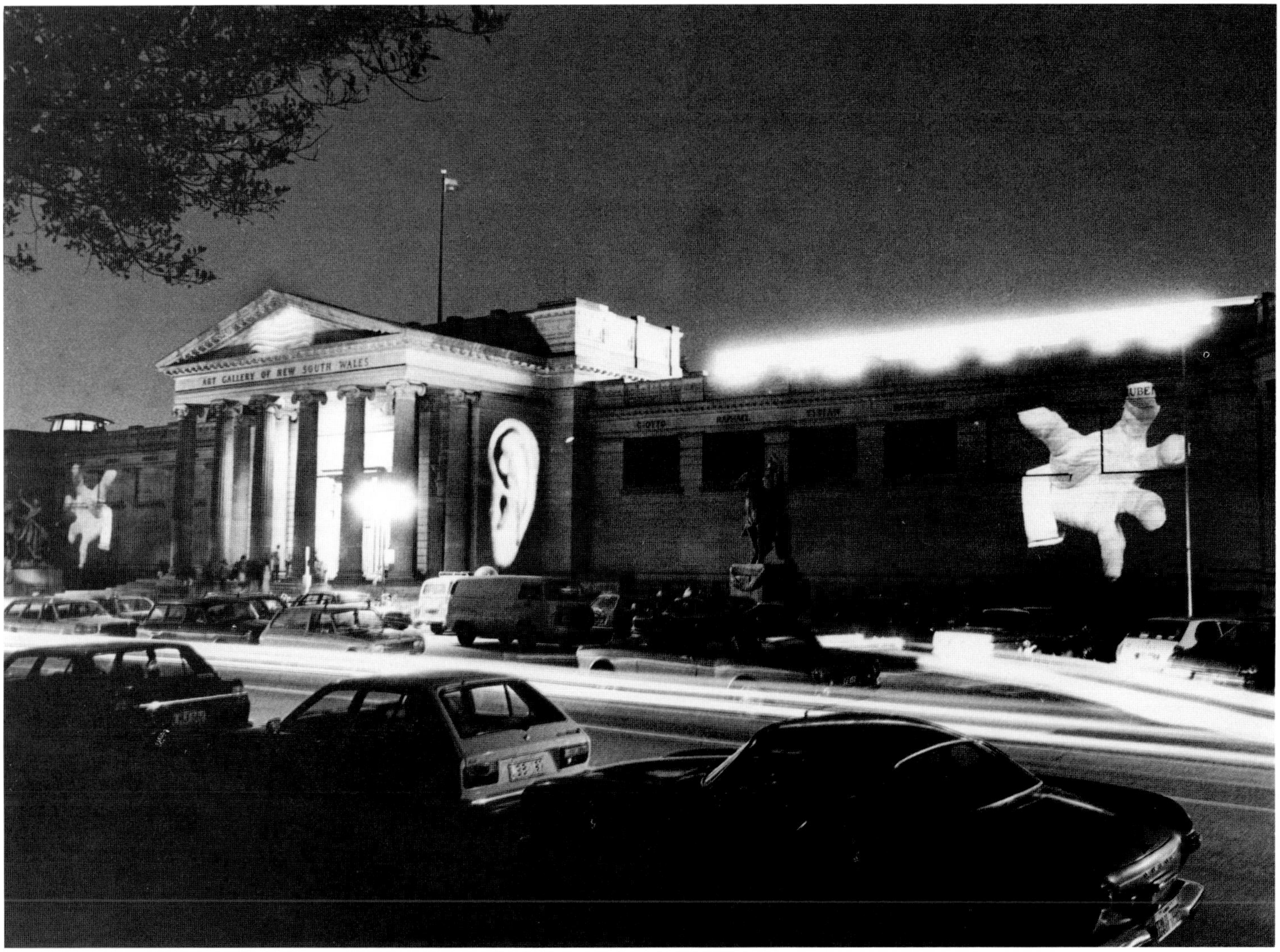
ART GALLERY OF NEW SOUTH WALES

25 *The Memorial Hall Projection*, 1983
∨ *Projection du Memorial Hall*, 1983
*La proiezione della Memorial Hall*, 1983

26 *The Stuttgart Main Train Station (Hauptbahnhof) Projection*, 1983
> *Projection de la gare centrale (Hauptbahnhof) de Stuttgart*, 1983
*La proiezione della stazione ferroviaria principale (Hauptbahnhof) di Stoccarda*, 1983

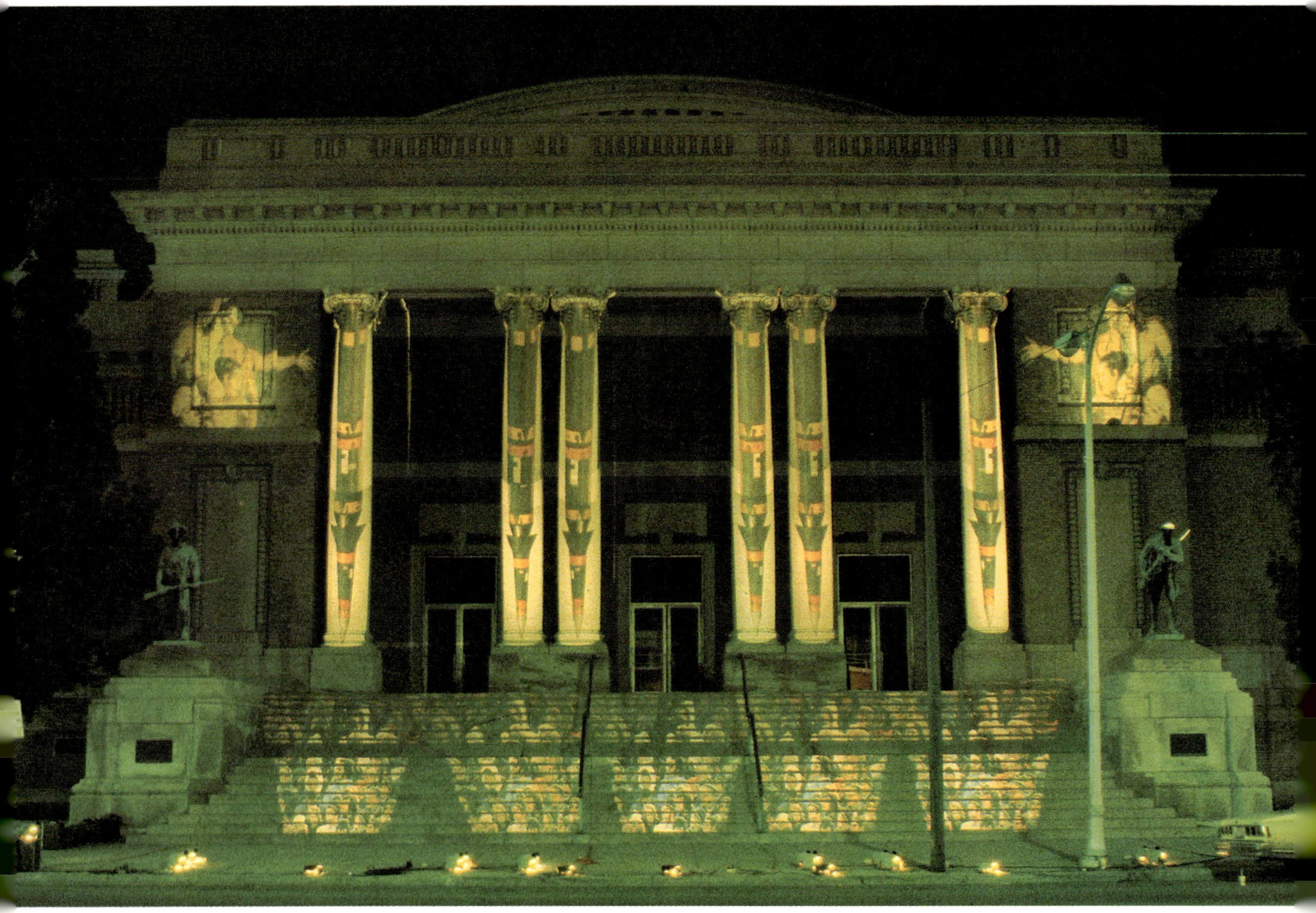

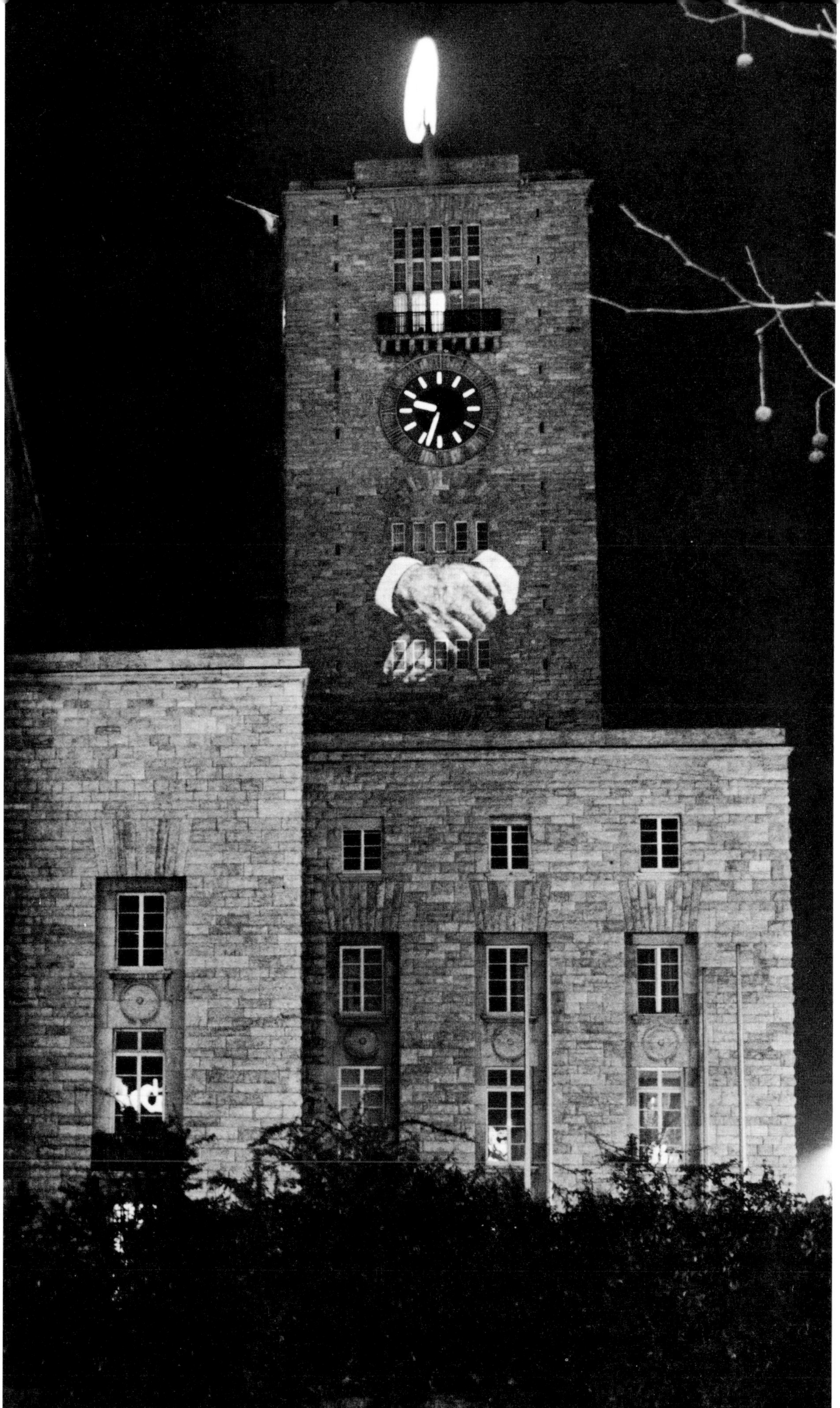

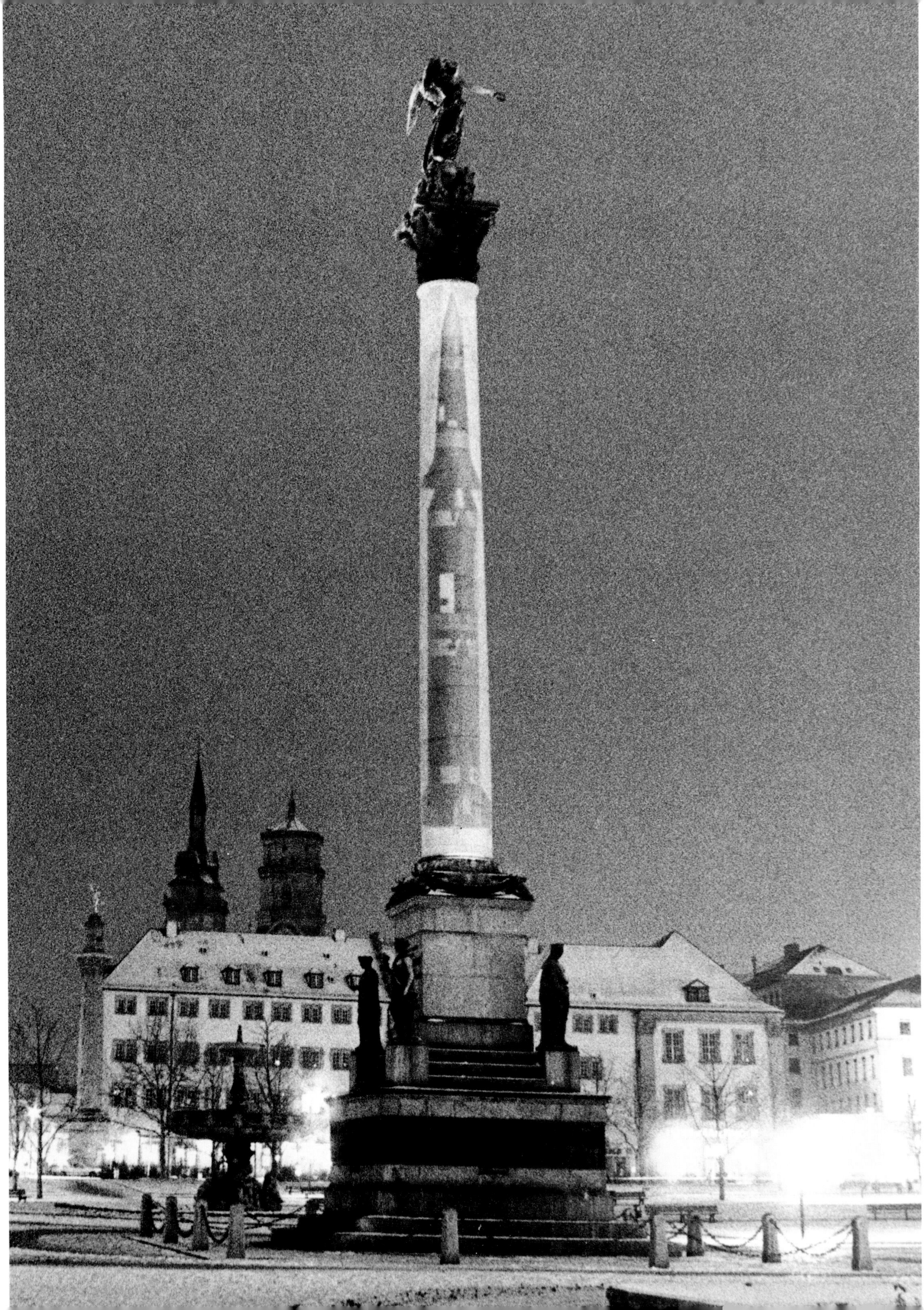

27 *The Victory Column Projection*, 1983
< *Projection de la colonne de la Victoire*, 1983
*La proiezione della Colonna alla Vittoria*, 1983

28 *The South African War Memorial Projection*, 1983
> *Projection du monument commémoratif de la guerre d'Afrique du Sud*, 1983
*La proiezione del Monumento commemorativo della guerra sudafricana*, 1983

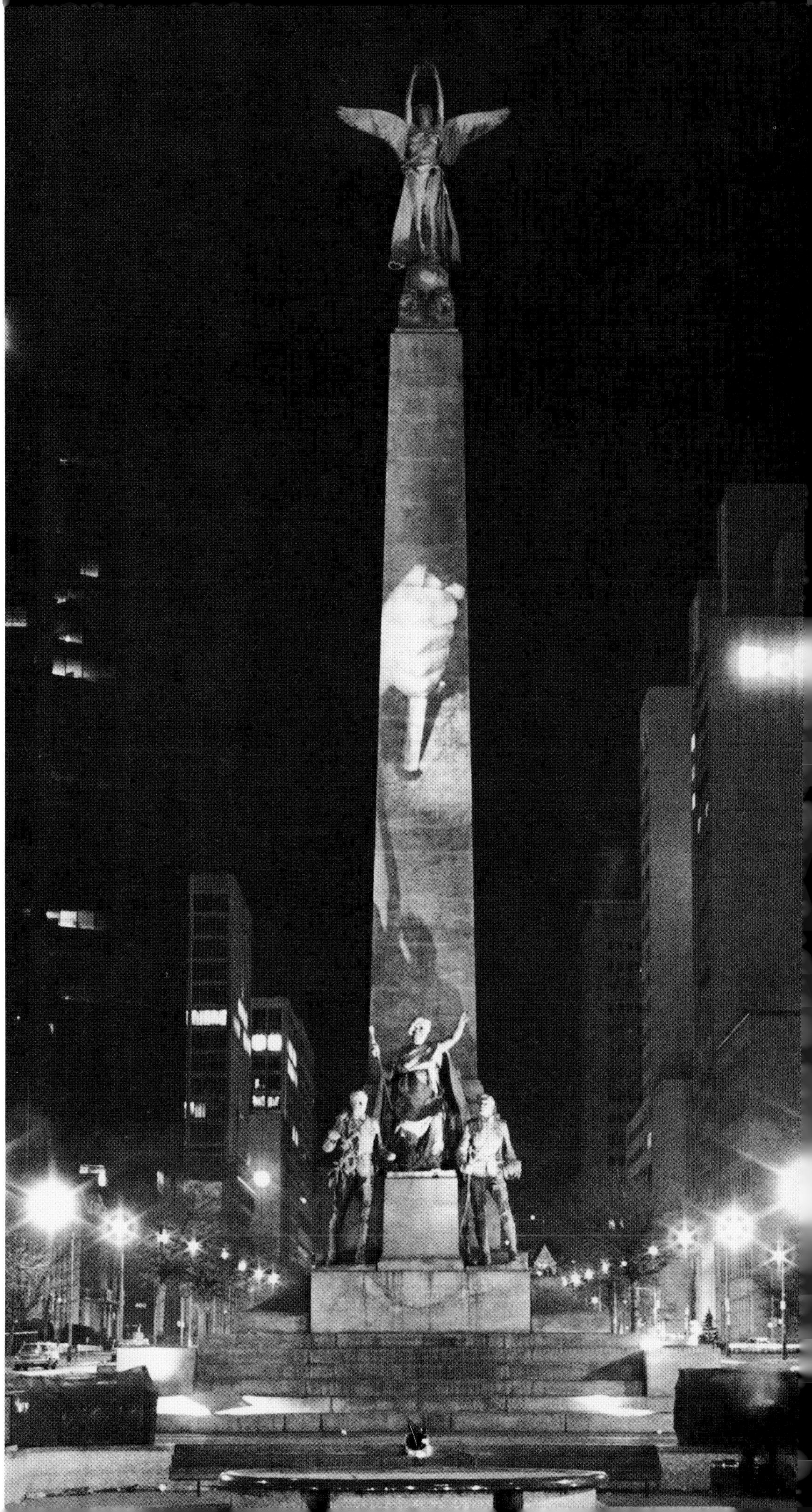

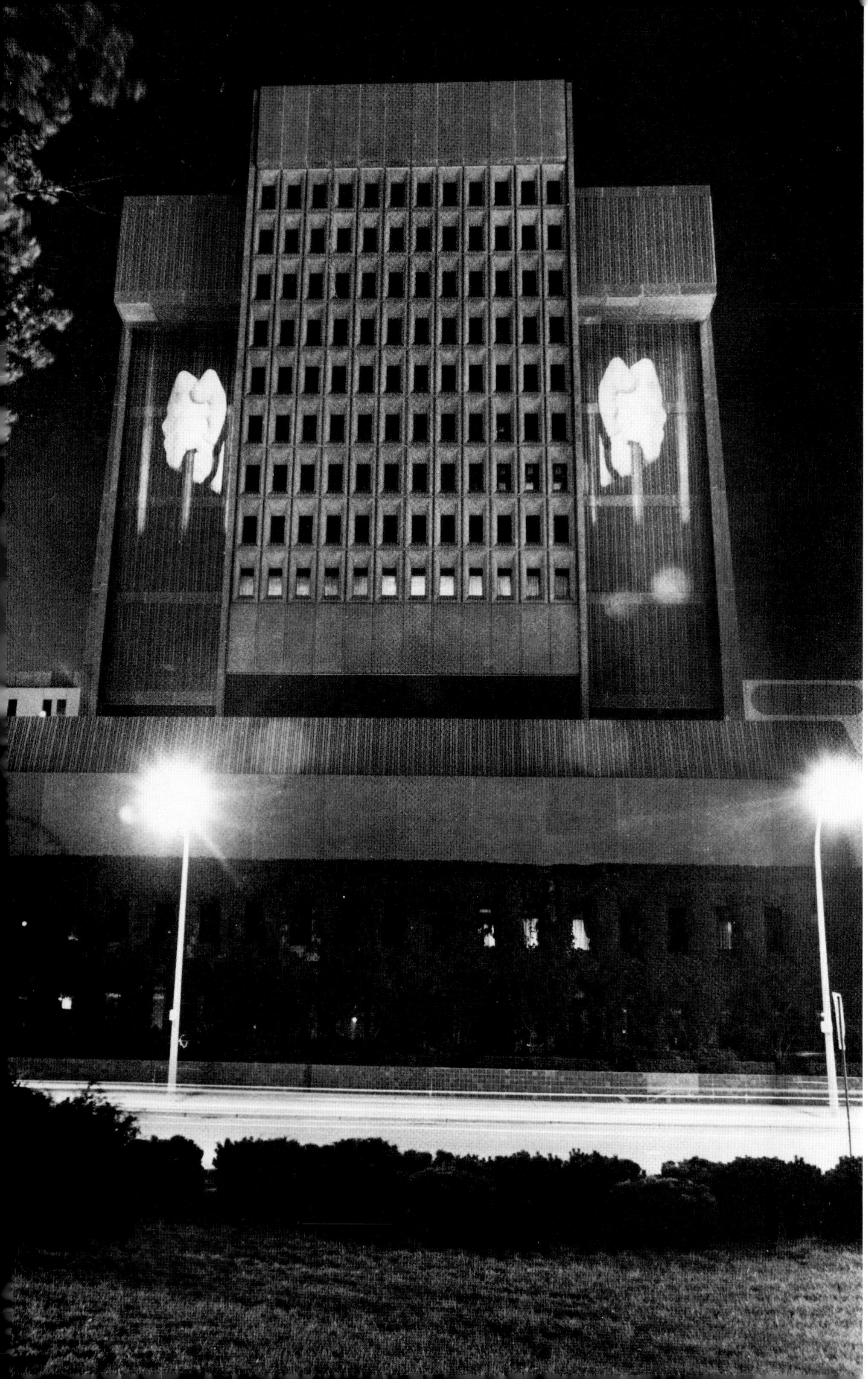

29 *The Federal Courthouse Building Projection*, 1984
*Projection du Palais de justice fédéral*, 1984
*La proiezione del Palazzo del Tribunale Federale*, 1984

30 *The Astor Building/New Museum Projection*, 1984/1985
*Projection de l'immeuble Astor/New Museum*, 1984/1985
*La proiezione del Palazzo Astor/New Museum*, 1984/1985

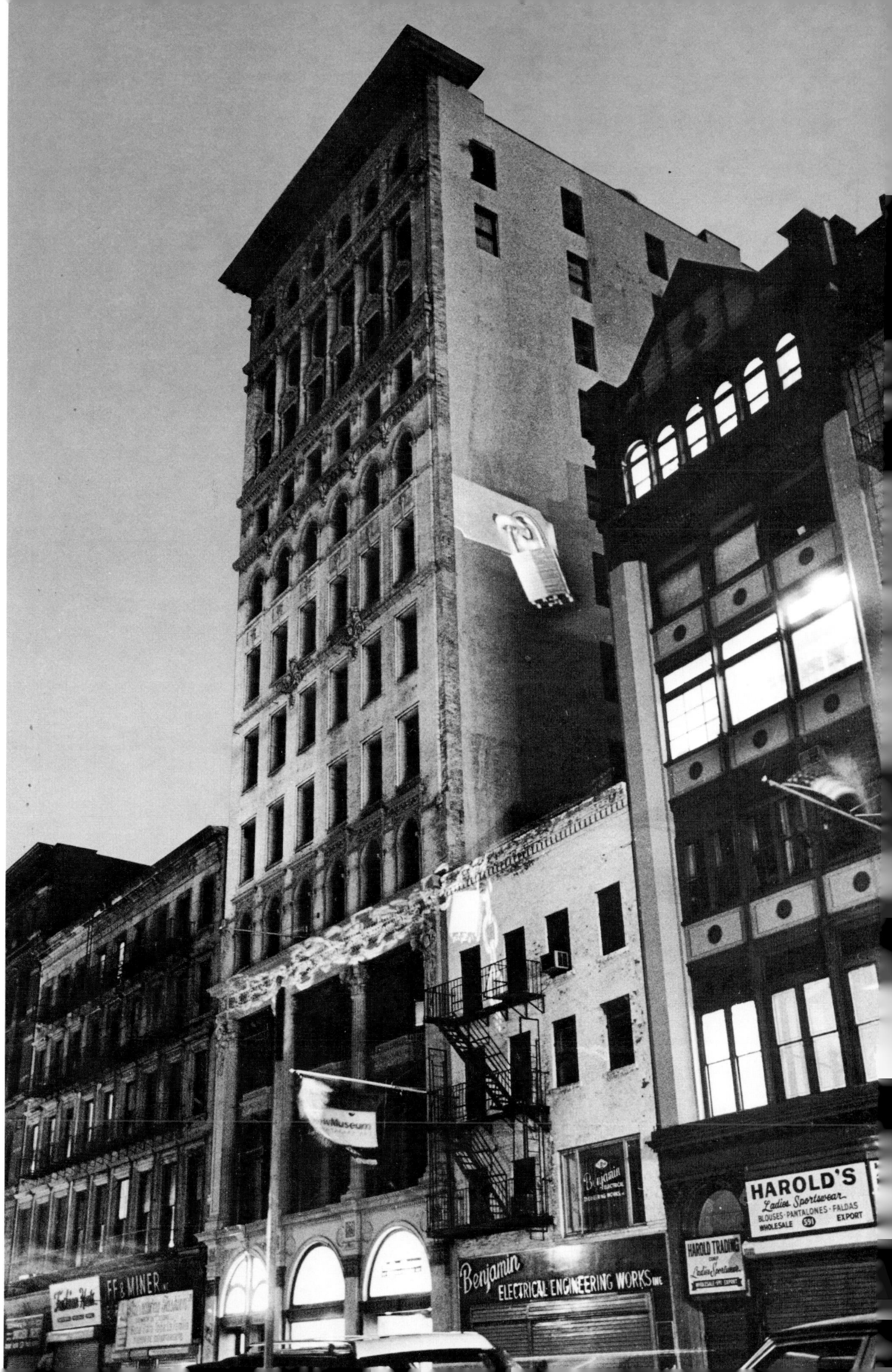

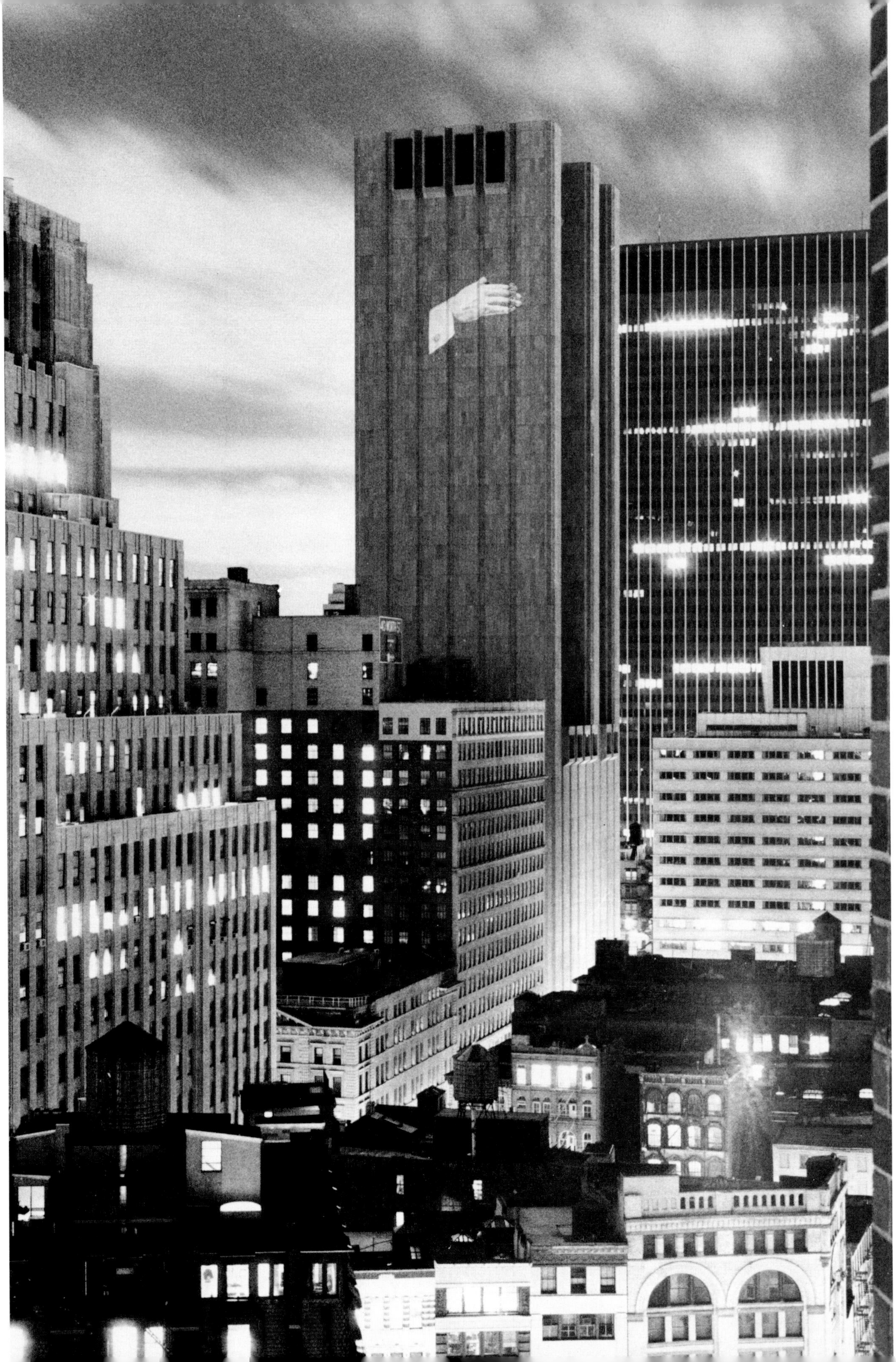

31 *The AT & T Building Projection*, 1984
< *Projection de l'immeuble de l'AT & T*, 1984
*La proiezione del Palazzo della AT & T*, 1984

32 *The Grand Army Plaza Projection*, 1984/1985
V *Projection de la Grand Army Plaza*, 1984/1985
*La proiezione della Grand Army Plaza*, 1984/1985

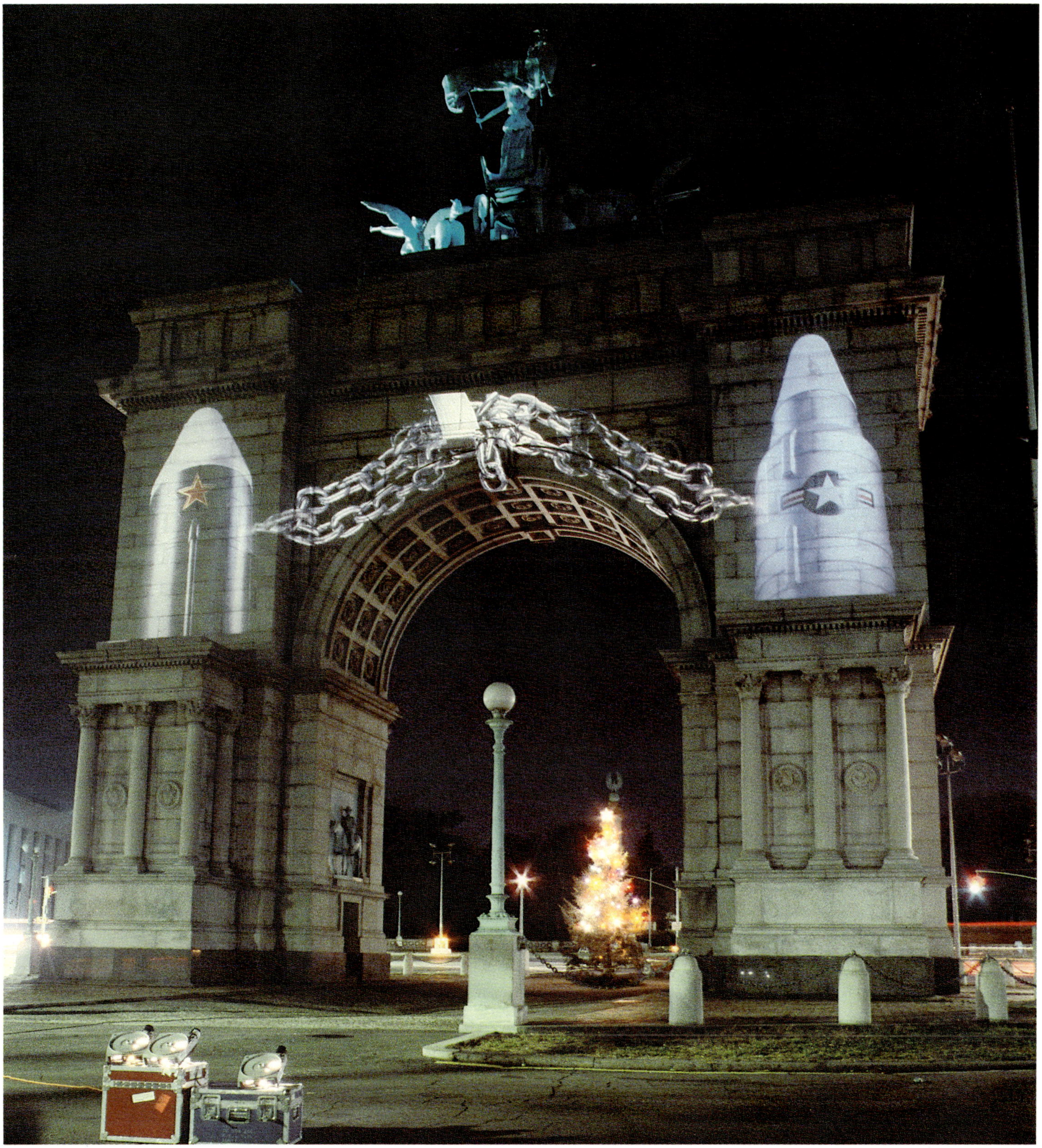

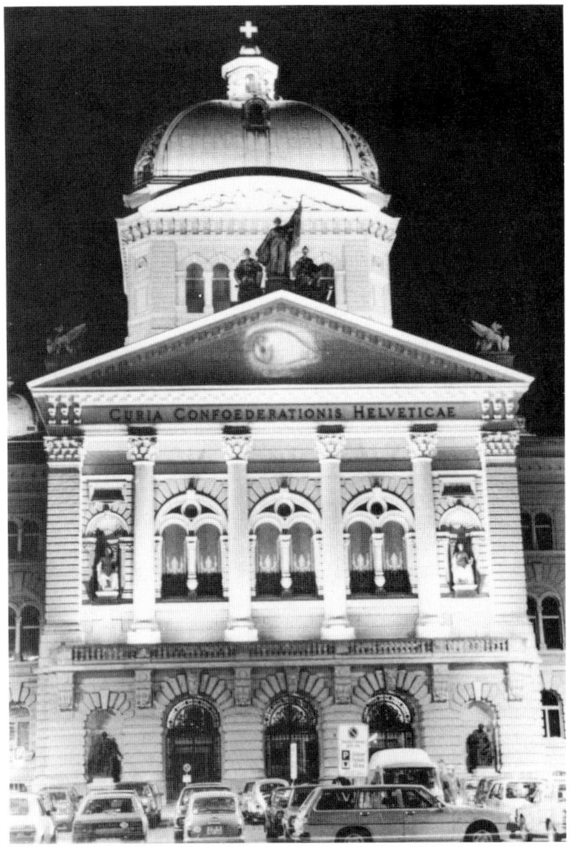
CURIA CONFOEDERATIONIS HELVETICAE

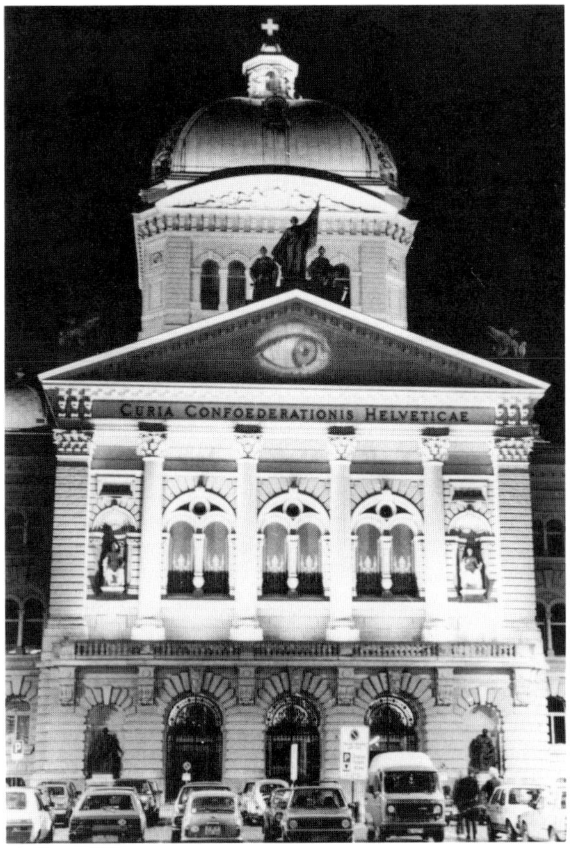
CURIA CONFOEDERATIONIS HELVETICAE

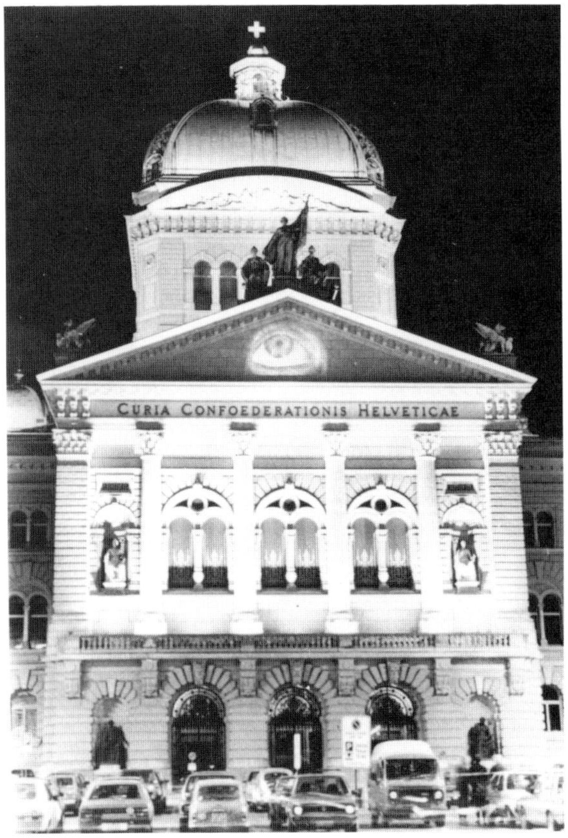
CURIA CONFOEDERATIONIS HELVETICAE

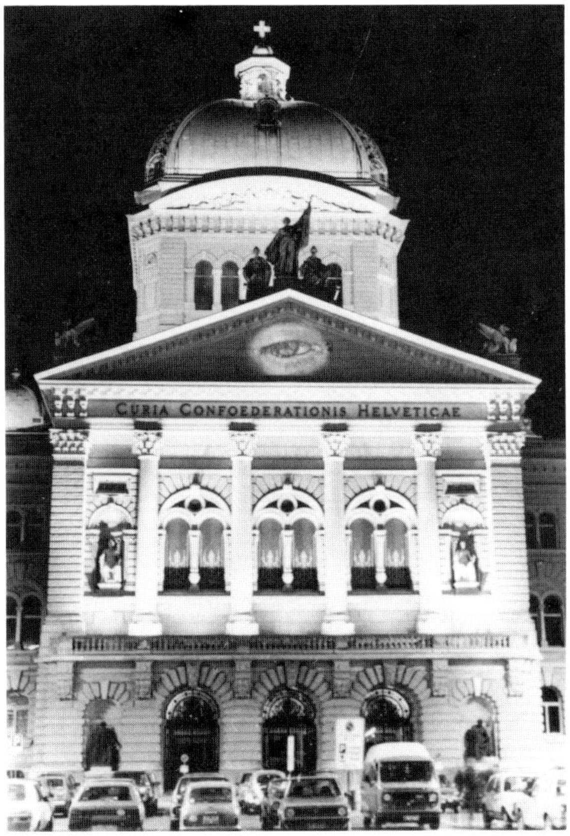
CURIA CONFOEDERATIONIS HELVETICAE

33 *The Swiss National Parliament Building Projection*, 1985
< *Projection de l'édifice du Parlement fédéral de la Suisse*, 1985
*La proiezione del Palazzo del Parlamento nazionale svizzero*, 1985

34 *The Royal Bank Building Projection*, 1985
∨ *Projection de l'immeuble de la Banque Royale*, 1985
*La proiezione del Palazzo della Royal Bank*, 1985

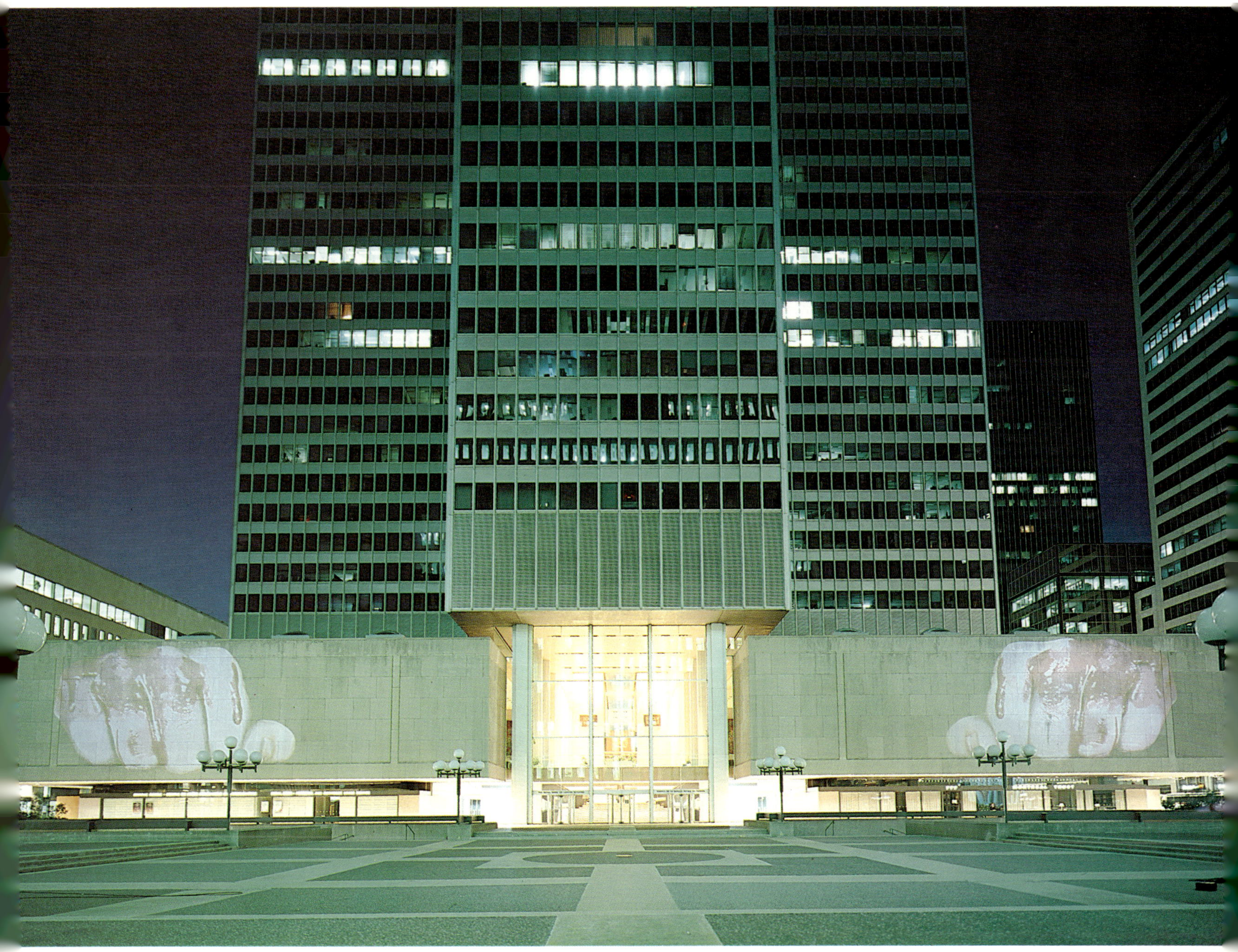

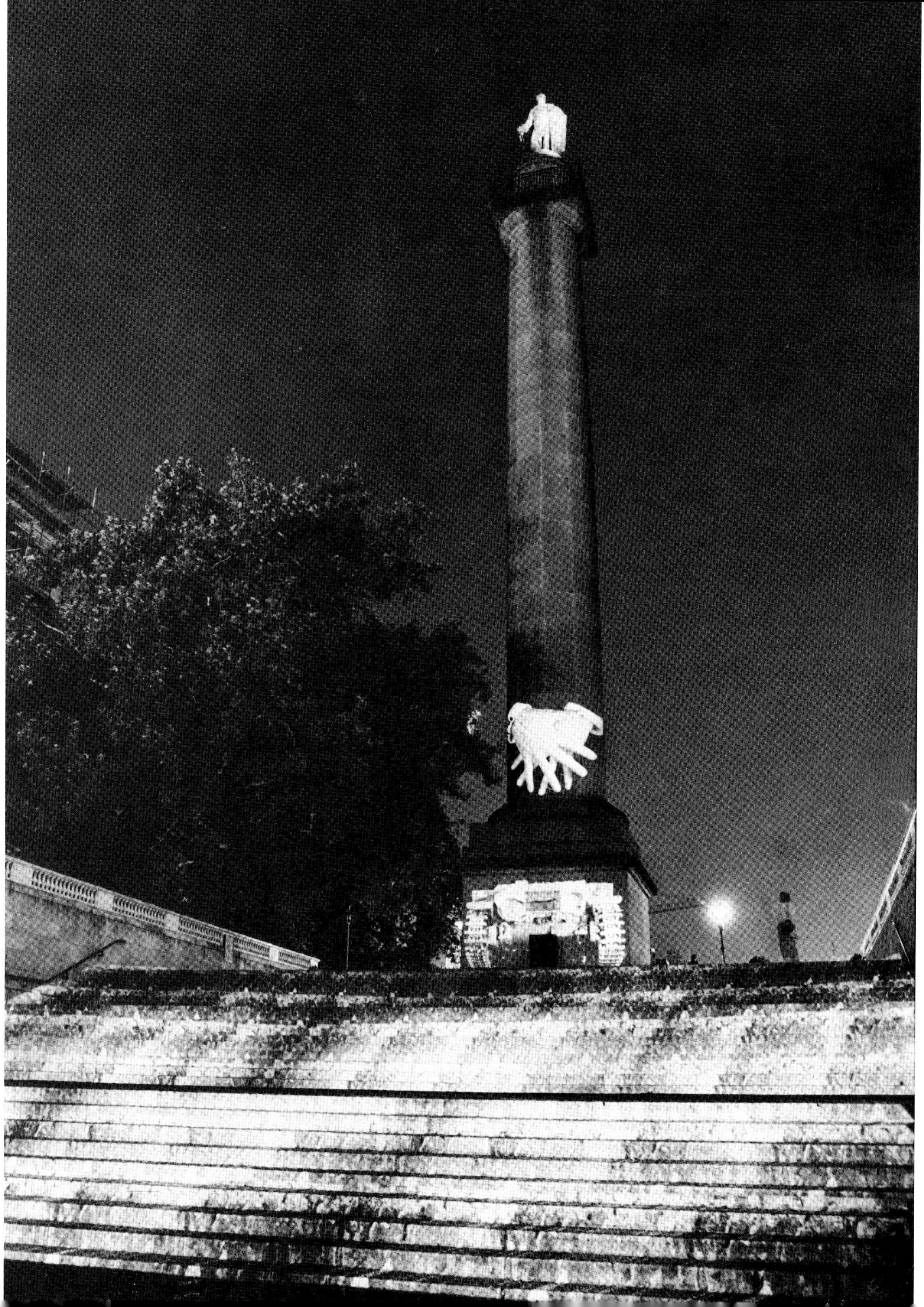

35 *The Duke of York Column Projection*, 1985
< *Projection de la colonne du Duc d'York*, 1985
*La proiezione della Colonna al Duca di York*, 1985

36 *The South African Embassy Projection*, 1985
V *Projection de l'ambassade sud-africaine*, 1985
*La proiezione dell'Ambasciata del Sudafrica*, 1985

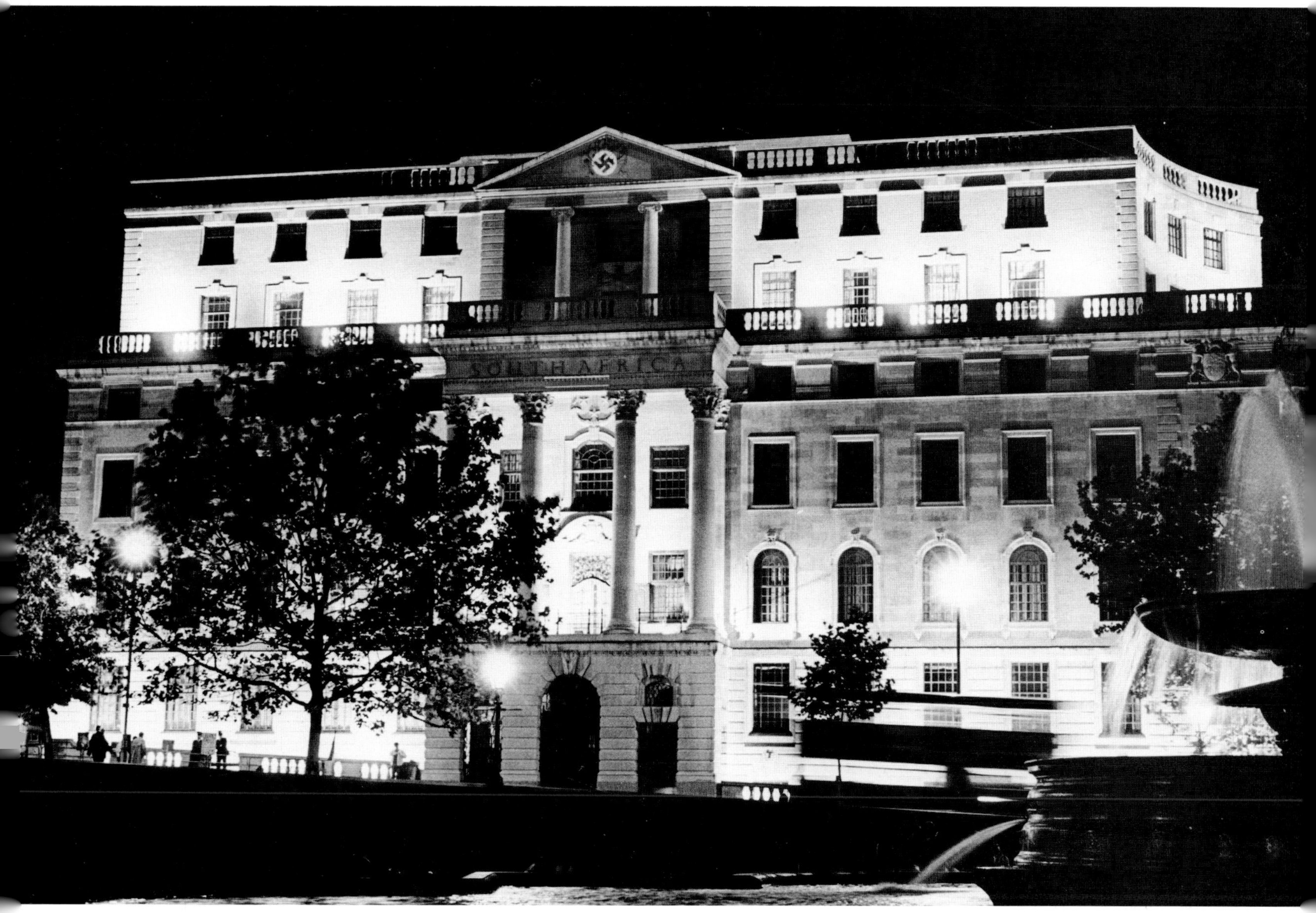

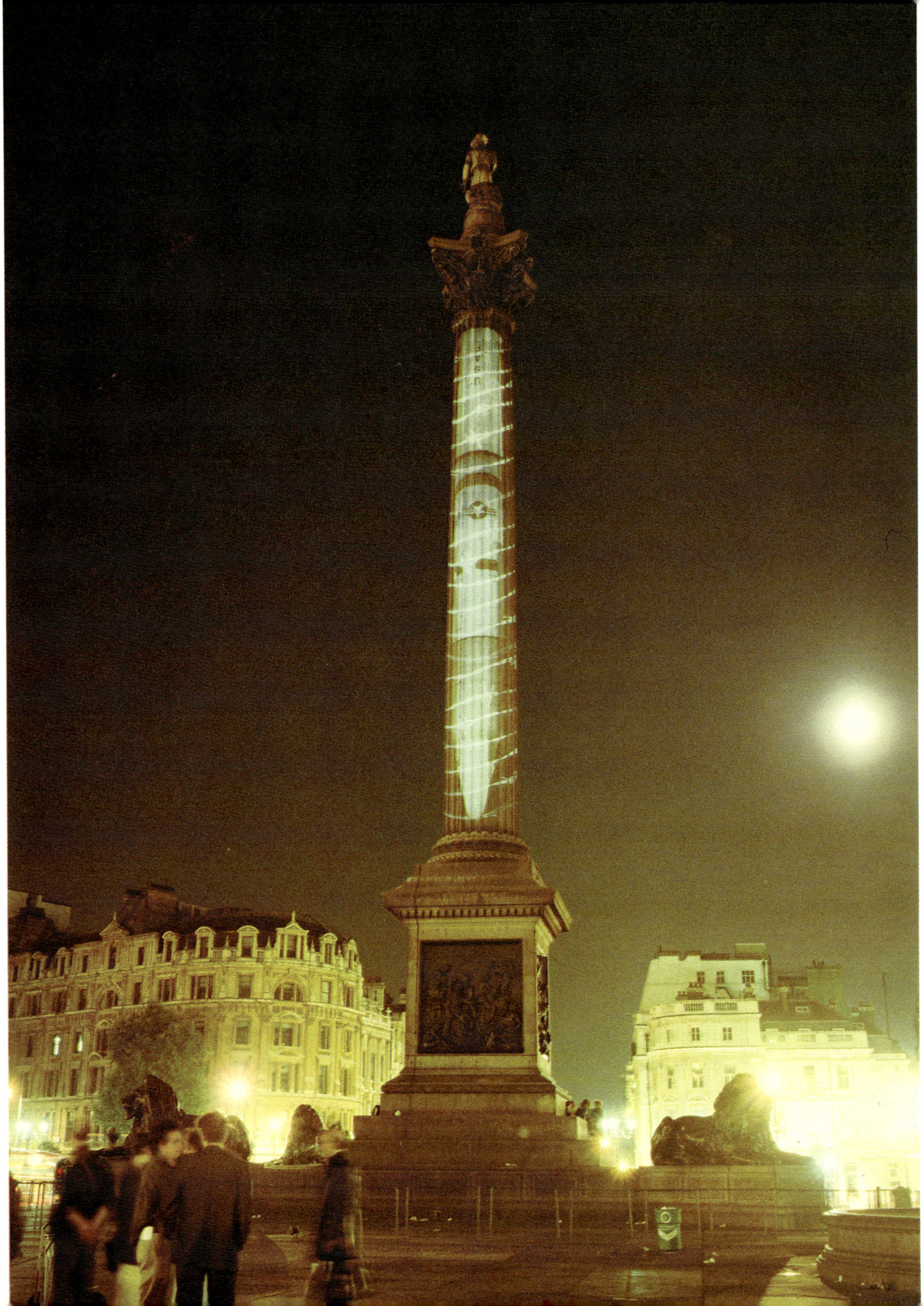

37 *The Nelson's Column Projection*, 1985
*Projection de la colonne de Nelson*, 1985
*La proiezione del Monumento a Nelson*, 1985

∨ Detail
Détail
Dettaglio

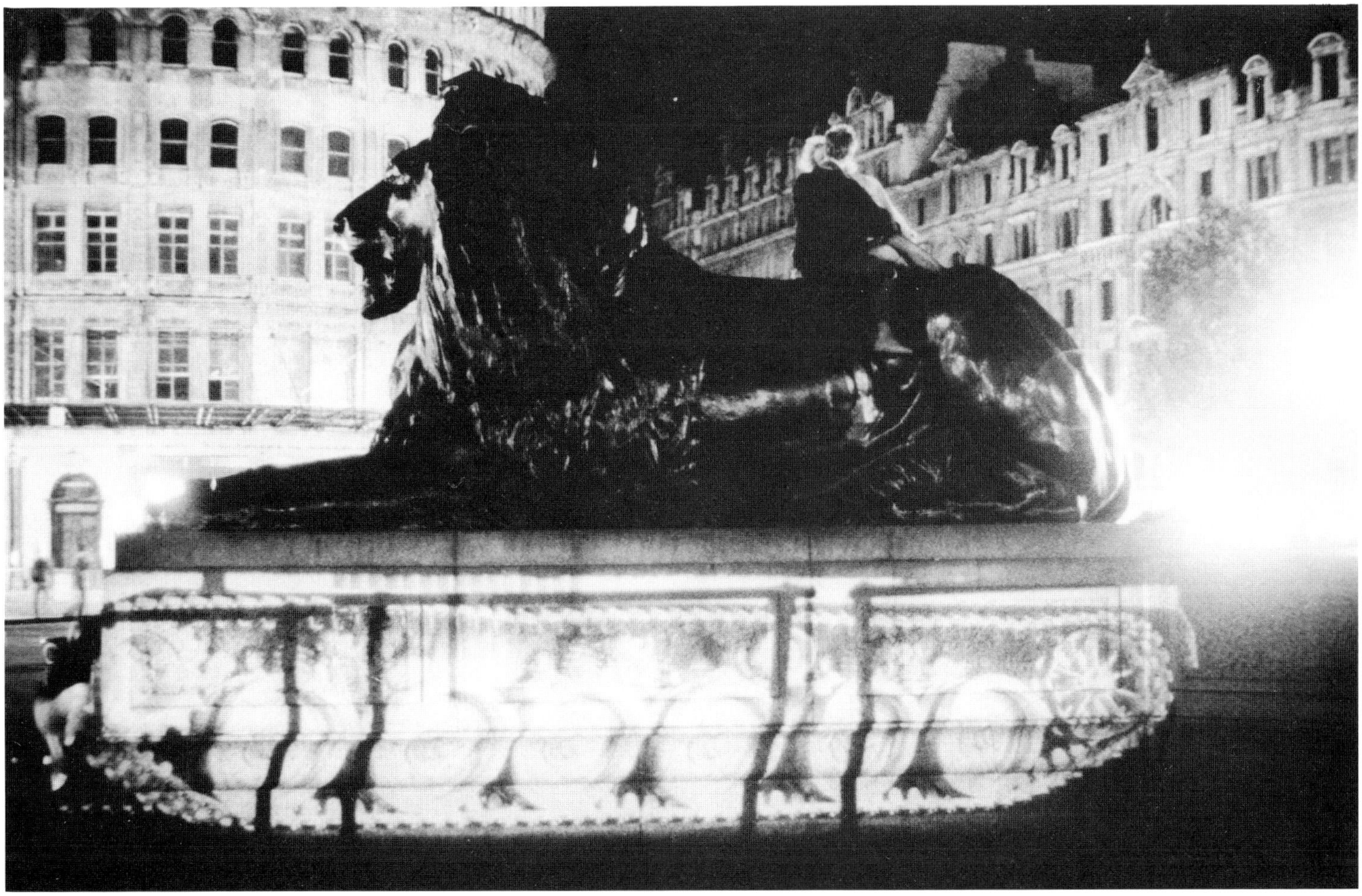

38 *The Derry Guildhall Projection*, 1985
*Projection du Guildhall de la ville de Derry*, 1985
*La proiezione del Derry Guildhall*, 1985

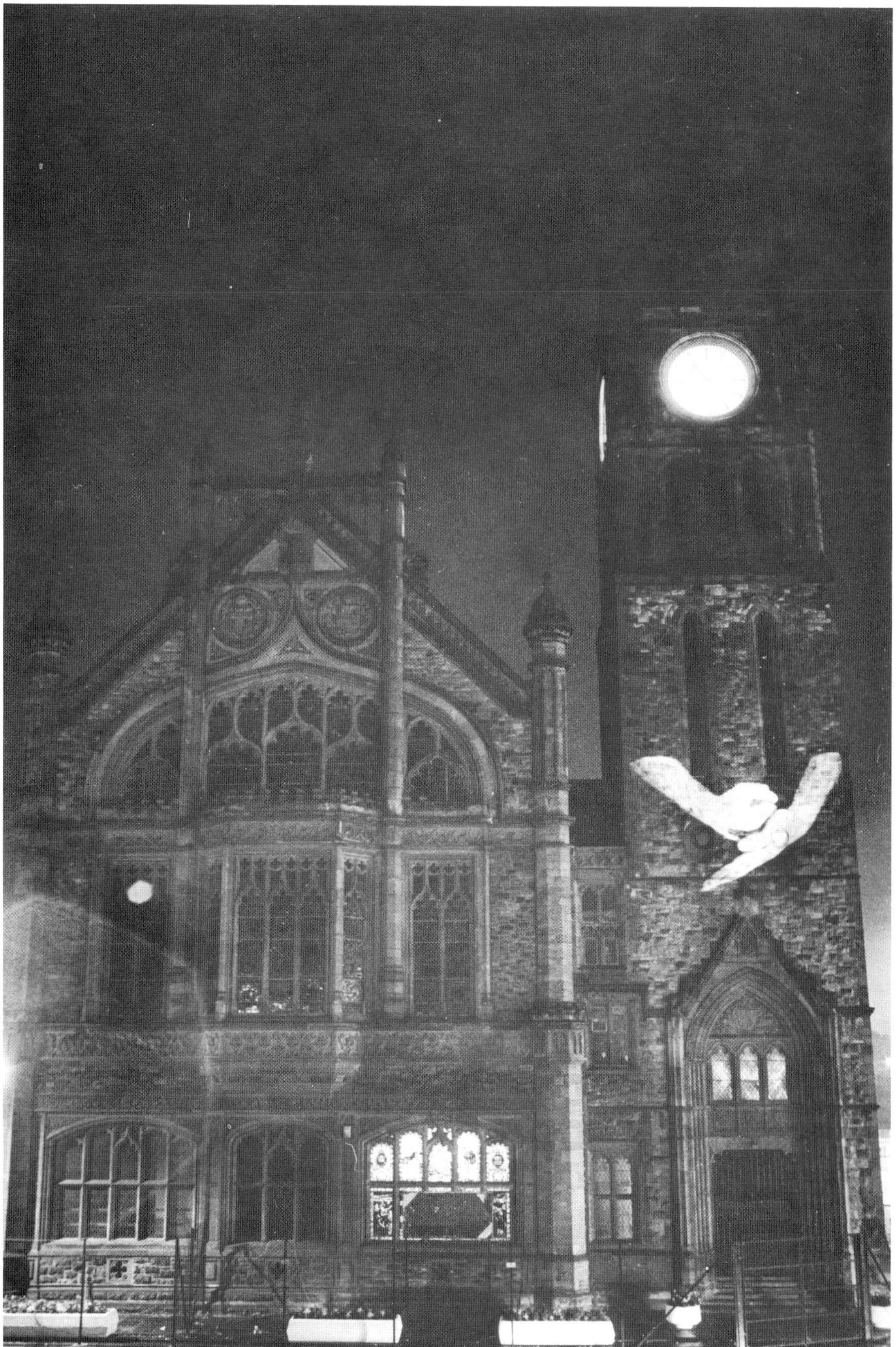

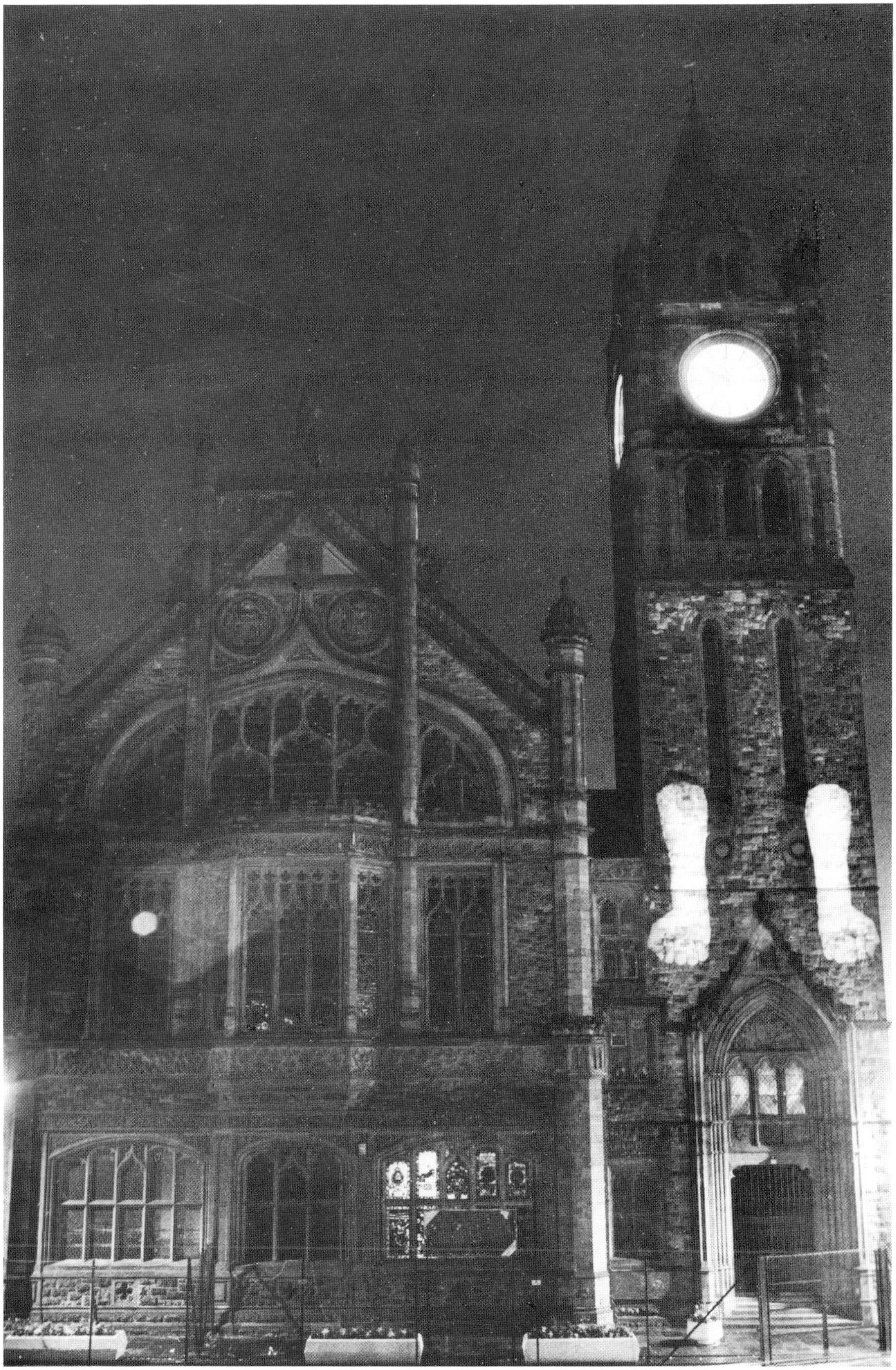

# Notes to the Plates

## Melvin Charney

1 *The Treasury of Three Rivers*, 1975
Wood construction
3.9 × 2.9 × 1.0 m
Installed at the Musée d'art contemporain, Montreal, for the exhibition *Québec 75*
The National Gallery of Canada, Ottawa

2 *The Houses of Sherbrooke Street*, 1976
Wood, steel, and concrete construction
16.4 × 15.8 × 12.0 m
Conceived for and installed on Sherbrooke and St. Urbain Streets, Montreal, June–July 1976
Commissioned by the Arts and Culture Programme of the XXI Olympiad

3 *Streetwork No. 2*, 1978
Coloured pencil and wax crayon on black-and-white photomontage
114.3 × 76.2 cm
Mr. and Mrs. Martin Zimmerman, Chicago

4 *Malevich Re-drawn*, 1978
Coloured pencil on Xerox
25.5 × 19.0 cm
Centre Canadien d'Architecture/ Canadian Centre for Architecture, Montréal

5 *Edifice: The Square in a Square*, 1979
Coloured pencil and wax crayon on black-and-white photograph
96.5 × 107.0 cm
Centre Canadien d'Architecture/ Canadian Centre for Architecture, Montréal

6 *A Chicago Construction*, 1982
Wood construction, partially painted
11.2 × 21.0 × 6.8 m
Conceived for and installed at the Museum of Contemporary Art, Chicago, May–September 1982

7 *Chicago Construction No. 3*, 1981
Coloured pencil and wax crayon on vellum paper
71.0 × 91.0 cm
Musée d'art contemporain, Montreal

8 *Toronto Construction No. 4*, 1982
Coloured pencil and wax crayon on black-and-white photograph
56.0 × 76.0 cm
Collection of the artist, Montreal

9 *A Toronto Construction*, 1982
Wood construction, partially painted
10.0 × 27.4 × 15.8 m
Conceived for and installed on King Street East, Toronto, June 1982–March 1983
Commissioned by Visual Arts Ontario

10 *Kingston Construction*, 1982
Conté and pastel on paper
75.3 × 105.5 cm
Agnes Etherington Art Centre, Queen's University, Kingston, Ontario

11 *A Kingston Construction*, 1983
Wood construction, partially painted
7.5 × 42.5 × 25.0 m
Conceived for and installed at the Agnes Etherington Art Centre, Queen's University, Kingston, Ontario, March–August 1983

12 *"Better if they think they are going to a farm ...,"* 1982
Coloured pencil on photomontage
43.0 × 53.0 cm
Conceived for Documenta-Urbana, *Documenta 7*. To be constructed on the Bahnhofplatz, Kassel, Federal Republic of Germany
Centre Canadien d'Architecture/ Canadian Centre for Architecture, Montréal

13 *"Better if they think they are going to a farm ..." No. 2*, 1982
Coloured pencil, conté, and pastel on paper
106.7 × 152.4 cm
Conceived for Documenta-Urbana, *Documenta 7*. To be constructed on Kurt-Schumacher Strasse, Kassel, Federal Republic of Germany
Canada Council Art Bank, Ottawa

14 *Pliny on My Mind No. 1 and No. 2*, 1983
Wood construction, partially painted
(1) 4.0 × 4.3 × 7.3 m
(2) 3.8 × 5.6 × 7.4 m
Installed at the Montreal Museum of Fine Arts for the exhibition *The Villas of Pliny and Classical Architecture in Montreal*, October–December 1983
Centre Canadien d'Architecture/ Canadian Centre for Architecture, Montréal

15 *Pliny on My Mind No. 1 and No. 2*, 1983
Coloured pencil on paper
99.0 × 114.0 cm
Centre Canadien d'Architecture/ Canadian Centre for Architecture, Montréal

16 *Pliny's Other Villa*, 1984
Pastel and conté on paper
56.7 × 76.0 cm
Department of External Affairs, Ottawa

17 *Fragments of the Forgotten City No. 6*, 1984
Conté and pastel on paper
56.0 × 56.0 cm
Centre Canadien d'Architecture/ Canadian Centre for Architecture, Montréal

18 *Fragments of the Forgotten City No. 14*, 1985
Pastel and conté on paper
35.0 × 28.0 cm
Collection of the artist, Montreal

19 *Way Station No. 6*, 1985
Oil pastel on paper
65.0 × 102.5 cm
Collection of the artist, Montreal

20 *Building Displacements No. 2 ... Study for a Construction at La Cité*, 1985
Pastel on paper
51.0 × 36.0 cm
Collection of the artist, Montreal

21 *From Laugier to Popova: Construction in Parts*, 1985
Pastel and conté on paper
104.5 × 171.5 cm
Centre Canadien d'Architecture/ Canadian Centre for Architecture, Montréal

22 *From Laugier to Popova: A Construction in Parts*, 1985
Wood construction
3.7 × 14.1 × 6.7 m
Installed at the Centre international d'art contemporain, Place du Parc, Montreal, for the exhibition *Aurora Borealis*, June–September 1985

## Krzysztof Wodiczko

23 *The Scotia Square Tower Projection*, Halifax, Nova Scotia, 1981

24 *The Art Gallery of New South Wales Projection*, Sydney, 1982
Changing images of hands showing a variety of "managerial gestures" were projected using four standard and one high-power slide projectors.
Organized for the opening of the *Sydney Biennale*.
Special thanks to Ian de Gruchy.

25 *The Memorial Hall Projection*, Dayton, Ohio, 1983
Images from David's painting *Lictors Returning to Brutus the Bodies of His Sons* (1789), as well as images of missiles and a crowd of people, were projected on the main façade using nineteen standard slide projectors located on the ground in front of the façade.

26 *The Stuttgart Main Train Station (Hauptbahnhof) Projection*, February 1983
The image was projected on the tower of the main train station using a Xenon-arc slide projector located on the roof of the station in front of the tower.
In conjunction with the exhibition *Künstler aus Kanada* organized by the Württembergischer Kunstverein, Stuttgart.
Special thanks to John Massey.

27 *The Victory Column Projection*, Schlossplatz, Stuttgart, February 1983
During the 1983 national election campaign in West Germany, the planned deployment of Pershing II missiles in Germany was the critical issue.

28 *The South African War Memorial Projection*, Toronto, 9 and 19 April 1983
Organized as part of an exhibition of Wodiczko's work at The Ydessa Gallery, Toronto.

29 *The Federal Courthouse Building Projection*, London, Ontario, September 1984
Images were projected on the façade using two high-power slide projectors located on the roof of the lower section of the building.
Organized by the London Regional Art Gallery.

30 *The Astor Building/New Museum Projection*, New York, 8 December 1984 and 6 February 1985
The upper image was projected on the ten-story section of the Astor Building that has been unoccupied for several years. The lower image was projected over the only occupied section of the building, the two floors owned by the New Museum of Contemporary Art.
Organized by the New Museum of Contemporary Art with the assistance of the 49th Parallel and the Hal Bromm Gallery, New York, on the occasion of the joint openings of the exhibitions *On View* and *Difference: On Representation and Sexuality* at the New Museum of Contemporary Art, New York.
Special thanks to François Alecque and Ian de Gruchy.

31 The *AT & T Building Projection*, Tribeca, New York, 2 November 1984
The projection took place during the 1984 Presidential campaign in conjunction with an exhibition at the Hal Bromm Gallery, New York, *Wodiczko: Completing Façades* (13 October–10 November 1984).
Organized by The Kitchen in cooperation with AT & T and with the assistance of the Lower Manhattan Cultural Council and the 49th Parallel, New York.

32 *The Grand Army Plaza Projection*, Brooklyn, New York, 31 December 1984/1 January 1985
The images were projected on the Memorial Arch using five modified slide projectors located on the ground in front of the arch. The projection coincided with the 1985 Brooklyn New Year's Gala fireworks display.
Organized by the New York City Parks Department, Prospect Park, with the assistance of Artists Space, the Hal Bromm Gallery, and the 49th Parallel, New York.

33 *The Swiss National Parliament Building Projection*, Bern, Switzerland, 12–14 April 1985
The eye projected on the pediment changed the direction of its gaze from the Swiss National Bank Building to the other banks of the Bundesplatz, from the ground (where the gold vault is located) to the sky.

34 *The Royal Bank Building Projection*, Place Ville-Marie, Montreal, 3 August 1985
Organized in conjunction with the exhibition *Aurora Borealis*, Centre international d'art contemporain de Montréal.

35 *The Duke of York Column Projection*, Waterloo Place, London, 29 and 30 August 1985
The Duke of York Memorial, part of Carlton House Terrace, is located on the Mall, the "royal route" between Buckingham Palace and Admiralty Arch, and is the beginning of a series of prominent historical monuments along Regent Street. The Steps of the Memorial are an important passage between Horse Guards Parade and Piccadilly Circus. The projection was timed to coincide with the closing of an official "son et lumière" event, which took place in Horse Guards Parade. Images of British mineworkers were projected onto the Steps. After the "son et lumière" ended, a large part of the audience left the area by walking through the Steps, thereby becoming part of the image of the projected crowds.
Since the original spotlight was not available, a special spotlight was installed as a part of the projection to illuminate the statue of the Duke of York at the top of the column. Six high-power slide projectors were located on the ground in front of the Steps. All of the projected images were visible from passing traffic in the Mall.
Organized by the Institute of Contemporary Arts and the Artangel Trust, London.

36 *The South African Embassy Projection*, Trafalgar Square, London, 31 August 1985
This projection coincided with another projection by Wodiczko on Nelson's Column, also in Trafalgar Square. South Africa House is the tallest and most brightly illuminated structure on the Square.
The projection, extensively photographed and reported by the press, was executed without the permission of either the City of London or South Africa House. It lasted two hours before it was stopped by the police. An anti-apartheid demonstration, protesting in particular the lack of British Government sanctions against South Africa, took place at the same time as the projection. The South African Embassy subsequently sent an official diplomatic note of protest to the Canadian High Commissioner at the Canadian Embassy in London, demanding an explanation.
Special thanks to Steven White.

37 *The Nelson's Column Projection*, Trafalgar Square, London, 27 and 30 August 1985
Six high-power slide projectors and the spotlight located in the centre of Trafalgar Square were used. The projection was televised by BBC Television.
Organized by the Institute of Contemporary Arts and the Artangel Trust, London.
Special thanks to Steven White.

38 *The Derry Guildhall Projection*, Derry, Northern Ireland, 4 September 1985
The Guildhall is situated outside of and facing the British-built Wall. Guns donated by London merchants are mounted on the Wall and trained on the Guildhall. Two images of hands were projected on the Guildhall using slide projectors mounted on the Wall.
Special thanks to Willy Doherty.

# Planches : Notices explicatives

## Melvin Charney

1 *Le Trésor de Trois-Rivières*, 1975
Construction en bois
3,9 × 2,9 × 1 m
Installée au Musée d'art contemporain de Montréal dans le cadre de l'exposition *Québec 75*
Musée des beaux-arts du Canada, Ottawa

2 *Les Maisons de la rue Sherbrooke*, 1976
Construction en bois, acier et béton
16,4 × 15,8 × 12 m
Conçue pour l'intersection des rues Sherbrooke et Saint-Urbain, à Montréal, où elle fut exposée en juin–juillet 1976
Œuvre commandée dans le cadre du Programme art et culture de la XXI^e^ Olympiade

3 *Streetwork n^o^ 2*, 1978
Crayon de couleur et crayon de cire sur photomontage en noir et blanc
114,3 × 76,2 cm
M. et M^me^ Martin Zimmerman, Chicago

4 *Malevitch redessiné*, 1978
Crayon de couleur sur xérocopie
25,5 × 19 cm
Centre Canadien d'Architecture/Canadian Centre for Architecture, Montréal

5 *Édifice : Le carré dans un carré,* 1979
Crayon de couleur et crayon de cire sur photographie en noir et blanc
96,5 × 107 cm
Centre Canadien d'Architecture/Canadian Centre for Architecture, Montréal

6 *Une construction de Chicago*, 1982
Construction en bois, partiellement peinte
11,2 × 21 × 6, 8 m
Conçue pour le Museum of Contemporary Art de Chicago, où elle fut exposée de mai à septembre 1982

7 *Construction de Chicago n^o^ 3*, 1981
Crayon de couleur et crayon de cire sur vélin
71 × 91 cm
Musée d'art contemporain, Montréal

8 *Construction de Toronto n^o^ 4*, 1982
Crayon de couleur et crayon de cire sur photographie en noir et blanc
56 × 76 cm
Collection de l'artiste, Montréal

9 *Une construction de Toronto*, 1982
Construction en bois, partiellement peinte
10 × 27,4 × 15,8 m
Conçue pour la rue King est, à Toronto, où elle fut exposée de juin 1982 à mars 1983
Œuvre commandée par Visual Arts Ontario

10 *Construction de Kingston*, 1982
Crayon Conté et pastel sur papier
75,3 × 105,5 cm
Agnes Etherington Art Centre, Université Queen's, Kingston (Ontario)

11 *Une construction de Kingston*, 1983
Construction en bois, partiellement peinte
7,5 × 42,5 × 25 m
Œuvre commandée par l'Agnes Etherington Art Centre, Université Queen's, Kingston (Ontario), où elle fut exposée de mars à août 1983

12 *« Il vaut mieux qu'ils croient aller à la ferme… »,* 1982
Crayon de couleur sur photomontage
43 × 53 cm
Conçue pour Documenta-Urbana, *Documenta 7*, et devant être construite sur la Bahnhofplatz, à Kassel, en République fédérale d'Allemagne
Centre Canadien d'Architecture/Canadian Centre for Architecture, Montréal

13 *« Il vaut mieux qu'ils croient aller à la ferme… » n^o^ 2*, 1982
Crayon de couleur, crayon Conté et pastel sur papier
106,7 × 152,4 cm
Conçue pour Documenta-Urbana, *Documenta 7*, et devant être construite rue Kurt-Schumacher, à Kassel, en République fédérale d'Allemagne
Banque d'œuvres d'art du Conseil des Arts du Canada, Ottawa

14 *Pline en tête n^o^ 1 et n^o^ 2*, 1983
Construction en bois, partiellement peinte
4 × 4,3 × 7,3 m; 3,8 × 5,6 × 7,4 m
Installée au Musée des beaux-arts de Montréal dans le cadre de l'exposition *Les Villas de Pline et l'architecture classique à Montréal*, qui fut présentée d'octobre à décembre 1983
Centre Canadien d'Architecture/Canadian Centre for Architecture, Montréal

15 *Pline en tête n^o^ 1 et n^o^ 2*, 1983
Crayon de couleur sur papier
99 × 114 cm
Centre Canadien d'Architecture/Canadian Centre for Architecture, Montréal

16 *L'Autre Villa de Pline*, 1984
Pastel et crayon Conté sur papier
56,7 × 76 cm
Ministère des Affaires extérieures, Ottawa

17 *Fragments de la Cité oubliée nº 6*, 1984
Crayon Conté et pastel sur papier
56 × 56 cm
Centre Canadien d'Architecture/
Canadian Centre for Architecture,
Montréal

18 *Fragments de la Cité oubliée nº 14*, 1985
Pastel et crayon Conté sur papier
35 × 28 cm
Collection de l'artiste, Montréal

19 *Chemin de la station nº 6*, 1985
Pastel à l'huile sur papier
65 × 102,5 cm
Collection de l'artiste, Montréal

20 *Déplacements d'édifice nº 2... Étude pour une construction à la Cité*, 1985
Pastel sur papier
51 × 36 cm
Collection de l'artiste, Montréal

21 *De Laugier à Popova : Construction en parties*, 1985
Pastel et crayon Conté sur papier
104,5 × 171,5 cm
Centre Canadien d'Architecture/
Canadian Centre for Architecture,
Montréal

22 *De Laugier à Popova : Une construction en parties*, 1985
Construction en bois
3,7 × 14,1 × 6,7 m
Installée au Centre international d'art contemporain de Montréal, dans le cadre de l'exposition *Aurora Borealis*, qui fut présentée de juin à septembre 1985

## Krzysztof Wodiczko

23 *Projection de l'immeuble de Scotia Square*, Halifax (Nouvelle-Écosse), 1981

24 *Projection de l'Art Gallery of New South Wales*, Sydney (Nouvelle-Galles du Sud), Australie, 1982
Au moyen de quatre projecteurs de diapositives standard et d'un projecteur très puissant, on a présenté différentes images de mains faisant « des gestes de direction ».
Organisée dans le cadre de l'inauguration de la *Biennale* de Sydney.
Nous remercions tout spécialement Ian de Gruchy.

25 *Projection du Memorial Hall*, Dayton (Ohio), 1983
Images d'un tableau de David (*Les Licteurs rapportent à Brutus les corps de ses fils*, 1789), de missiles et de la foule projetées sur la façade au moyen de dix-neuf projecteurs de diapositives standard placés sur le sol, devant la façade.

26 *Projection de la gare centrale (Hauptbahnhof) de Stuttgart*, République fédérale d'Allemagne, février 1983
Projection sur la tour de la gare centrale au moyen d'un projecteur de diapositives à arc au xénon placé sur le toit de la gare, face à la tour.
Présentée conjointement à l'exposition *Künstler aus Kanada*, organisée par le Württembergischer Kunstverein, de Stuttgart.
Nous remercions tout spécialement John Massey.

27 *Projection de la colonne de la Victoire*, Schlossplatz, Stuttgart, République fédérale d'Allemagne, février 1983
Le projet de déploiement de missiles Pershing II en Allemagne a été le thème central de la campagne électorale de 1983 en République fédérale.

28 *Projection du monument commémoratif de la guerre d'Afrique du Sud*, Toronto, les 9 et 19 avril 1983
Organisée dans le cadre d'une exposition de l'œuvre de Krzysztof Wodiczko à l'Ydessa Gallery de Toronto.

29 *Projection du Palais de justice fédéral*, London (Ontario), septembre 1984
On a projeté des images sur la façade au moyen de deux projecteurs de diapositives très puissants placés sur le toit de la partie basse de l'immeuble.
Organisée par la London Regional Art Gallery.

30 *Projection de l'immeuble Astor/New Museum*, New York, le 8 décembre 1984 et le 6 février 1985
L'image supérieure était projetée sur la section de dix étages de l'immeuble Astor, inoccupée depuis plusieurs années. L'image inférieure était projetée sur la seule partie occupée de l'immeuble, les deux étages appartenant au New Museum of Contemporary Art.
Organisée par le New Museum of Contemporary Art avec l'aide du centre 49e Parallèle et de la Hal Bromm Gallery, de New York, à l'occasion de l'inauguration conjointe des expositions *On View* et *Difference : On Representation and Sexuality* au New Museum of Contemporary Art, à New York.
Nous remercions tout spécialement François Alecque et Ian de Gruchy.

31 *Projection de l'immeuble de l'AT & T, Tribeca, New York, le* 2 novembre 1984
Tenue au cours de la campagne présidentielle américaine de 1984, dans le cadre d'une exposition de la Hal Bromm Gallery de New York, *Wodiczko : Completing Façades*, présentée du 13 octobre au 10 novembre 1984.

Organisée par The Kitchen, en collaboration avec la société American Telephone and Telegraph, et avec l'aide du Lower Manhattan Cultural Council et du centre 49e Parallèle.

32 *Projection de la Grand Army Plaza*, Brooklyn (New York), le 31 décembre 1984 et le 1er janvier 1985
Les images ont été projetées sur l'arc de triomphe au moyen de cinq projecteurs de diapositives modifiés placés sur le sol, devant le monument. La projection coïncidait avec le feu d'artifice du Gala du Nouvel An 1985 de Brooklyn.

Organisée par le New York City Parks Department (Prospect Park), avec le concours d'Artists Space, de la Hal Bromm Gallery et du centre 49e Parallèle.

33 *Projection de l'édifice du Parlement fédéral de la Suisse*, Berne, du 12 au 14 avril 1985
L'œil projeté sur le fronton fixait dans un premier temps l'immeuble de la Banque nationale suisse, pour se tourner ensuite vers les autres banques de la Bundesplatz, depuis le sol (où se trouve la réserve d'or) jusqu'au ciel.

34 *Projection de l'immeuble de la Banque Royale*, place Ville-Marie, Montréal, le 3 août 1985
Organisée parallèlement à l'exposition *Aurora Borealis*, présentée au Centre international d'art contemporain de Montréal.

35 *Projection de la colonne du Duc d'York*, place Waterloo, Londres, les 29 et 30 août 1985
La colonne du Duc d'York, à Carlton House Terrace, est située sur le *Mall*, la route royale reliant le palais de Buckingham et l'Arc de l'Amirauté, et est le premier d'une série de monuments historiques de premier plan qui se dressent le long de Regent Street. Les marches conduisant au monument constituent un passage important entre Horse Guards Parade et Piccadilly Circus. La projection coïncidait avec la fin d'un spectacle « son et lumière », qui avait eu lieu place Horse Guards Parade.

Comme le projecteur habituel n'était pas utilisé, on a installé un projecteur spécial pour éclairer la statue du duc d'York, au sommet de la colonne. Six projecteurs de diapositives très puissants étaient placés sur le sol, devant les marches. Du *Mall*, les passants pouvaient voir toutes les images projetées.

Organisée par l'Institute of Contemporary Arts et l'Artangel Trust, de Londres.

36 *Projection de l'ambassade sud-africaine*, Trafalgar Square, Londres, le 31 août 1985
Cette projection a coïncidé avec une autre projection de l'artiste, sur la colonne de Nelson, également sur Trafalgar Square. La Maison de l'Afrique du Sud est l'immeuble le plus élevé et le plus illuminé de Trafalgar Square.

La projection, qui a fait l'objet de reportages aussi nombreux que détaillés, a eu lieu sans la permission ni de la municipalité ni de la Maison de l'Afrique du Sud. Elle a duré deux heures, avant que la police y mette fin. Une manifestation anti-apartheid avait lieu au même moment, relativement à l'absence de sanctions de la Grande-Bretagne contre l'Afrique du Sud. Par la suite, l'ambassade d'Afrique du Sud a envoyé une note de protestation officielle au haut-commissaire du Canada, à l'ambassade canadienne de Londres, exigeant des explications.

Nous remercions tout particulièrement Steven White.

37 *Projection de la colonne de Nelson*, Trafalgar Square, Londres, les 27 et 30 août 1985
On s'est servi de six projecteurs de diapositives très puissants et du projecteur situé au centre de Trafalgar Square. La projection a été télévisée par la B.B.C.

Organisée par l'Institute of Contemporary Arts et l'Artangel Trust, de Londres.

Nous remercions tout spécialement Steven White.

38 *Projection du Guildhall de la ville de Derry*, Irlande du Nord, le 4 septembre 1985
Le Guildhall fait face à la muraille édifiée par les Britanniques. Des canons donnés par des marchands londoniens sont installés sur la muraille et braqués sur le Guildhall. Deux images de mains ont été projetées sur le Guildhall au moyen de projecteurs de diapositives placés sur la muraille.

Nous remercions tout spécialement Willy Doherty.

# Illustrazioni: Note esplicative

## Melvin Charney

1 *Il tesoro di Trois-Rivières*, 1975
Costruzione in legno
3,9 × 2,9 × 1,0 m
Installata nel Musée d'art contemporain, Montreal, per l'esposizione *Québec 75*
National Gallery of Canada

2 *Le case della via Sherbrooke*, 1976
Costruzione in legno, acciaio e cemento
16,4 × 15,8 × 12,0 m
Studiata ed installata per l'incrocio fra le vie Sherbrooke e St. Urbain, Montreal, giugno–luglio 1976
Ordinata dal « Programma di Arti e Culture delle XXI Olimpiadi »

3 *Streetwork No. 2*, 1978
Matita a colori e pastello cerato su fotomontaggio in bianco e nero
114,3 × 76,2 cm
Sig. Martin Zimmerman e Signora, Chicago

4 *Malevich ridisegnato*, 1978
Matita a colori su Xerox
24,5 × 19,0 cm
Centre Canadien d'Architecture/ Canadian Centre for Architecture, Montréal

5 *Edificio: il quadrato in un quadrato*, 1979
Matita a colori e pastello cerato su fotografia in bianco e nero
96,5 × 107,0 cm
Centre Canadien d'Architecture/ Canadian Centre for Architecture, Montréal

6 *Una costruzione in Chicago*, 1982
Costruzione in legno, parzialmente pitturata
11,2 × 21,0 × 6,8 m
Studiata ed installata nel Museum of Contemporary Art, Chicago, maggio–settembre 1982

7 *Costruzione in Chicago No. 3*, 1981
Matita a colori e pastello cerato su carta pergamena
71,0 × 91,0 cm
Musée d'art contemporain, Montreal

8 *Costruzione in Toronto No. 4*, 1982
Matita a colori e pastello cerato su fotografia in bianco e nero
56,0 × 76,0 cm
Collezione dell'artista, Montreal

9 *Una costruzione in Toronto*, 1982
Costruzione in legno, parzialmente pitturata
10,0 × 27,4 × 15,8 m
Studiata ed installata per la via King East, Toronto, giugno 1982–marzo 1983
Ordinata da Visual Arts Ontario

10 *Costruzione in Kingston*, 1982
Conté e pastello su carta
75,3 × 105,5 cm
Agnes Etherington Art Centre, Università di Queen's, Kingston, Ontario

11 *Una costruzione in Kingston*, 1983
Costruzione in legno, parzialmente pitturata
7,5 × 42,5 × 25,0 m
Studiata ed installata al Agnes Etherington Art Centre, Università di Queen's, Kingston, Ontario, marzo–agosto 1983

12 *« E' meglio se pensano che stanno andando verso una tenuta agricola... »*, 1982
Matita a colori su fotomontaggio
43,0 × 53,0 cm
Studiata per Documenta-Urbana, *Documenta 7*. Da essere costruita sulla Bahnhofplatz, Kassel, Repubblica Federale della Germania
Centre Canadien d'Architecture/ Canadian Centre for Architecture, Montréal

13 *« E' meglio se pensano che stanno andando verso una tenuta agricola... » No. 2*, 1982
Matita a colori, conté e pastello su carta
106, 7 × 152, 4 cm
Studiata per Documenta-Urbana, *Documenta 7*. Da essere costruita sulla Kurt–Schumacher Strasse, Kassel, Repubblica Federale della Germania
Canada Council Art Bank, Ottawa

14 *Pensando al Plinio No. 1 e No. 2*, 1983
Costruzione in legno, parzialmente pitturata
(1) 4,0 × 4,3 × 7,3 m
(2) 3,8 × 5,6 × 7,4 m
Installata nel Musée des beaux-arts de Montréal, per l'esposizione *Les Villas de Pline et l'architecture classique à Montréal*, ottobre–dicembre 1983
Centre Canadien d'Architecture/ Canadian Centre for Architecture, Montréal

15 *Pensando al Plinio No. 1 e No. 2*, 1983
Matita a colori su carta
99,0 × 114,0 cm
Centre Canadien d'Architecture/
Canadian Centre for Architecture,
Montréal

16 *L'altra villa di Plinio*, 1984
Pastello e conté su carta
56,7 × 76,0 cm
Ministero per gli Affari Esteri,
Ottawa

17 *Frammenti della città dimenticata No. 6*, 1984
Conté e pastello su carta
56,0 × 56,0 cm
Centre Canadien d'Architecture/
Canadian Centre for Architecture,
Montréal

18 *Frammenti della città dimenticata No. 14*, 1985
Pastello e conté su carta
35,0 × 28,0 cm
Collezione dell'artista, Montreal

19 *Stazione secondaria No. 6*, 1985
Pastello ad olio su carta
65,0 × 102,5 cm
Collezione dell'artista, Montreal

20 *Spostamenti edilizi No. 2... Studio per una costruzione a La Cité*, 1985
Pastello su carta
51,0 × 36,0 cm
Collezione dell'artista, Montreal

21 *Da Laugier a Popova: costruzione in parti*, 1985
Pastello e conté su carta
104,5 × 171,5 cm
Centre Canadien d'Architecture/
Canadian Centre for Architecture,
Montréal

22 *Da Laugier a Popova: una costruzione in parti*, 1985
Costruzione in legno
3,7 × 14,1 × 6,7 m
Installata nel Centre international d'art contemporain, Place du Parc, Montreal, per l'esposizione *Aurora Borealis*, giugno–settembre 1985

## Krzysztof Wodiczko

23 *La proiezione del Palazzo della Scotia Square*, Halifax, Nuova Scozia, 1981

24 *La proiezione della Art Gallery of New South Wales*, Sydney, Australia, 1982
Vengono proiettate, a mezzo di quattro proiettori convenzionali di diapositive e di uno ad alta potenza, varie immagini di mani che fanno dei « gesti manageriali ».
Organizzata per l'apertura della *Sydney Biennale*.
Un ringraziamento speciale va a Ian de Gruchy.

25 *La proiezione della Memorial Hall*, Dayton, Ohio, 1983
Facendo uso di diciannove proiettori convenzionali di diapositive situati di fronte alla facciata principale dell'edificio, vengono proiettate delle immagini prese dal dipinto di Davide *I littori portano a Bruto le salme dei figli* (1789), nonchè immagini di missili e di una folla.

26 *La proiezione della stazione ferroviaria principale (Hauptbahnhof) di Stoccarda*, febbraio 1983
L'immagine viene proiettata sulla torre della stazione ferroviaria principale usando un proiettore di diapositive a arco di xeno situato sul tetto della stazione di fronte alla torre.
Organizzata dal Württembergischer Kunstverein, Stoccarda, in occasione dell'esposizione *Künstler aus Kanada*.
Un ringraziamente speciale va a John Massey.

27 *La proiezione della Colonna alla Vittoria*, Schlossplatz, Stoccarda, febbraio 1983
Nel corso della campagna elettorale del 1983 nella Germania occidentale, il dibattito verteva sulla possibile installazione in Germania dei missili Pershing II.

28 *La proiezione del Monumento commemorativo della guerra sudafricana*, Toronto, 9 e 19 aprile 1983
Organizzata come parte di una esposizione delle opere di Wodiczko alla Galleria Ydessa in Toronto.

29 *La proiezione del Palazzo del Tribunale Federale*, London, Ontario, settembre 1984
Le immagini vengono proiettate su una facciata dell'edificio facendo uso di due proiettori di diapositive ad alta potenza situati sul tetto della parte bassa dell'edificio stesso.
Organizzata dalla London Regional Art Gallery.

30 *La proiezione del Palazzo Astor/New Museum*, New York, 8 dicembre 1984 e 6 febbraio 1985
L'immagine superiore viene proiettata sulla sezione di dieci piani del Palazzo Astor che è stata mantenuta vuota per parecchi anni. L'immagine inferiore viene proiettata sull'unica sezione del palazzo che è occupata, cioè sui due piani di proprietà del New Museum of Contemporary Art.
Organizzata dal New Museum of Contemporary Art con l'aiuto del 49th Parallel e la Galleria Hal Bromm di New York in occasione delle aperture

congiunte delle esposizioni *On View* e *Difference: Representation and Sexuality* al New Museum of Contemporary Art di New York.
Un ringraziamento speciale va a François Alecque e Ian de Gruchy.

31 *La proiezione del Palazzo della AT & T*, Tribeca, New York, 2 novembre 1984
La proiezione ha luogo durante la campagna presidenziale del 1984 in occasione di una esposizione alla Galleria Hal Bromm di New York dal titolo *Wodiczko: Completing Façades* (13 ottobre–10 novembre 1984).
Organizzata da « The Kitchen » in collaborazione con la AT & T (American Telephone and Telegraph) e con l'aiuto del Lower Manhattan Cultural Council e il 49th Parallel di New York.

32 *La proiezione della Grand Army Plaza*, Brooklyn, New York, 31 dicembre 1984/1 gennaio 1985
Le immagine vengono proiettate sull'Arco Commemorativo facendo uso di cinque proiettori per diapositive modificati. Questi vengono posti sul terreno di fronte all'Arco. La proiezione ha coinciso con i fuochi artificiali per il Gala di Capodanno di Brooklyn 1985.
Organizzata dal New York City Parks Department, con l'aiuto di Artists Space, della Galleria Hal Bromm, e del 49th Parallel, New York.

33 *La proiezione del Palazzo del Parlamento nazionale svizzero*, Berna, Svizzera, 12–14 aprile 1985
L'occhio proiettato sul frontone cambia la direzione dello sguardo andando dall'edificio della Banca nazionale svizzera alle altre banche della Bundesplatz, e poi da terra (nel punto dove è situata la camera di sicurezza contenente l'oro della Nazione) al cielo.

34 *La proiezione del Palazzo della Royal Bank*, Place Ville-Marie, Montreal, 3 agosto 1985
Organizzata in occasione della esposizione *Aurora Borealis*, Centre international d'art contemporain de Montréal.

35 *La proiezione della Colonna al Duca di York*, Waterloo Place, Londra, 29 e 30 agosto 1985
Il Monumento al Duca di York, che fa parte di Carlton House Terrace, è situato sulla Mall, la « strada reale » fra il Palazzo di Buckingham e l'Arco dell'Ammiragliato. Esso è il primo di una serie di monumenti storici importanti situati lungo la Regent Street. I Gradini del Monumento sono un passaggio importante fra la Horse Guards Parade e Piccadilly Circus. La proeizione avvenne in coincidenza con la chiusura di un avvenimento ufficiale « son et lumière », che ebbe luogo nella Horse Guards Parade. Sui Gradini furono proiettate delle immagini di minatori inglesi in sciopero. Subito dopo che il « son et lumière » fini, gran parte della folla cammino sui Gradini, diventando così parte dell'immagini della folla proiettata.
Siccome non era disponibile il reflettore originario, fu installato uno speciale riflettore come parte della proiezione per illuminare la statua del Duca di York in cima alla colonna. Sei proiettori ad alta potenza furono sistemati sul terreno di fronte ai Gradini. Tutte le immagini proiettate potevano essere vedute dalla gente che passava attraverso il Mall.
Organizzata dal Institute of Contemporary Arts e dal Artangel Trust, Londra.

36 *La proiezione dell'Ambasciata del Sudafrica*, Trafalgar Square, Londra, 31 agosto 1985
Questa proiezione è coincisa con un'altra proiezione di Wodiczko sul Monumento a Nelson, anch'esso in Trafalgar Square. La Casa del Sudafrica è la costruzione più alta ed illuminata più intensamente di tutta la piazza.
La proiezione, fotografia ripetutamente e descritta nella stampa, fu fatta senza ne' il permesso della Città di Londra ne' quello della Casa del Sudafrica. La proiezione duro due ore prima che fosse interrotta dalla polizia. Nel corso delle proiezione ebbe luogo una dimostrazione anti-apartheid, di protesta in particolare per la mancanza di applicazione di sanzioni da parte del Governo britannico contro il Sudafrica. L'Ambasciata del Sudafrica inviò in seguito una nota diplomatica ufficiale di protesta al Delegato canadese presso l'Ambasicata canadese in Londra, con la quale si chiedevano delle spiegazioni.
Un ringraziamento speciale va a Steven White.

37 *La proiezione del Monumento a Nelson*, Trafalgar Square, Londra, 27 e 30 agosto 1985
Vengono usati sei proiettori ad alta potenza ed un riflettore nel centro di Trafalgar Square. La proiezione è stata teletrasmessa dalla televisione BBC.
Organizzata dal Institute of Contemporary Arts e dal Artangel Trust, Londra.
Un ringraziamento speciale va a Steven White.

38 *La proiezione di Derry Guildhall*, Derry, Irlanda del Nord, 4 settembre 1985
Il Guildhall è situato al di fuori del Muro costruito dagli Inglesi e di fronte ad esso. Dei cannoni donati da mercanti di Londra sono montati sul Muro e puntati verso il Guildhall. Due immagine di mani vengono proiettate sul Guildhall usando dei proiettori di diapositive montati sul Muro.
Un ringraziamento speciale va a Willy Doherty.